Book one describes the obstacles to
and effects of spirit □ that purges & cleanses
that purges & cleanses
Book TWO — about God's visit — made
possible by the purge   pg 26

JOHN OF
THE CROSS
FOR TODAY:
The
Dark Night

Books by Susan Muto

Approaching The Sacred: An Introduction to Spiritual Reading

John of The Cross for Today: The Ascent

Blessings That Make Us Be: A Formative Approach to Living the Beatitudes

Celebrating the Single Life: A Spirituality for Single Persons in Today's World

The Journey Homeward: On the Road to Spiritual Reading

Meditation in Motion

Renewed at Each Awakening: The Formative Power of Sacred Words

Pathways of Spiritual Living

A Practical Guide to Spiritual Reading

Steps Along the Way: The Path of Spiritual Reading

Womanspirit: Reclaiming the Deep Feminine in Our Human Spirituality

With Adrian van Kaam

Aging Gracefully

Am I Living A Spiritual Life?

Caring for The Caregiver

Commitment: Key to Christian Maturity

Formation Guide: Becoming Spiritually Mature

Harnessing Stress: A Spiritual Quest

Healthy and Holy Under Stress: A Royal Road to Wise Living

The Participant Self

Power of Appreciation: A New Approach to Personal and Relational Healing

Practicing the Prayer of Presence

Songs for Every Season

Stress and the Search for Happiness: A New Challenge for Christian Spirituality

JOHN OF THE CROSS FOR TODAY: *The Dark Night*

Susan Muto

Companion to *John of the Cross for Today: The Ascent*

AVE MARIA PRESS   NOTRE DAME, INDIANA 46556

Acknowledgments and permissions:

Scripture texts used in quotes are those found in *The Collected Works of St. John of the Cross*, translated by Kieran Kavanaugh, O.C.D. and Otilio Rodriguez, O.C.D. Copyright © 1979, 1991 by Washington Province of Discalced Carmelites. ICS Publications, Washington, DC. Used with permission of the publisher.

Scripture texts, other than those mentioned above, are taken from the *New American Bible with Revised New Testament* Copyright © 1986 by the Confraternity of Christian Doctrine, Washington, DC, and are used by permission of the copyright owner. All rights reserved.

Excerpts from *The Collected Works of St. John of the Cross*, translated by Kieran Kavanaugh and Otilio Rodriguez. Copyright © 1979, 1991 by Washington Province of Discalced Carmelites. ICS Publications, Washington, DC. Used with permission of the publisher.

Excerpts from *The Collected Works of Teresa of Avila: Volume One* translated by Kieran Kavanaugh and Otilio Rodriguez. Copyright © 1976 by Washington Province of Discalced Carmelites. ICS Publications, Washington, DC. Used with permission of the publisher.

Excerpts from *He Leadeth Me* by Walter J. Ciszek, SJ. Copyright © 1975 Doubleday, New York, NY. Used with permission of the publisher.

Excerpts from *Tales of St. Francis: Ancient Stories for Contemporary Living* by Murray Bodo, OFM. Copyright © 1988 Doubleday, New York, NY. Used with permission of the publisher.

Excerpts from *Story of a Soul*, translated by John Clarke, O.C.D. Copyright © 1975, 1976 by Washington Province of Discalced Carmelites. ICS Publications, Washington, DC. Used with permission of the publisher.

Imprimatur:

The Most Reverend Donald William Wuerl

Bishop of Pittsburgh

The nihil obstat and the imprimatur are declarations that this work is considered to be free from doctrinal or moral error. It is not implied that those who have granted the same agree with the contents, opinions, or statements expressed.

Given this 14th day of January, 1994.

International Standard Book Number: 0-87793-532-7

Library of Congress Catalog Card Number: 94-71727

Cover and text design by Eizabeth French

Printed and bound in the United States of America

This book is dedicated to
family members and friends
who have shown me that
the dark nights in life
are times of sheer grace.

Contents

Acknowledgments

Since the publication of my book on *The Ascent of Mount Carmel* in 1991, many people have encouraged me to continue the work begun there by writing a companion text to *The Dark Night*. I thank them all for their faith and support. I acknowledge, especially in this regard, the invaluable help I received from my mentor, friend, and colleague, Father Adrian van Kaam, C.S.Sp., Ph.D., whose works pertaining to the "transcendent self" connected perfectly with St. John's mapping of the soul's journey to God.

Audiences and students of spiritual literature here and abroad have helped me by their insightful questions and obvious love for the mystics to refine the theoretical and practical findings of this book.

I am most grateful to Ave Maria Press and its excellent publishing staff for encouraging me to complete this book during its years of preparation and for guiding its publication. I am grateful also to the Institute of Carmelite Studies in Washington, D.C., for allowing me to use in citations the revised 1991 translation by Kieran Kavanaugh, O.C.D., and Otilio Rodriguez, O.C.D., of *The Collected Works of St. John of the Cross*. Theirs is a remarkable contribution to our understanding of the life and writings of a spiritual master whose influence is perhaps more significant today than in any previous time in history.

I would be remiss not to acknowledge the prayers and support I have received from the Epiphany Association as a whole and particularly from two members of our staff: my administrative assistant, Marilyn Russell, whose advice I sought and whose help I received on all technical aspects of production, and Karen Holttum, whose tireless efforts to ready the manuscript will never be forgotten.

To one and all who enabled the dream of this book on *The Dark Night* to become a reality, I offer sincere and loving thanks.

And, as I noted in *The Ascent*, I would like you to join me in thanking God for giving us the gift of St. John of the Cross, who more than any writer I know has named the unnameable and filled the darkness with light divine.

Editor's Note

There are several parts in the body of literature authored by the great Spanish mystic, St. John of the Cross, which deal with achieving what he calls "perfection" or "union with God through love."

There is the famous drawing by which he illustrated his teachings on achieving this union for his sixteenth century contemporaries, primarily Carmelite nuns and friars. It shows Mount Carmel, the metaphorical place of union, and the pitfalls along a path to its summit.

The other components are:

The Dark Night, an eight-stanza allegorical poem in which he describes his search and testifies to his joys at reaching union with the Beloved.

The Ascent of Mount Carmel, a commentary on how a seeker ascends the Mount. It is written from the perspective of one who has made the journey and in looking back can point out the obstacles to those who follow. In *The Ascent of Mount Carmel* he focuses on how those seeking God can actively purify themselves through their own efforts.

And *The Dark Night*, in which he continues his teaching on reaching mystical union, offers an incomplete commentary on the poem, and provides insight on how those seeking union are passively purified by God.

In both of these works St. John frequently uses the term "dark night" to refer to the obstacle-strewn path up Mount Carmel—the way to union with God.

Although often treated as two different works, *The Ascent of Mount Carmel* and *The Dark Night* are integral to one another, focus on "the dark night" as a difficult path to perfection, and form the whole treatise that the mystic promised in the first chapter of *The Ascent of Mount Carmel*.

This note—admittedly an oversimplification of this body of the saint's writings—is intended only to provide a context in which to read this book, as well as the author's prequel, *John of the Cross for Today: The Ascent* (Ave Maria Press, 1991).

Introduction

December 14, 1991. This date marked the end of the 400th anniversary year commemorating the life and death of St. John of the Cross and celebrating with the whole church the efficacy of his ascetical-mystical genius. In the epilogue of my book, *John of the Cross for Today: The Ascent*, I promised to provide a companion text to *The Dark Night*. I bring to this commentary long years of research and teaching in the field of literature and spirituality.

As in *The Ascent*, it is my intention in this sequel also to encourage a slowed down, dwelling, almost line-by-line meditative reading of the text many consider to be St. John's true masterpiece. In it I adopt an approach that is formative rather than informative. This emphasis, pioneered so profoundly by my colleague and mentor, Adrian van Kaam, C.S.Sp., Ph.D., asks the reader to be receptive to the message of the text in its multifaceted meaning.

I often compare formative reading to what happens when light passes through a prism and reveals a rainbow of colors. Such reading risks remaining flat if it is not done in a spirit of prayer and thanksgiving. To be formative it has to evoke personal and shared memories and experiences. I believe that Christians of all persuasions can benefit from the insights St. John offers into the secret chambers of contemplative love for God. One can blend and balance what is relevant to spiritual formation in his work with what is uniquely pertinent in one's own faith tradition. Much depends on the ability to trace foundational themes of spiritual deepening.[1]

When these are disclosed through the art and discipline of formative reading, we will enjoy moments of profound resonance with the master's message. Certain words, phrases, and paragraphs may evoke ancient longings in us for a life of uncompromising union with God. There are times when we shall encounter equally profound resistances to insights and ideas, examples and directives, that appear to ask too much of mere humans. At other times the poetry of

prayer will soar to such a height of intensity that it may be
more than mind and heart can bear. Then, too, when we
behold in the mirror held up by the master the scope of our
sinfulness, we may feel a shudder running along our spine.
How could we who have been called by God to such high
planes of love settle for the paltry promises of self-centered
pride!

The counsels of the master do not mince words, no more
than do the sayings of Jesus. The pilgrimage to the mount
toward which St. John leads us is not meant for wimps but
for stalwart women and men. The climb upward to liberation
through abandonment to God's loving and allowing will
cannot be made by persons accustomed to sipping only the
watery soup of soap opera spirituality. One following the
route to freedom through obedience, of restoration through
renunciation, has to feed on the solid food of faith, and on
the bread and wine of Jesus' own body and blood.

Many today who seek a spiritual life succumb to the
propaganda of New Age gurus who promise instant salvation through one or the other technique of self-actualization.
They are prone to run from the cross as fast as fireflies from
flame. St. John not only embraces the cross with joy; he says
we can never climb to the mountaintop of union with the
Divine unless we take up the cross and follow Christ with
courage. Only if we lift high the cross in abandoned faith,
unfailing hope, and selfless love can we escape prisons of
doubt, despair, self-hate, and prejudice. To face the suffering
symbolized by the cross is paradoxically to be set free from
the paralyzing illusion of self-sufficiency. It is to see in cruel
suffering an invitation to compassion. It is to behold in
darkness the faint glow of a greater light.

The night of sadness that never seems to end, the day of
depletion that drags on mercilessly, the crisis that tears us
asunder like cracked glass—all such occasions that stretch
our faith to the limit are, in reality, our greatest teachers. We
would be less able to walk in the truth of who we are without
the grace of these detachments. Outside of the dark night, St.

John says, it is virtually impossible to attain the secret wisdom of contemplation. Sheer observation shows us that a life bound to pleasure, possession, and power as ultimates tends to keep us fixated at the level of narcissistic infancy. The disorientation caused by sin puts us on the wrong course. We may enjoy the good life in the worldly sense, but its fruits never last. All the while we are in pursuit of the wrong goals, we miss the perennial delights, the grace and peace, associated with a mature spiritual life.

Though he holds out to us the tantalizing vision of eternal joy, it is not St. John's place to mitigate the difficulty entailed in ascending the mount. Many are the times when we shall want to turn back. Reading certain portions of *The Dark Night* will leave us feeling as if we are in an icy shower on a frosty morning when the furnace refuses to fire. We will long for the comforts of the valley. We will shun the cold blasts of bracing mountain air. But the master does not flinch. He invites us to press on, to run the race with Christ in the lead until we cross the finish line (cf. 2 Tm 4:7). There Jesus waits for us, arms outstretched in love. He desires nothing more than that we share in his glory for eternity. To glimpse what God has in store for those who love the Mystery with all their might is sufficient reward for the reader who wills to be continually formed in the divine image.

In a society that would confine the life of the spirit to occasional practices of private piety, one might wonder what a mystic and spiritual master like St. John has to say to the masses. It is a challenge to reconstruct in contemporary language—while remaining faithful to the parlance of this classic—its timely and timeless counsels to sincere seekers. St. John's probing analysis of our dark nights has to appeal as much to Carmelites in monasteries as to laity in the marketplace. It is to the foundational, formative themes of the text that we must turn. We have to dive deep. We dare not stay on the surface because we need to know what this great guide teaches more in our era than perhaps in any previous age.

Pastors and people in the pews, married and single persons, parents and teachers, executives and laborers, the well-to-do and the indigent, adults and youth face perilous times of transition to the year 2000.

The "dark night" is no longer a metaphor we can take or leave, a quaint symbol or the title of an old book. It is our unique and universal reality. It is a description of our world, our neighborhood, our family life. It is about pain and loneliness, anxiety and grief.

The dark night afflicts the parent of an addicted teenager as well as the victim of violence and disease. It touches every woman and man laid off from work. It affects single persons, both young and old, who are unable to pay their monthly bills. It etches its lines into the face of the woman whose husband deserts her after twenty-five years of marriage as well as the spouse who confesses to infidelity. The dark night is friendship betrayed, trust destroyed, abuse inflicted. It is the biologist beholding a beautiful lake in which no fish can live. It is Rachel weeping for her children, Mary at the foot of the cross, Anne Frank, Edith Stein, and Etty Hillesum being transported to concentration camps and certain death.

It is out of this social and personal experience of the dark night that we can once again be enlightened by the writings of St. John of the Cross.[2] The dark night is not distant from us; it is as near as our own backyard. The child with no place to call home, the bored teenager tempted to take drugs, the parent with a list of a thousand things to do and no time to relax are living in the nights of suffering only God knows. We all journey into the night in one way or another. We all seek the guidance St. John has to offer us today. When the center cannot hold, when, as the poet William Butler Yeats says, mere anarchy is loosed upon the world,[3] we are then ready to listen, if not with quiet attention, then with mounting desperation, to wise counsels from a Doctor of the Church. When the rhetoric of the world no longer rings true, we know that what we need to hear are not secular slogans but the sayings of a real spiritual master.

1

Walking the Narrow Way to Union With God

(Prologue to *The Dark Night*)

The Dark Night

One dark night,
fired with love's urgent longings
—ah, the sheer grace!—
I went out unseen,
my house being now all stilled;

In darkness, and secure,
by the secret ladder, disguised,
—ah, the sheer grace!—
in darkness and concealment,
my house being now all stilled;

On that glad night,
in secret, for no one saw me,
nor did I look at anything,
with no other light or guide
than the one that burned in my heart;

This guided me
more surely than the light of noon
to where he was awaiting me
—him I knew so well—
there in a place where no one appeared.

O guiding night!
O night more lovely than the dawn!
O night that has united
the Lover with his beloved,
transforming the beloved in her Lover.

Upon my flowering breast
which I kept wholly for him alone,
there he lay sleeping,
and I caressing him
there in a breeze from the fanning cedars.

When the breeze blew from the turret,
as I parted his hair,
it wounded my neck
with its gentle hand,
suspending all my senses.

I abandoned and forgot myself,
laying my face on my Beloved;
all things ceased; I went out from myself,
leaving my cares
forgotten among the lilies.

As we embark upon this arduous journey under the guidance of grace, who of us would dare to step foot on a path so narrow, to follow a way so constricting to our customary comforts, were the goal not so splendid? What we seek is nothing less than union with God. This quest requires a faith so strong, a hope so uncompromising, a love so lasting that already in this life we attain a foretaste of what awaits us fully in eternity.

To survive and thrive spiritually through the dark nights of sense and spirit, we need to know, first of all, how to conduct ourselves. What must we do to cooperate with all that God is already doing in us? Secondly, what are the obstacles to and the conditions characteristic of persons who have reached the mount of perfection?

The Night as Transforming

At the onset of this lifelong walk with the Lord, it is wise to meditate on the song of suffering and joy that prefaces the two books often entitled *Ascent-Dark Night*. The first stanza of the poem on which St. John bases his books begins with the unforgettable line: "One dark night ... ."

This is no ordinary night. It is not like the night I wandered away from the company gathered in our backyard to be alone for a little while under an overcast sky unbroken by bright stars or the sheen of a summer moon. The dark night is not a portion of time that passes either noticed or unnoticed. It is a powerful symbol of a formation event that affects one physically, emotionally, and spiritually. Under the impact of this transforming night, one may feel bodily fatigue or affective isolation, but neither tiredness nor melancholia can account for the transcendent power that overtakes the seeker of God one dark night.

Each word in this symbolic phrase stimulates the minds and hearts of persons in love with the Mystery we name God. The symbol of darkness points beyond the biography of its author to capture something of the incomprehensibility of the sacred. It may have been inspired by St. John's imprisonment in the Carmelite monastery of Toledo, but its implications are far-reaching. Anyone who can recall the day, the hour, the occasion when God entered his or her life and took charge knows the deeper meaning of the night.

This period of time, of long or relatively brief duration, may be for some as dramatic as the future saint's incarceration and escape from a prison cell; for others the conversion may occur in a series of small assents to God's call. Whatever the case may be, the night in question throws a veil over one's ability to understand what is happening. One has no choice but to proceed in faith. Memories of what used to be fade in comparison to the anticipation of what is to come. All one can do is to inch forward on filaments of hope. The courage to let God be God in one's life, especially in the night, stems from love purified of self-centered desires. This love guides one more surely than sunshine at high noon.

The Night as Awesome

The second line of the poem says that the seeker was "fired with love's urgent longings." No courtly lover would win fair lady were he not on fire with hot coals of affection. So it is when one's entire being longs for union with God. One's body or mind may protest against having to say "yes" to yet another call to snap out of a current course of action or inertia; one's sense of functioning furiously while accomplishing little worth mentioning may cause one to step dangerously close to the quicksand of depression. We need not fear falling backward, provided we submit these protests and resistances to the energizing fire of love that urges us forward to new heights of surrender, to new depths of longing.

St. John managed to escape the physical and mental prisons that threatened to deprive him of God's company and obscure God's plan for his life. We, too, must break asunder the bonds of vital gratification and functional satisfaction that pose as ultimate sources of happiness.[1] It takes the fire of transcendent inspirations and aspirations to melt the chains of complacency, the fetters of failure, that prevent us from trusting the sheer grace of God drawing us toward liberation and redemption.

Of this grace the poet can only utter a sound, "ah!" This exclamation is like an intake of breath in the face of an amazing mystery that is beyond words. It is literally the "ah!" of "awe." This disposition of the heart is innate to human beings made in the image and likeness of God.[2] Without awe the potency for transcendence remains dormant. Without wonder we would not be distinctively human.

The poet, ordinarily so prolific, can find no word beyond this exclamation to capture his immense relief, in a sense his disbelief, that the love he feels for God pales in comparison to the love God has for him. God's care is unconditional; it does not depend on our being perfect or sinless. God comes to us where we are with all the quirks and quagmires of our personality. That is why this outpouring of sheer grace evokes in us, as it did in St. John, the "ah!" of "awe."

Such love is too wonderful for words. It is too large a portion for puny mortal minds to fathom. The mystery and immensity of divine love is truly awesome. Were we to grasp only a sliver of it, it would already be too much to bear. Hence the poet offers no explanation, only an exclamation, only an "ah!" That becomes the best prayer possible. It is like a fiery arrow that aims beyond the reaches of reason to fields of faith where God prepares a veritable banquet to welcome the weary hunter.

A similar experience gripped another Doctor of the Church, St. Catherine of Siena. In her *Dialogue* she asks what she ought to say before the supreme magnificence, the immeasurable abyss, of the eternal majesty of God:

> I shall stutter, "A-a," because there is nothing else
> I know how to say. Finite language cannot express
> the emotion of the soul who longs for you infinite-
> ly. I think I could echo Paul's words: The tongue
> cannot speak nor the ear hear nor the eye see nor
> the heart imagine what I have seen! What have you
> seen? "I have seen the hidden things of God!" And
> I—what do I say? I have nothing to add from these
> clumsy emotions [of mine]. I say only, my soul, that
> you have tasted and seen the abyss of supreme
> eternal providence.[3]

Returning to St. John, the poet writes that he goes forth into the night unseen by anyone, for God is now taking the lead. Grace has sparked the longings that enable him to leave behind all that was less than God. It would seem as if this adventure of the spirit is possible only for an escape artist! To be a secret agent for the eternal, one has to sneak away unseen from the ties of temporal, purely sensual or spiritual attachments; one has to be ready and willing to move with the drum rolls of detachment from all that is less than God

toward all that awaits one in the "More Than" that constitutes union with God.

The Night as Reforming

To go out unseen does not mean to obviate the senses or
to dull the spirit. We must go to God as whole persons. The
heresy of dualism finds no room in St. John's reservoir of
formation wisdom. What we must go out unseen from are
illusions of fulfillment based on the false premises posed by
human pride. It puts forth pleasure, possession, and power
as ultimate. This triple disorientation takes us off course. It
plays on that in us which is weak and prone to sin. To reorient
ourselves on the right path is the work of grace. On our part,
we must respond to these spirit-filled leadings, moving gently, unseen as it were, to a place where it is possible to see our
life from a spiritual or transcendent point of view.[4]

Faith grows stronger through the trials of this transforming experience. We begin to understand what God really had
in mind for us from the start. We discern as through a sudden
clearing in a dark cloud who we are called to be. Eventually
we may come to realize that the nights of sensate deprivation
and ego-desperation are not events to lament but occasions
to celebrate being released by sheer grace from prisons of our
own making. The night that seemed on the surface to be
without rhyme or reason is no longer beheld as blinding but
as guiding. We can see that the night, even the darkest hour,
is actually brighter than the sight of the rising sun.

In this night where one has to undergo much sensual and
spiritual reformation, it is doubly necessary that seekers
draw close to God. The miracle of transformation for which
one searches tirelessly is a true mystical union between us
and God, a union that is nearer than we might think.

St. John's vision of what happens next is nothing short of
amazing. It is as if God—the almighty, the Most High—becomes again like the babe of Bethlehem, who lays his head
on his mother Mary's breast. She caresses him gently while
the child sleeps in peace, cooled by a breeze from the swaying

cedars. This intimate scene parallels that of a lover resting in sweet intimacy in the arms of the beloved. The tender imagery through which the poet chooses to convey the mystery of mystical marriage confirms the truth that God's name is Emmanuel, the One Beyond Us Who Is Now With Us.

This seeing in unseeing, this knowing in unknowing, offers the seeker a glimpse of what lasts beyond the vicissitudes of this life. To see with eyes of faith, one's inner house must be cleared of clutter. The pain one might have to endure to grow spiritually mature leaves one not bitter but better. On the plateau of presence to the transcendent, the wild winds of desire are as still as tall palms before a tempest. In this stillness one can hear God knocking at the door. The losses one has had to endure make one ready to listen at a new level of appreciative appraisal.[5]

Proceeding to the Land of Likeness in Darkness

The key motifs of this provocative stanza are thus longing and listening. The seeker under the urgent promptings of love longs to shed his or her old self with its childish deceits and to listen to the invitations of grace in the hush of an empty house. The second stanza repeats these themes while emphasizing the conditions under which one can best heed God's call.

To be sure, it is necessary to proceed in darkness. We do not know for a long while where God is leading us nor do we comprehend the extent of the changes asked of us. We only accept that we have no choice but to follow the promptings of grace in dialogue with the truths of our Christian faith and formation tradition. We listen in darkness, but we do not feel insecure. The opposite is true. We feel secure enough to climb up and down the secret ladder of love blindfolded! There is no need for anyone to know what is transpiring nor could we explain it were they to ask.

Another condition that facilitates this deeper listening is to proceed, as it were, in disguise. It may appear to the casual observer that the seeker is the same as everyone else, but this is not true. One operates under a mantle of faith in a culture that promotes disbelief as realism; under a cloak of hope in a society that defends doubt as wisdom; under a veil of love in a world that condones prejudice as class consciousness. Thus one moves under the guise of darkness away from the land of unlikeness toward a place where it is possible to let go of these deceptions, to cease resisting the subtle prompt-ings of grace, and to forget our futile fears. God wants us to live in carefree abandonment amidst lilies of the field that neither toil nor spin but whose splendor rivals the finest artist's rendering (cf. Mt 6:28).

The concealment essential to this walk with the Lord to the land of likeness becomes paradoxically an arena of revelation. In the stillness we are able to listen intently to a word of truth. High on the ladder of love, we are able to see the promised land where providence has been leading us. We can feel the breeze that blows gently across the turret, suspending our senses in their natural functions while elevating them supernaturally. Thus grace reforms and trans-forms our spiritual faculties, readying intellect, memory, and will to taste and see and touch here on earth something of what God has in store for us in eternity.

In Book One of *The Dark Night*, St. John intends to com-ment on the obstacles to and the effects of this spiritual housekeeping that purges or cleanses sense and spirit to make way for God's visit, an event described more fully in Book Two. The first stanza of his poem will require a lengthy exposition of the meaning of purification in the sensory part of the soul, whereas the commentary on the second stanza will explain in more detail the meaning of spiritual purga-tion. The resulting stanzas on which St. John does not com-ment, at least not in *The Dark Night*, address the fruits of this purification in terms of spiritual illumination and of union with God through love. These themes are treated by the saint in his other masterpieces on the life of the spirit—*The Spiritual Canticle* and *The Living Flame of Love*—for which I hope to write companion texts in the future.

St. John reminds us that the lines of the poem itself were recited by one who had already been brought by grace to union. In his commentary on them he is working retrospectively—going backwards—to rehearse the severity of the trials and conflicts that led him to choose the narrow way that leads to life eternal (cf. Mt 7:14).

Though God can draw one in an instant to total transformation, such is not the usual course grace takes. The ordinary way is to walk the long road of formation and reformation until one begins to behold the promised land of sublime union with God. The joy that awaits one does not remove the pain of the walk. Due to the nature of this narrow path, it calls for great courage to continue along it. One who has walked the way is able to look back with no regrets. His or her joy is contagious. That one has advanced so far is cause enough to be radiantly happy, for no other experience can rival that of pure and perfect love.

The dark night refers in this first stanza to the narrowness of the road on which one must walk to reach the highway to heaven. Having trod this path and survived to tell the tale is a source of genuine delight. The sadness initially felt is turned to a gladness one would not trade for any amount of worldly consolation.

With God's grace, we shall attempt to walk the road to Mount Carmel with St. John at our side. Though at times we shall be sorely tempted to seek shelter from the rain of truth from which no falsehood can hide, we shall be aided in midnight moments by a skilled and gentle master who has been to that place where no one save God appears. He wants us to go as far as grace will carry us. He asks for no fee but faith. He does not want us to look at him but at the Holy Spirit, who is the director of directors. Even when our intellect grows dim and our memory dull, he wants us to trust the light that burns in our heart. However dense the darkness, it will illumine the way that leads to lasting union with our gracious God.

2

The Imperfections of Beginners

(*The Dark Night*, Book One, Chapter 1)

A familiar proverb suggests, "Do as I say, don't do as I do." What is St. John saying in *The Dark Night*? And how, in our limited way, can we respond to what the Spirit prompts us to do? While being faithful to our call, while in no way trying to duplicate the actions of the saint, in what way can we, with the help of grace, cultivate the dispositions of faith-deepening he teaches?

Responding to God's Initiative

The symbol of the dark night gives rise to what I call true retrospective disclosures. This evocative phrase calls to mind the pain of an unexpected setback, a partnership betrayed, a series of events that made us feel as if the cross would never be lifted. Each time we are drawn by circumstances beyond our control into yet another phase of enforced detachment, into yet another desert of ego-desperation, we sense with trepidation the encroaching darkness.

The night of spiritual aridity often feels endless. It can come upon us in small, oft-repeated "lights out" experiences or for prolonged periods that stretch faith to the limit. Such was the case with Teresa of Avila who, in "The Book of Her Life," reports a dry spell lasting eighteen years.[1] She could not pray without the help of a book. She was also sorely tempted to abandon prayer once and for all.

What are we to do amidst the confusion and ambiguity we feel spreading through us like fog on a moonless night?

Must our faith be tested in the fire of woundedness and vulnerability? How is it possible when we are dying daily to trust without doubt in Christ's victory over death?

Despite our misgivings, nothing can replace the purging fire many mystics view as both necessary and good. Faith grows stronger. Hope soars on eagle's wings. Love is rekindled by urgent longings. We feel torn between the fear of a life lived without nearness to God and the fascination of what it might mean to pass through the dark night and be transformed. Much to our surprise, in the midst of outer turmoil and uncertainty, we may suddenly grow still. A hush falls over our inner house. Try as we might, we know that no human effort can compel this passage beyond the darkness into the dawning of a new day. This initiative belongs to God.

To go beyond or more deeply into these times of felt purgation, we have to be content to feel lost, seemingly without any definite direction. We have to make frequent acts of faith. All we can do is to wait upon the power of grace to lead us to a secure place where we ourselves cannot go. At such times we rely on the inspirations of the Holy Spirit, and on the living witness of holy people, to see us through. We trust that we shall be kept safe from all harm, that God is on our side, that faith overcomes despair.

Certain shifts occur during these dark night experiences that remain a mystery to the probing mind. As we shall see, to abandon oneself to the ultimate benevolence of God, even when one's well-being appears to be threatened by a profound transcendence crisis, can be a blessing. Both during and after such spiritual earthquakes, we may see for the first time that darkness, humanly speaking, is like the dawn's first light, spiritually speaking.

Waiting Upon the Power of Grace

Drawn by grace away from a style of living that is overly attached, caught in self-centered concerns, and fearful of failure makes us sad at first. But this feeling soon gives way to a new-found gladness. We are grateful to the Most High for having liberated us from encapsulation in "little beyonds." The night of painful transformation that seemed to separate us from the "Beyond" now becomes the space of grace wherein the lover is united with the Beloved. Whereas previously we may have felt only the absence of God, we now feel lifted up in quiet faith by a felt awareness of the divine presence.

In a word, the night that may have been perceived initially as threatening has become a much needed opening to the transcendent. The dissonance of the darkness has given way to the consonance of the dawn. The disintegration of sensate attachments and less-than-spiritual understandings is seen as but a stage along the way to a fuller disclosure of God's will. That of us which was isolated from the transcendent has undergone a profound purification—so much so that we feel reintegrated in the transcendent. The wounding that once seemed so harsh is now beheld as the delicate touch of a gentle hand. What began as a futile attempt to control the quake now becomes an opportunity to stay quiet.

Rather than wait for an expected outcome, one is content to wait upon the workings of grace and to anticipate in faith, hope, and love its good results. Growth at this level of spiritual maturing is not of our doing. It is due to the power of grace. This awareness is humbling to the intellect, calming to the memory, gentling to the will. The way at this point no longer seems complex. It involves abandoning ourselves in childlike simplicity to the benign goodness of our gracious Lover. We let go of the demand for instant, predictable solutions and our now aborted projects of self-salvation. We come to rely on the transcendent. Our "control center" turns itself off. We turn instead to our saving Lord. We make a firm act of faith, knowing that faith is the only proximate means of union with God. We leave our cares forgotten among the lilies.

Walking Along the Narrow Way

The first chapter of Book One of *The Dark Night* is about what happens when we begin this serious walk with God. It concerns the move away from spiritual mediocrity for the sake of setting out on a journey into the unknown land of intimacy with the Mystery.

Following the promptings of grace, we must freely take the first step. We must overcome our fear and make the leap of faith. On the way that leads to union with God, on the road to love, we must let go of the illusion of perfection. We will always need help. The goal to be reached happens only because the generosity of God knows no bounds. The question is: Are we receptive to the ocean of grace in which we are swimming like fish in the sea, whether we know it or not?

To make this journey to the land of likeness means for most of us being led by grace through an entanglement of severe trials and conflicts. This is so, explains St. John in the Prologue, because the way to eternal life is narrow, especially to us who are accustomed to the wideness of an "anything goes" world. The road is dark because we shun self-denial. Used to self-indulgence, caught in the net of narcissism, we find it hard to accept that the delightful life of love between us and God has to begin with the pain of death. We would like to leap by a single bound to the mount of contemplation without having to pass through the valley of negation of self-centeredness, but this is impossible.

If we follow Christ's teachings in this regard and witness his life, we realize that there is no other method than mortification. There is no other way to journey to God than by passing through the dark night of faith. In the twilight of our lives, when defenses drop and we feel worn out by the futility of our own efforts to find happiness, we are more ready to confront the deceptions that have so far entrapped us. We then have no choice in the midnights but to recognize how worldly we have become, how inordinate our desires for everything but God are, how vulnerable we feel in the face of sly, demonic seductions.

St. John names the world, the flesh, and the devil as the three enemies with which we shall have to wrestle in the dark night. Only when all three are lulled to sleep in the house of the senses can we experience the release of spirit that liberates us for a new life of faith, hope, and love in conformity to Christ.

Entering a New Phase of Spiritual Maturity

Let us review once more the opening stanza of the poem with which St. John begins this first chapter of his commentary. The words he chooses are stark and spare: "One dark night ... ." From whence comes the darkness of this stage of the spiritual journey? Its source is not this or that experience of personal loss, frustration, or worry. This night marks the beginning of a new phase of spiritual maturity. Its principal agent is the Holy Spirit. It is God's own grace that draws us into this dark night. God is the initiator of this transformation. The Spirit takes the lead in moving us from an imperfect, baby-step way of walking to the confident stride of a person not about to be deterred from his or her goal. It is exactly the tension of transformation that causes us to suffer. More than anything, our way of prayer is undergoing profound alteration. One way of knowing God is ending, another is beginning, and living in the between-time is not easy to endure.

St. John, therefore, describes us as "beginners," not because we have never prayed before but because we must be taught by the Spirit to pray in a new and deeper way. In the light of where we are being led, our imperfections constitute a veritable litany of passions and practices in need of profound reformation. "Beginners" are simply identified by the saint as those who practice meditation. Only passage through the passive night of the senses will place us on another plateau of prayer—that experienced by "proficients," who are well along the way to contemplation, indeed who are not far from the place of the "perfect" or those who enjoy union with God. This is understood by St. John as participant transformation in the life of the Trinity through the mediation of the Christ-form in the core of our being.[2]

With pastoral solicitude and the gentle yet firm dispositions characteristic of a true spiritual father, St. John holds up a mirror in which we beginners can view ourselves standing, as it were, naked before God, alone with the Alone. His reason for so doing is to offer an explanation of the nature of this night so that we do not shun the work involved in the transition to transcendent transformation. The saint makes no attempt to hide the turmoil this state entails. Both explicitly and implicitly he shares his experience of having gone through it himself and of having directed many others along the way.[3] That is the reason he is able to shed light on why God allows this "dark night" form of direction to happen and why it is so effective.

Stripping Away Illusions of Self-Sufficiency

What do we see in the mirror the saint places before us? Without doubt, our weaknesses come into view. We wonder if we are being faithful to our divine life call, if our ministry is secretly self-serving, if people see behind the mask of self-sufficiency how feeble, fickle, and frustrated we feel. While we may see a mess in the mirror, the master assures us, as if he were looking over our shoulder and shaking his head at such self-deprecating remarks: "Take courage ... if you were oblivious of your misery, how could you appreciate God's mercy?"

Our potential for contemplative prayer begins with the longing we feel to place ourselves entirely in God's hands. This is what it means to return to the center of our humility as the surest starting point for our pilgrimage to the mount.[4] This surrender usually means that we cannot escape suffering through a rather intense dark night experience. As our illusions are stripped away, we cannot help but suffer. We can only trust that in our weakness God will be our strength (cf. 2 Cor 12:9-10). Christ will be our rock, our fortress, our stronghold, the one in whom we trust and on whom we can rely for everything (cf. Ps 18:2). The Holy Spirit will prepare a dwelling place for us in which we shall experience in due course the delights of divine intimacy. As St. John says:

> ... God nurtures and caresses the soul, after it has
> been resolutely converted to his service, like a
> loving mother who warms her child with the heat
> of her bosom, nurses it with good milk and tender
> food, and carries and caresses it in her arms (DN
> I:1 [2]).

With this kind of care, why be concerned? It offers all that
we need to make progress initially. As time passes, another
strategy on the part of parents has to be brought into play if
one is to move from childhood to adulthood. St. John explains this way as well:

> ... as the child grows older, the mother withholds
> her caresses and hides her tender love; she rubs
> bitter aloes on her sweet breast and sets the child
> down from her arms, letting it walk on its own feet
> so that it may put aside the habits of childhood and
> grow accustomed to greater and more important
> things (DN I:1 [2]).

St. John understands not only the path to maturity in
Christ but also the stages of psychological growth. His comparison of God to a loving mother is most fitting. Just as God
enables us to grow in our relationship with him, so a good
mother offers her child many occasions for learning how to
love. She gives birth to her child not once but many times
over. She wants him or her to learn from mistakes what
makes for a meaningful life. She knows that satisfaction is
possible only through self-giving. Similarly, in doing good
for others, we receive in return much more than we give. We
both feel embraced by the tender love of God. We know when
we help others it is only because God holds both of us in the
palm of his hand.

Seeing Signs of Progress Though We Are Still Imperfect

As we move away from false securities and journey
toward the land of likeness, it feels right to spend longer and

longer periods of time in prayer. Our appreciation of what God has done for us helps us to pray always (cf. 1 Thes 5:17). Paradox abounds at this point on the path to full friendship with the Divine. For example, doing penance by listening patiently to an aging parent instead of quickly dismissing her becomes easier. Fasting not only from food but from always expecting things to go our way makes us feel happy. Receiving the sacraments worthily and conversing about spiritual things brings us joy, even if it does not make us popular.

That from which we derive great profit is not sloth and lack of follow-through but diligent practice of our faith and perseverance. All of this constitutes progress, to be sure, but there is still a problem. It resides not so much in our intentions, which are good, but in the way in which we perform good deeds and devotions. This way, according to St. John, is still weak and imperfect. There is too much of *us* in what we do, not enough of God. We need to reform our motives, if not our actions. There is still a lot of inner work left for us to do in response to the forming, reforming, and transforming power of grace.

All too often what is moving us to walk the way of perfection is not our love for the God who consoles but our dependency on the consolations of God. We see these as signs of progress. We are like children who pretend they are growing in self-giving but who really do good for the sake of receiving rewards. Their love is bound up with what they get rather than with what they give.

These deep roots of narcissism can be purged only in the dark night of faith. There the focus is not on personal satisfaction but on obedience to God. To arrive at this point in the process of spiritual growth requires a lot of reconditioning. Only with time and the humble attempt to stay responsive to the pace of grace can we grow more and more in conformity to Christ. It takes time to acquire what the saint calls the habits of perfection, just as it takes a concert pianist years to attain the skill to be named a virtuoso. She had first to master

musical scales, then to overcome a thousand faults and imperfections, and finally to play with confidence.

Acknowledging Our Sins

At this point of our walk with the Lord, the main problem
is to reform our motivation for making the journey. Conversion
is necessary. We must shift from the practice of virtue because
of the satisfaction we find in it to the desire to do good for God's
sake, whether or not we receive any visible reward. What
prevents us from making progress are the obstacles or imperfections described in our Christian faith and formation tradition as the "seven capital sins."[5] These, says St. John, are what
hinder beginners from becoming proficients.

Like children who wail when parents try to put away
their security blankets, so beginners tend to resist walking
through the desert of detachment. Be that as it may, there is
no way out—only a way through. These imperfections must
not take the place of transcendent ideals. Any one of these
sins can throw us off course. Taken together they block our
ascent to union with God.

Is it any wonder that St. John teaches us to embrace the
dark night? Its benefits will be evident as we proceed. We
could compare its purifying effect to what it feels like to take
a brisk shower after a tortuous drive through a maze of
detours when one is covered with dust and can't wait to feel
clean. As we look at what hinders our becoming children of
light, who walk with our God (cf. Eph 5:8), we must admit
that the dark night is the doorway to eternal delight. Renunciation of lesser goods is the royal road to liberation and true
love of God, self, and others.

3

The Prison of Pride

(*The Dark Night*, Book One, Chapter 2)

Amidst the upsets of everyday existence, its failures, fixations, and finiteness, we long for an experience of consonance with the Mystery of all that is. The most universal of desires is that for loving union with the Divine. We want to be freed from the dissonance of a life that feels like Humpty Dumpty falling off the wall. As the nursery rhyme says, not all the king's horses nor all the king's men could put that silly egg together again.

Pride Retards Spiritual Progress

What in us prolongs this unhappy state of disintegration? What prevents us from making progress, from entering the promised land of peace and joy? What is at the root of our broken hearts and depreciative feelings? Why are we so unhappy? What makes us settle for so little when the Spirit calls us to so much more? Since when did we come to believe that half a life is enough?

The cause of this deception has plagued humanity since the Fall. It is "spiritual pride." It is a form of egocentricity, far more subtle than mere boasting or the penchant to want to control everything. This is the fault that perverts the transcendence dynamic. It turns us away from Christ and toward our own autonomy. It halts progress on the road to holiness like potholes on a country lane.

Not surprisingly, spiritual pride often poses as humility. It is an aberration to which beginners are especially prone. Their fervor and diligence in regard to such spiritual practices as reading holy texts, fasting in moderation, making retreats, saying vocal prayers, or practicing meditation harbors a secret "I-can-do-it" mentality. One feels proud of being so pious.

A holier-than-thou type appears to have it made. What kills the quest for deepening is the blinding power of complacency. We focus on our religiosity or our charitable donations as if these represent profound spiritual accomplishments. We treat grace as we would a game played for merits or demerits. Good works gain rewards. So many merits bring a person to the portals of heaven, so many demerits to the door of hell. In this game the "saved" feel obliged to teach the how-to's of righteous living to the "unsaved." The spiritually proud like to show off in the presence of others. Though they assume a posture of effacement, they still manage to call attention to themselves. Christ is, as it were, left in the dust of their drive to show others ways of holy living they have not yet learned themselves.

Signposts of Spiritual Pride

A sure sign of spiritual pride is harsh judgment of those who do not practice "my" kind of devotion. I feel superior because "they" have not had experiences of the Almighty similar to mine. They do not yet deserve the privileges God has given to me. St. John cites as a good example of such hypocrisy the story of the Pharisee and the Publican told in the gospel of Luke (18:11-12). Remember which of the two went home justified in the eyes of God.

This imperfection of pride posing as humility easily succumbs to demonic seduction. As in the Garden of Eden, so in the holiest of places, the Tempter lurks, forever playing on the weak points of pride and presumption. The tactics used to pull one away from Christ are hard to detect because they look so like the real thing. St. John says that this bad spirit increases one's zeal and makes one double up on good works without examining one's motives. It is as if I am the only right and good person around. Others are power-hungry or lazy or out to make a name for themselves—not I.

As St. John reminds us, if our hearts are not purified of such false motivations, the works they promote are not only worthless in God's eyes, they may severely retard the work of salvation. Perverted virtue is the greatest vice. It collects envy and jealousy around itself like green moss on stone. I feel a little twitch inside myself when anyone appears more holy than I or receives a compliment for the compassion they show. I appear to agree with others about the virtues they display, but I cannot resist pointing out—of course, in "fraternal admonition"—a few of their faults. In fact, I feel obliged to detract from their acclaim whenever an occasion arises. I cannot stand it when they receive the attention I deserve! Both scripture (Mt 7:5) and the master (DN I:2 [2]) warn that such judgmental behavior is reprehensible in God's eyes and must be rejected.

The person ensnared in the net of spiritual pride moves from one strategy to another to protect the veneer of vanity. When, for example, a spiritual guide or confessor expresses disapproval of one's actions, not I, but she or he, have to be mistaken. Not I, but they lack the first semblance of sanctity, namely, an ability to esteem a person like myself, who is so obviously ahead of them in holiness! To prove my point I set out to find someone who does understand, a person who will see immediately how well-meaning I am. I want him to offer me the confirmation I crave to continue my mission. I want her to tell others of the good I do since I would look immodest were I to boast about it.

St. John says that proud, pious persons can sense when they are in the presence of a wise director, who can spot these self-assertive strategies. From such a person one flees as from death. If flight, especially in a small community, is not feasible then the hostility one feels may surface more openly. Pride dons more subtle disguises. One boldly makes resolutions aimed at personal and communal reformation and is full of clever excuses for not being able personally to keep them. It becomes customary to promise great results and to make refined excuses when little or nothing is actually done.

Always the situation "out there" or others in the group are to blame for these failures—never I. Others cannot see what a noble person I am, how hard-working and devout. I feel as persecuted as Jesus was. To show people who are envious of me how much I am suffering, I may begin to move more slowly, as if carrying a heavy cross on my shoulders. I may develop the custom of sighing deeply, of loud praying, of walking quickly with eyes downcast. One moment I feel besieged by God to be a savior to the sick of soul, the next finds me ready to be a martyr.

As if such tricks to gain attention were not bad enough, one's pride falls further into the snare set by the Seducer. As St. John says, "... sometimes, with the assistance of the devil, they experience raptures, more often in public than in private, and they are quite pleased, and often eager, for others to take notice of these" (DN I:2 [3]).

The anonymous author of *The Cloud of Unknowing*, a spiritual director of the fourteenthth century, an English mystic whose insights we can trust, is as adept at detecting these pretenses of pride as is St. John. He describes tongue-in-cheek a similar scene involving the behavior of pseudo-contemplatives:

> The eyes of some of them are so set in their heads as though they were sheep suffering from the brain disease, and were near death's door. Some of them hold their heads on one side as though a worm were in their ears. Some squeak instead of speaking normally, as though there were no breath in their bodies. Hypocrites tend to behave like this. Some again are so eager and quick to say what they think that they gurgle and splutter in their throats; which is what heretics are wont to do, and those who with their presumption and cleverness stubbornly hold fast to their error ... these unseemly and inordinate gestures have such control over the

man that makes them that he cannot stop them even when he wants to. So I maintain that they are signs of pride, of outlandishness, of exhibitionism and an inordinate desire for knowledge. In particular they are true tokens of moral instability and mental restlessness, and they indicate a lack of acquaintance with the exercises described in this book. The reason why I mention so many of these illusions here in these chapters is that he who undertakes this exercise can consider them, if he will, in order to put his own work to the test.[1]

More Subtle Signs of This Imperfection

St. John's probing analysis of pride continues. He writes with the genius of one who understands the human condition as thoroughly as Houdini understood magic tricks. The saint must have known that such a person feels compelled to be the "pet" of his or her spiritual director. Anyone else who gains favor becomes the target of envy because "I" want to be in the center of his or her attention. This competitive bent contributes to the leveling mentality and hypertension that often kills creativity and health in a community.

When and if qualms of conscience plague such prideful types, they are too embarrassed to confess them. So dependent have they become on looking good in the eyes of others that they prefer maintaining a posture of sweet innocence. They first compose in their head a script that sounds good and then follow it when confessing their sins. They prefer not to speak from the heart. In this way they think they will keep their reputation intact and pull the wool over their confessor's eyes.

Though a person of St. John's wisdom and experience could not be fooled so easily, someone less astute may miss the message written between the lines of this compulsion to appear in a favorable light. Suspicion ought to be aroused, the saint says, when people strive willfully to appear better than they are and especially when they use the sacrament of

penance "to excuse themselves rather than accuse themselves" (DN I:2 [4]).

The game goes on because pride does not easily loosen
its grip. St. John reports that one may choose another priest
to whom to tell one's sins so that a regular confessor will
assume one has no major faults at all. Supporting this ploy is
the prideful desire to appear holy—at any price. In the softest
of tones, with modest whispers, such persons hesitantly
share examples of good deeds they have done in Christ's
name, examples that make their acts appear greater than they
are. What else but the fire of inner purification, what else but
an inescapable confrontation with the truth of a dark night
experience, could explode the grid of defenses one has
created and draw one to the liberating deserts of repentance
and humility?

Onset of Reformation Via Self-Examination

One sign that a shift may be occurring is making light of
the good one does, sharing it at most with a soul friend, and,
in the end, considering it of no importance since to Christ
alone belongs the glory.

The following insights ought to signal to oneself or to the
person to whom one is accountable that spiritual pride may
be what is retarding progress to union with God. I would like
to present these thoughts of St. John's in a question format to
enhance sincere self-examination in the light of the transcendent.

1. Do I consciously or unconsciously tend to minimize
my faults, to dismiss them as one would a slight smudge
on an otherwise sparkling mirror?

2. Though I make light of my sins, am I secretly discouraged by them? As a result, do I become impatient
with myself, desiring to be holy in a day? Do I become
the brunt of self-anger, pushing against the pace of grace
in my life and unwittingly slipping into a fault worse
than the first?

3. Do I live in unfocused anxiety, wondering if I am forgivable and worrying excessively because God does not seem to be helping me, no matter how hard I try? Am I inclined as a result to seek harsher and harsher means of mortification, even to resort to physical measures under my own counsel, willing to do whatever it takes from fasting to flagellation to get rid of my imperfections?

4. What motivates me? Is it God's beckoning grace or my inordinate desire to feel personal peace and to be done with these human foibles? People in this state of resistance and confusion, says St. John, "fail to realize that were God to remove their faults they might very well become more proud and presumptuous" (DN I:2 [5]).

5. Do I find it as unpleasant to offer praise to someone as it would be to eat a mouthful of sawdust? By the same token, do I seek ways to call attention to myself and to receive praise? Is my need for such confirmation noticeably insatiable?

St. John seems to know firsthand how serious these imperfections can be in some people and how much harm they may do. People are at different places in these beginning stages and have to be guided accordingly. While one person may be in more trouble and another less, there are, according to the saint's experience, few if any beginners who do not fall into one or the other of these traps, especially in the early flush of fervor.

Deeds and Decisions Facilitating Reform

What may help beginners to reform their ways is to consider, by contrast, how a person emulating the humility of Christ might behave. Here we see an entirely different picture. Using the analogy of a game of chess, Teresa of Avila says in "The Way of Perfection":

The queen is the piece that can carry on the best battle in this game, and all the other pieces help. There's no queen like humility for making the King surrender. Humility drew the King from heaven to the Womb of the Virgin, and with it, by one hair, we will draw him to our souls. And realize that the one who has more humility will be the one who possesses him more; and the one who has less will possess him less. For I cannot understand how there could be humility without love or love without humility; nor are these two virtues possible without detachment from all creatures.[2]

When humility becomes the seed of one's Christ-centered growth, it is obvious that a person places little importance on the good deeds he or she accomplishes. One simply does what is necessary. One does not dwell on feelings of self-satisfaction but on the call of Christ. If the truth were told, one tends to see others as much better than oneself. If any envy is present, it is what St. John calls "holy envy," that is, a desire to model and match another's service to God.

The more zealous one becomes, the more aware one is of being utterly dependent on God. The more good one does, the less adequate one feels one's service of God to be. Others may lavish praise on us for this or that worthwhile deed, but we derive less and less personal satisfaction from such attention since the real doer is not I but Christ in me. We want to do everything for God; yet we feel, regardless of what or how much is accomplished, we have done pitifully little.

Persons drawn by grace to act only for the greater glory of God often feel embarrassed by the attention they receive. All that moves them, all that holds their attention, is loving solicitude for God's will. This desire for obedience so absorbs their energy that they hardly notice what others around them do or do not achieve. If they are sensitive to anything, it is that others are probably doing more for the Lord and doing it better than they.

It is as if we develop an inner radar system that bleeps whenever we come into proximity with an enemy submarine named *S.S. Pride*. To counter a possible attack, it is important to think of ourselves—in comparison to the Divine Master whom we serve—as "small potatoes." To avoid being the brunt of others' jealousy, it is best that people hear us saying, and meaning it, that what we do is not that important.

"It's all in a day's work," my grandmother, an accomplished gardener, used to say. She made light of a number of remarkable accomplishments, like turning clay into fertile ground. She gave the honor to God. Whenever people praised her, she found it hard to believe they would make such a fuss over produce that clearly came from the bounty bestowed by a loving God. She would smile and accept graciously her neighbors' compliments, but the fuss they made was funny to her. What mattered was making them happy, giving away all but what she needed for the family.

Signs of the Shift From Pride to Humility

St. John gives the following indicators to show when and if we are moving out of range of pride's explosive power into the spiritually safe zone of humility.

1. We experience docility or the ability to be taught by whomever or whatever offers us lessons for life. We become adept in meekness or the virtue of allowing ourselves to be God-molded or shaped by grace into a more perfect likeness to the one in whose image we have been made (cf. Gn 1:26-27).

2. How different docility is from the pretense that we are omniscient. When we are full of ourselves and another adult, or even a child, tries to teach us something, we snatch the words out of their mouth as if we knew what they wanted to say ahead of time. Humility resists such indelicacy.

3. Far from posturing their importance, humble persons have to be called forth by the community to teach.

Were it up to them, they would flee, as did the desert fathers and mothers, to a sanctuary of solitude.[3] They are, moreover, ready to listen to advice and follow a different road if the one they are on takes them away from Christ.

4. It is hard for persons striving to live in humility to trust completely in their own appraisals. They tend always to consult with elders lest the illusions lurking in them due to pride gain ascendancy once more.

5. One sure sign of maturity is our capacity to rejoice and be genuinely happy when others receive praise. This is followed in short order by a renewed desire on our part to serve God as well as others seem able to do.

6. The fact is, we consider our own good deeds to be relatively insignificant and dislike anyone broadcasting them. We believe that for the most part they are not really worth mentioning—not even to a confessor or a soul friend. What would be more interesting to bring up is the number of times we have missed the mark and have had to rely totally on the mercy of God.

7. Humble people prefer to speak of their vices more than to brag about their virtues. They would rather seek direction from an objective person who concentrates less on what they do and more on who they are.

Such pure and simple souls, in St. John's experience, are pleasing to God. They become epiphanies of the Most High, messengers of the Beyond, without knowing it. They are temples of the Holy Spirit, content to live the hidden life of Jesus of Nazareth. God moves these good people to decrease so that Christ in them, their true treasure, may increase and manifest himself to others, not because of their importance but because he is greater than their imperfections. Such is the grace God gives to the humble.

Witnesses to This Way

Such people seem to attract to themselves like-minded others. Is this not the story of great founders of religious orders and spiritual guides like Francis of Assisi in medieval times and Francis Libermann in the modern era? Around them people gathered to serve God and to show others how to grow beyond self-centeredness. From accounts of their lives,[4] we learn that when they did make a mess of things, as the best of us are wont to do, they did not turn their mistakes into tragic dramas. They suffered what occurred with humility and docility. St. Francis, for example, had to apologize at the end of his life to "Brother Ass," his body, for having treated it so harshly. He was fearful that others would imitate his actions without having received the grace that prompted him to such austerity. What matters most are such attitudes as awe before God and hope in his promises, dispositions of the heart the saints wanted their followers to emulate.

Few seekers learn as quickly as these saints did to root their spiritual lives in the fertile soil of humility. The tentacles of pride spread far and wide. It is like a giant octopus. Pride strangles initiatives and tempts us to feel complacent in the face of this or that accomplishment; it prompts us to cling to the lie of self-salvation; it weakens our reliance on grace while we continue to presume on God's mercy; it dampens the desire to give ourselves to the service of God without advertising our accomplishments.

These are a few of the reasons why more radical measures are required. In due course, St. John concludes, the time will come for "God [to place] these souls in the dark night so as to purify them of these imperfections and make them advance" (DN I:2 [8]).

4

The Triple Trap of Avarice, Lust, and Anger

(*The Dark Night*, Book One, Chapters 3, 4, 5)

I remember a woman in our neighborhood who could never throw anything away. Her parents, middle-class people who had survived the Great Depression, had instilled in her a save-and-conserve mentality. This collector tendency led to a full-blown character disorder. She was full of fears. Everyone who came to the door was thought to be a potential thief. People were sent by the devil to persecute her because they envied her possessions. An avaricious streak dense as a vein of coal made her reluctant to share so much as a glass of water with a stranger. We neighbors tried to be kind, but she was suspicious of our attention. Her only goal in life was to guard her precious things. When she died, the police found her body wedged between paths in her apartment created by piles and piles of old newspapers and magazines, pathetic evidence of her inability to part with anything.

Avaricious Deformation

This example of a person's greedy grasp of tangible possessions may shed light on why St. John of the Cross targets as a great obstacle to spiritual growth the capital vice of avarice. This deformative disposition counteracts the nonpossessive, detached posture of a pilgrim seeking to discard excess baggage so as to run freely and swiftly to God. Avarice also breeds in one's heart, like bacteria in toxic waste, a nervous discontent. No matter how many blessings God sends one's way, there is no peace in the avaricious person.

Clinging to every consolation, collecting spiritual feelings as if they were souvenirs of bygone days, these barriers to grace begin to occupy most of one's time. Just as a child who receives a toy, after assuring his harassed parents it is all he ever wants, plays with it for a few days and then begs for the next gadget advertised on TV, so collectors of spiritual goods desire to possess more of the same.

Discontent prevails because one clearly places more value on the consolations of God than on the God who consoles. One does not see spiritual goods as pointers to the divine giver but as ends in themselves, as status symbols associated with self-declared advancements in sanctity. Spiritually avaricious people, despite their claims to the contrary, never seem happy. They are not content with the gains and losses that come their way from the hand of God. The more they brag about being the recipients and possessors of lavish blessings, the less they exude deep transcendent peace. On the contrary, as St. John says, they are "peevish because they don't find the consolation they want in spiritual things" (DN I:3 [1]).

Once, after having given a talk at a conference on spirituality open to the public, I went into the cafeteria to have a cup of coffee. Two people who turned out to be brother and sister approached me with gleaming eyes to report that for the past two years they had been traveling around the country in their van to see for themselves every site where reported apparitions of the Blessed Virgin Mary had occurred. With them they had a large plastic box that contained dried blades of grass, small stones, scrapings from asphalt pavements, and other assorted trinkets they reverenced as one would first-class relics. All the items had been collected, stored in the box, and carefully labeled. They had at least ten more trips planned for the coming year.

I thought of these two "eager religious beavers" in the context of St. John's cautions pertaining to spiritual greed. Clearly their box of apparitional paraphernalia was a prized possession. They said, "For no amount of money in the world would we part with it."

My impression was that they felt far advanced in the spiritual life. They would have been sorely offended had I suggested that they suffered from a typical imperfection of beginners. In the saint's words, they "... never have enough of hearing counsels, or learning spiritual maxims, or keeping them and reading books about them" (DN I:3 [1]). There was no doubt in my mind that the box of "relics" they showed me was more important to these seekers than any form of self-denial. Neither of them took time to verify the validity of a sighting. They jumped in their van and drove to the "holy place" as soon as possible after "it" had happened.

I ventured to ask what the poverty of spirit, about which I had been speaking that morning, meant to them. They appreciated Jesus' blessing of the poor in spirit and his promise that they would see God. Wasn't that the same as seeing apparitions? Didn't it prove that they had been the recipients of special graces? Everything in the box was worthy of veneration, wasn't it?

Grasping, Greedy Hearts

Hearing the intensity of their voices, I knew my cautions would go unheeded. The contents of the box had become for them not merely pointers to a Higher Power but magical objects in themselves. Like the novices described by St. John, so this couple, without knowing it, suffered from "possessiveness of heart":

> ... they weigh themselves down with over-decorated images and rosaries. They now put these down, now take up others; at one moment they are exchanging, and at the next re-exchanging. Now they want this kind, now they want another. And they prefer one cross to another because of its elaborateness. Others you see who are decked out in *agnusdeis* and relics and lists of saints' names, like children in trinkets (DN I:3 [1]).[1]

The objects of one's interest, collected under the guise of spiritual avarice, pose a major obstacle to poverty of spirit. It is as if one is so discontented with *who* one is that one has to collect things to prove *that* one is.

There was an elderly lady in my parish who made and then elaborately decorated dresses and robes for a small statue of the Child Jesus. She would count and recount the articles of clothing she sewed to be sure no one had tampered with them. She even hoarded the gift of her handiwork and would share it with no one. I wonder to this day—much as I admired her talents as a seamstress—if she was aware of the inner meaning of her devotion to the Christ Child or if her only interest was to make garb so intricate that it absorbed more of her attention than the Divine Master it was meant to adorn.

It is St. John's contention that true devotion comes from a detached heart freed from avaricious claims on grace. One should know the difference between sacred objects and images and the Holy Other they represent. The fruit of interior detachment is freedom from any and all forms of inordinate attachment. One's desire for these things in themselves has to be renounced if one is to be released from the prison of possessiveness. Lacking this kind of radical letting go, one risks not reaching the higher ranges of spiritual maturity. Keeping one's eyes fixed on things rather than on the Transcendent to which they point is a stumbling block on the road to liberation.

St. John apparently knew a person who was as content to venerate a cross made out of blessed palm and held fast by a pin as one lavishly decorated. Overcoming the obstacle of avarice enabled him to attend to the true object of his devotion: Christ crucified. Another person St. John knew had a rosary made from the spinal bones of a fish. The material out of which the beads were carved had nothing to do with the efficacy of the prayers she said. In neither of these instances were the devotees so foolish as to base their devotion on avaricious attachment to special ornaments. What they valued were not these objects as such but the openness to God's grace their veneration made possible.

Greediness Blocks Friendship With God

In our time the age-old wisdom taught by St. John offers food for thought. It is sad to see how shrines at Lourdes or Fatima, Assisi or Avila, become breeding grounds for greed. Pilgrims have to fight their way through rows of buyers and sellers hawking their wares to get to the places of worship. It is tempting when avarice is so evident to attach more importance to visible reminders of piety than to invisible graces. The best cure for greedily grasping good works, says St. John, is to keep our eyes fixed only on God and on being God's friend. Of what worth are bunches of belongings if they prevent us from being united with God? Only through renunciation can we move from the confines of avarice to the freedom of self-giving. Then we become people for whom:

> Their pleasure is to know how to live for love of God or neighbor without these spiritual or temporal things. As I say, they set their eyes on the substance of interior perfection, on pleasing God and not themselves (DN I:3 [2]).

On our own it is neither possible to practice such poverty of spirit nor to implement its invitation to selfless love. We need the aid of grace. The vice of avarice often poses as a virtue. We are prone to place more value on created things than on their Creator and to call this kind of self-centeredness stewardship! That is why grace places us in the passive purgation of the dark night so that we may see the light. We are much too weak to exercise the kind of wisdom that would enable us to possess material or spiritual things while not being possessed by them.

Through our own efforts we are unable to handle the twisted logic that justifies greed. Only grace can unlock the trap of avarice. It snaps shut precisely because it disinclines us to share what we have with others. It attaches us inor-

dinately to consolations, as if they were proof of our special-
ness in God's eyes. It keeps us as complacent as "fat cats" that
only growl when they are being fed.

To let go of greed and give to others are necessary steps
on the way to the perfection of love. It is St. John's contention
that no matter how much we try to overcome this obstacle
on our own we cannot actively purify our hearts from the
stain of avarice. This purgation is a gift. The fire that cleanses
us may be dark, but it gives off warmth and light. It is of this
paradox that the saint promises to speak in upcoming chapters (cf. DN I:3 [3]).

Lustful Addictions to Spiritual Feelings

If spiritual avarice promotes, among other things, inordinate attachment to images rather than admiration for their
divine source, then spiritual lust, an equally great obstacle to
union, fosters the proclivity to be possessive of sensual experiences of the sacred. In short, one who is spiritually lustful
tends to reduce love's longings for God to the senses rather
than lifting the senses chastely and respectfully to God. Lust
of this sort often leads one to a fever pitch of fanatic fervor.
How does this happen and why is it so addictive?

Because we are a body-mind-spirit unity, it is not unusual
for us to feel sensual stirrings in the midst of spiritual exercises. When one is falling in love with God, when one like the
Samaritan woman is learning to worship in spirit and in truth
(cf. Jn 4:4-42), one can hardly prevent the arousal of sensual
affections. These might include feelings of warmth, short
intakes of breath, fleeting waves of emotion. This can happen
bodily when we are spiritually in the stillness of contemplative prayer or when we are receiving the sacrament of
penance or meditating after reception of the eucharist. St.
John calls these movements "impure," not because they are
mean or dirty but because they may slow down our ascent
to God in purity of heart. These feelings may arise from any
one of three causes:

1. *Sensory Gratification.* This occurs every time we eat a good meal, sleep deeply, lose a few pounds, hug someone. We may derive similar pleasure from a silent retreat, a slowly read passage from scripture, a moment of intimate and intense prayer. Our senses and our spirits are uplifted and refreshed by such exercises and experiences, some more so and some less, depending on which part of our nature is touched. Our spirit, our higher or transcendent "I," to use a term of Adrian van Kaam, aspires to God, soaring upward in delight as would a pilot whose glider plane catches a thermal current and takes off like a bird in flight. How marvelous it feels to be in the company of our good and loving God.

This feeling flows naturally into our lower or pretranscendent self and therein, suggests van Kaam, lies a potential problem. It would be comparable to what happens when distilled water, freed of all impurities, is mixed with water running from a faucet. While actively engaged in prayer, a well-meaning person may be surprised, displeased, and upset when he or she passively, without willing it, feels the upsurge of a sensual desire for physical love or imagines a sexual encounter or remembers some impure acts or movements for which one has long ago repented.

St. John says this very thing happens frequently at the time of holy communion (cf. DN I:4 [2]). Reception of the eucharist evokes joy and gladness, for we are immersed in an exchange of love, in a heart-to-heart encounter with Christ, who grants this grace and freely gives himself to us as our lover, savior, friend. In this exchange, our senses find their own level of satisfaction. One may experience a welling up of tears or a flush of warmth and peace. We are, insists the saint, a unity of body and soul. What we receive is, therefore, appropriate to the mode of its reception.

Our spirit may be inspired by the Holy Spirit, for example, to persevere in fidelity to the promises we made to God while, for whatever reason, our bodily senses may feel, as far as this intention is concerned, both dry and exhausted.

The difficulty St. John addresses does not concern these natural movements in themselves but the imperfect response to what occurs in the sensory dimension of our human life form. We can unwittingly start to lust after spiritual feelings, attaching much too much importance to them. We can make them signs of progress instead of passing phases that flood the minds and hearts of beginners as well as those who are advanced.

These imperfections influence our receptivity to grace. Because grace builds on nature, the sensory part of our being must be reformed through the purgation of the dark night. Like fire deliberately set to clear and cultivate a field, so the passive night of the senses purifies us of these infirmities and initiates a necessary reversal:

> Then the spiritual part of the soul rather than the sensory part receives God's spirit, and the soul [the whole person] thus receives everything according to the mode of the spirit (DN I:4 [2]).

To use van Kaam's terms, transformation by grace enables our pretranscendent vital and functional spheres to become servants of the transcendent. In the process un-spiritual lust loosens its grip on our capacity to follow the leadings of grace rather than our own grandiosity.

2. *Demonic Seduction.* There may be times when we would like to dismiss or demythologize altogether the reality of the demonic, but sheer observation of the human condition and of our own state of being makes us think twice. While the violence and unrest reported in the headlines ought to be enough to convince us that something is amiss, the surest validation of the presence of the Tempter is the turmoil we feel within—what St. John terms "rebellions." The saint is aware of how subtly the devil plays upon our own coercive obsessions, especially in the realm of vitalistic drives and passions. A prime time for attack is when we are at prayer. The onslaught of disquieting thoughts, disturbing images, and the excitation of sensual feelings, memories, and

fantasies seems to proliferate. To pay attention to these is to open the portals of our already fallen hearts to the wiles of the fallen one, whose only intention is to do us great harm.

These inner battles are exhausting and confusing to beginners. They are duped into believing that their cause is not demonic seduction but praying as such. Fearing what goes on in their minds when they try to meditate, they grow slack in their devotions, thus playing right into the devil's hands. Others, also trying to avoid the warfare within, commit the grave mistake of giving up on prayer entirely. Observing that such lustful feelings seem to worsen when they pray, they conclude it is best to stop.

Teresa of Avila had to cope with this seductive distortion in her own prayer life. She tells of her decision to persevere in spite of the devil's insidious suggestion that prayer itself was her problem:

> This was the most terrible trick the devil could play on me, under the guise of humility: that seeing myself so corrupted I began to fear the practice of prayer. It seemed to me that, since in being wicked I was among the worst, it was better to go the way of the many, to recite what I was obliged to vocally and not to practice mental prayer and so much intimacy with God, for I merited to be with the devils. And it seems to me that I was deceiving people since exteriorly I kept up such good appearances. Thus the convent where I resided was not at fault. For in my craftiness I strove to be held in esteem, although I did not advertently feign Christianity. In this matter of hypocrisy and vainglory, praise God, I don't recall ever having offended him knowingly, because at the first urgings I felt so much sorrow that the devil ended up with a loss and I with a gain. And so in this matter he never tempted me very much. Perhaps if God had permitted me to be tempted in this regard as severely as in other things, I would also have fallen.

> But his Majesty up till now has preserved me in this. May He be blessed forever! Rather, I grieved very much over being held in esteem since I knew what was down deep in my heart.[2]

As St. Teresa discovered, the devil is prone to excite waves of lusty illusions exactly when one is at prayer and hence less functionally occupied than when one is busy with work. The end result of the seduction would be to convince one to abandon prayer. Thus, in the name of expelling lustful thoughts and desires, one cuts oneself off from the grace that alone can quell them and rechannel this libidinal energy upward in aspirations for the sacred.

The thoughts upon which the Tempter plays roam free and wild. Some concern spiritual consolations; others focus on affections for counselors who have been of help. Instead of setting these perusings aside and returning to peaceful prayer, one tries to resist them directly, not daring to look at anything or to think lovingly of anyone. This harsh exercise in self-protection proves to be futile. The more we fight such distractions the less likely are they to dissipate. By contrast, the more we let go of flights of fancy and rely on grace, the closer we come to dampening the fires of lust.

The alternative is extremely disconcerting. So affected are some persons by the number and kind of impure thoughts that plague them that they sink into self-pity, anger, and despondency. They are afflicted by what the diagnostics of St. John's day termed "melancholia." He must have encountered many such sad cases in his hours of direction, for he writes of them with great compassion. So profound is their suffering and sense of remorse over what they may foolishly conclude is an unforgivable sin, that beginners forfeit their freedom. They start to believe that the devil has access to their free will and that they have no power to resist or prevent this invasion. They become obsessed by the seductive insinuations of an alien power that continues its attack despite the intensity of one's efforts to resist.

It is as if one is caught in a triple bind: the thoughts that one would keep hidden from God are the same thoughts that one must turn over to God though they make one feel utterly abject and worthless before God. Freedom from the shackles of such melancholia is unlikely, concludes the saint, unless God leads one, with all one's sadness and confusion, into the dark night. There grace flows into the farthest recesses of one's heart, depriving it of its capacity to dwell on anything but God, and casting aside—as one would useless trash— any thoughts or temptations the devil deploys to stop this ascent.

3. *Fear of Feelings.*   As if this battle with the demonic were not enough to exhaust one thoroughly, one must cope with yet another onslaught, namely, the upsurge of impure feelings aroused by the very fear one has of them. This fear can be so great it erodes one's faith and prevents one from placing personal weaknesses before God for healing and forgiveness. Just when one thinks the warfare has subsided, the thoughts against which one has inwardly fought loom up, evoking the anxiety that no progress has been made. Rather than accepting the remembrance of past mistakes in equanimity, relying upon the ever present infinite mercy of God, one becomes self-accusative, thereby restarting the vicious cycle of discouragement, depression, and demonic seduction.

The fault which concerns St. John has less to do with sin as such and more with the delicate constitution of people for whom consolations received in prayer immediately arouse pleasurable, corporeal feelings to which they become inordinately attached. Hence,

> they immediately experience a lust that so inebriates them and caresses their senses that they become as it were engulfed in the delight and satisfaction of that vice ... (DN I:4 [5]).

It may be that involuntary arousals in the sexual sphere occur simultaneously with the spiritual uplifts one receives.

The accuracy of St. John's analysis seems to indicate that he has dealt with persons whose biological make-up ("their humors and blood") are whipped into a frenzy of sorts by any change. He notes similar reactions when they are angry or agitated by other disruptions or afflictions.

Such volatile characters need wise and balanced, gentle yet firm, spiritual guidance if their energetic temperaments are to be channeled in the direction of theocentric love rather than reduced to the exercise of egocentric lust. The master observes how troubleshooters tend to show off when carrying on spiritual conversations or doing good works. They exhibit their dramatic gifts in calculated ways, depending on whomever is present. They take vain satisfaction in the impression they make. St. Teresa's description of the nuns entertaining knights in the parlor of the convent of the Incarnation is a classic rendition of this facet of spiritual lust. As she writes in her autobiography:

> Now then, I engaged in these conversations thinking that since this was the custom, my soul would not receive the harm and distraction I afterward understood comes from such companionship. It seemed to me that something as general in many monasteries as this visiting would not do me any more harm than it did others who I saw were good. I did not consider that they were much better and that what was a danger for me was not so much so for others, for I doubted that there was always some kind of danger—but at least there was some waste of time. While I was once with a person, the Lord at the outset of our acquaintance desired to make me understand that those friendships were not proper for me and to counsel and give me advice in the midst of such thorough blindness.
>
> With great severity, Christ appeared before me, making me understand what He regretted about the friendship. I saw Him with the eyes of my soul

more clearly than I could have with the eyes of my body. And this vision left such an impression on me that, though more than twenty-six years have gone by, it seems to me it is still present. I was left very frightened and disturbed, and didn't want to see that person any more.[3]

Appraising the Origins of Spiritual Lust

All such actions are for St. John by-products of spiritual lust. This grave obstacle to union with God "generally accompanies complacency of the will" (DN I:4 [6]). It is a short step from such apparently innocent flirtations to the more serious mistake of playing favorites. Then one begins to acquire, albeit innocently, a spiritual affinity to or liking for a particular individual, another sister, a confessor, a visitor. Such attractions, however naively begun, may become more and more preoccupying. One may refer to them as gifts of God, only the God who gave them is soon given second place to the attraction. According to St. John, such liaisons are more often than not lustful rather than purely spiritual in origin. How does one know what is really happening? The criterion for appraisal is clear:

> This lustful origin will be recognized if, on recalling that affection, there is remorse of conscience, not an increase in the remembrance and love of God (DN I:4 [7]).

The opposite is true when one's affection, let us say for a friend, is uplifting, inspiring, and spiritual. A sure test of transcendence is that this human love fosters growth in the love of God. When one thinks of the beloved or remembers graced moments together, one thanks God for this gift and loves the divine giver all the more. This human love, wonderful as it is, evokes in one a deeper desire for God, who alone can fulfill the longing of the human heart. Thus by growing in spiritual friendship, to use this example, one grows in friendship with God.

Like attracts like. Good increases as the goodness of God's spirit is offered room in us to grow. When love loses its God-oriented course, lust may take the reins with contrary effects. The greater the sensual vice, the less room there is for God's spirit to guide us from within.

When remembrance of God as good and loving begins to fade, inordinate attachments to "lesser gods" are likely to increase. Soon enough the embers of God's eternal embrace turn into ashes. The heart grows as cold as a frozen waterfall. The love one once felt for God is forgotten as the remembrance of other loves gains ground. Moments of remorse flash before the mind's eye like neon signs seen from the window of a moving train, but the temptation of lust is too powerful to resist. If left unchecked, this vice can wipe away all but the firmest traces of pure love.

Yet St. John is not without hope. It is never too late to turn our life around. We must return to God, repent, and acknowledge our need for help. We must detonate the tough walls of willfulness we have built around our hearts. Love wants to lead us back to the land of likeness. As soon as we let go of our selfish agendas and offer God our love, something freeing happens. What grows cold are the lustful affections that kept us from God. Compared to where we are being led by God, what used to preoccupy our attention is gladly relinquished. Our inner self senses a lessening of this spiritual battle, but it is only the dark night that can put these loves in proper order. What this night does is to strengthen the love we have for God while putting in their place the lesser loves lust has duped us into making ultimate.

Deformations Due to Spiritual Anger

For beginners this kind of purification can be a sobering experience. In fact, it is likely to arouse a third tempting trap: that of spiritual anger. Its arousal is directly proportionate to the Spirit's urging that one give up the strong desire for consolations as if these were the trademarks of holiness. It is inevitable as one moves toward Christian maturity that one has to accept the passing nature of initial uplifts and delights. Just because the savor of spirituality is less spicy, it does not mean that the meal God offers is any less nourishing. Quite the contrary is true. When Christ carried his cross, he was bereft of felt satisfactions. He was neither sensually nor spiritually consoled. Hanging in disgrace, he acknowledged the pain of feeling abandoned by God (cf. Mt 27:46), but this only served to strengthen his pledge of obedience to the Father.

When anger replaces appreciation, no peace is possible. Hence spiritually angry persons become peevish. They are impatient and upset by the least thing. Nothing seems to satisfy them. They become unbearable in family, parish, or community. Few can put up with them suggests St. John, especially if and when they experience some pleasant sensation in prayer. Immediately they focus on it, and then feel angry at themselves and God when in a short while the sensory resonance ceases and they are left "vapid and zestless, just as a child is when withdrawn from the sweet breast" (DN I:5 [1]).

The feeling of being abandoned by God is not pleasant, but it does pass provided we imitate Christ and abandon ourselves to the Mystery.[4] We must not give in to the "demons" of discouragement, dejection, and depression. These three "D s" sap our courage. They weaken our will to choose the abundant life Jesus promised us—the life of encouragement, trust, and hope. It is because these "D s" put up such strong defenses against the appeal of the Spirit that we must be led by God into "the dryness and distress of the dark night" (DN I:5 [1]).

There is another deformation due to spiritual anger that can be particularly fatal in a community. This facet has about it the self-righteousness Jesus condemned in the Pharisees. It is named by the saint "indiscreet zeal." An angry, holierthan-thou type of person would be inclined to lash out at others and to judge them harshly because of their sins. Like a volcano spouting lava, such people feel obliged at every turn to angrily admonish sinners while at the same time placing themselves on pedestals of virtue. They behave without any spiritual meekness whatsoever. Angry would-be saints cannot be messengers of the mercy of God. The wrath of their own need to feel superior causes them to arouse in already weakened people debilitating fears of a tyrannical God they have somehow irredeemably offended.

It is likely, predicts St. John, that the tables will one day turn. The anger so viciously directed at others will backlash upon oneself. Behind this obstacle lurks the bully of perfectionism. One feels increasingly incensed by the simplest faults and failings. Such people become angry with themselves. No matter how hard they try it is never enough. They are forever driven to whip themselves into shape with an "unhumble impatience," to use St. John's term. In fact, he says, "So impatient are they about these imperfections that they would want to become saints in a day" (DN I:5 [3]).

How to Temper Spiritual Anger

Self-anger, if not anger at God, stirs up a veritable soup of distress when a proliferating list of plans, projects, and spiritual resolutions fails to materialize. Lacking humility and the wisdom to rely on grace rather than on their own compulsion to be perfect, such people start to distrust themselves as much as to wonder if God really intends to answer their prayers. Like a dieter who goes up and down on the scale, "the more resolves they make the more they break" (DN I:5 [3]). This futile course ends in failure and fuels spiritual anger. It grinds down like grain in a mill the gentle posture of patient presence. One refuses to wait upon God's will in love and trust until such time as God shows one what to do and where to go on his or her walk of faith.

Until spiritual anger can be tempered by meekness, until one allows himself or herself to once more be molded and formed by God—as a potter works pliant clay—one cannot hope to make much progress. Thus the remedy one needs can only be found in the purgation of a dark night experience.

Here the balance will return between zealously running after felt signs of progress and patiently waiting, often in dryness, upon the Word. In some persons the thermometer of zeal has to be lowered lest the steam of anger shoot forth like a geyser; in others the flame of love has to be relit in the darkness of the night.

5

Debilitating Obstacles of Spiritual Gluttony, Envy, and Sloth

(*The Dark Night*, Book One, Chapters 6 and 7)

Because eating can be so pleasurable, we attribute to it great importance, both socially and from the viewpoint of sheer physical survival. Film masterpieces like *Babette's Feast* portray with wit and pathos the connection between savoring abundant food and celebrating self-revelatory togetherness around a table.

The film depicts the unpretentious lives of Martina and Phillipa, two sisters, pledged to keep alive the memory of their minister father and to maintain the faith community he had begun years ago. Weekly they serve to the sullen gathering of simple faithful a dense, sour broth with black bread, a fitting symbol of their usually joyless mood. One evening there comes a knock on the door. It is Babette, a French woman, a refugee, seeking shelter and in need of work. The sisters take her into their house as a servant and teach her to cook and serve the terrible soup. She does so humbly, fitting into their lives for ten long years, showing the humility of a lowly servant who does not complain when she is excluded from their table. Her unassuming presence is a silent source of edification, her joy often the only bright light in their day. Then comes the extraordinary news that she has won a lottery in her home country yielding 10,000 francs, a small fortune. The sisters are sure she will leave them, for her new wealth can set her free.

Instead of departing as mysteriously as she had come, Babette decides to prepare for her new friends and family a feast, the likes of which they had never seen. It will be in honor of their dead father's memory. She imports every imaginable delicacy from France—from turtles to truffles—and invites townspeople to the banquet table. There a transformation takes place. A slow release of the spirit occurs in synchronization with each course that delights the palate. By evening's end the conversation is flowing as freely as the champagne and cordials. When the guests depart they cannot contain the enjoyment they feel in one another's company. In the courtyard under a starry sky old and young, woman and man, join hands, circle in dance, and sing hymns to the goodness of God.

Exhausted in the kitchen, Babette can feel nothing but the contentment of a cook who has fed her guests in body, mind, and spirit. The sisters, however, feel sad because they know she will now depart. Then Babette announces matter-of-factly that she has spent all the money she won on the feast. The sisters are stunned. They tell her she will once again be destitute and dependent. With dignity in her voice, Babette reveals the deep truth that an artist is never poor.

In the theater where I saw the film, there was not a dry eye in the house. Everyone broke into spontaneous applause. Human goodness had won over gluttony and greed.

Deceptive Grip of Gluttonous Gratification

Addiction to food, physically speaking, can be comparable to clinging to spiritual goods as if one's prayer life depended on finding fulfillment on this lower level of gratification. Spiritual gluttony, according to St. John of the Cross, is a serious obstacle to advancement in Christian maturity. It is a vice few, if any, beginners can avoid. It erects a formidable wall that blocks our walk of faith. It contains as many traps as a magician's bag of tricks.

As with any addiction, be it to food or to a chemical substance, the attraction one feels to spiritual food is deceptive. How could something so bad for you make you feel, at least momentarily, so good? Whereas the consequences can be disastrous, the course we take to satisfy an addiction can be a delight, albeit a deceptive one. Why should a glutton stop at one dish of chocolate fudge ice cream when he or she can prolong the fun by consuming an entire quart? If one drink gives an alcoholic a lift, why not down a few more shots and stay high? Addiction is dangerous for many reasons but surely one is that it pushes a person toward higher and higher levels of tolerance. One needs larger amounts of the substance in question to feel "good."

By way of analogy, St. John applies the dynamics of psycho-physical addiction to the experience of beginners inebriated with the consolations they receive at the start of a serious spiritual life. People caught in the grip of such gluttony are prone to use religious practices to procure as a first aim the warm glow that makes them feel as if they are advancing in sanctity.

Just as the phenomenon of tolerance brings one to the point where the substance imbibed no longer gives one the same buzz and hence one needs more of it to get high, so are upstarts on the way to union inclined to want to "up the dosage" of consolations. Their tendency is to "strive more for spiritual savor than for spiritual purity and discretion" (DN I:6 [1]). They forget that the journey homeward is not about pleasing self but about serving God in purity of heart. What they ought to concentrate on is the detection of hindrances to union. What they ought to do is to call on God continually for help.

Learning to Recognize Spiritual Gluttony and Let Go

Just as addicts must learn that no person or thing can satisfy them totally, so beginners on the way must learn to make relative even the loftiest spiritual feelings, consolations, and delights. One acknowledges God's gracious granting of these favors while letting them go. To absolutize their importance, to make them the be-all and end-all of the life of the spirit, is to place oneself in the position of going to any extreme to procure them.

Say that every time Mary Jo feels alone she finds an excuse to eat. As long as her mouth is full, she feels worthwhile. Though she hates herself when she gains weight, in the throes of her irrational need for food she will do whatever it takes—from hiding cookies to eating on the sly—to indulge her addiction.

No tip at the track, however much of a long shot, seems unreasonable to Guy, an addicted gambler. The thought that he will win this time, if not the next, drives him to the betting window. As he passes his last ten dollar bill to the teller, he is beyond the bounds of reason. The urge that maybe this is it gets the best of him.

Spiritual gluttons behave in a similar fashion. They violate the happy medium in which virtue resides and in the light of which lasting joy is attained. Such people will go to any lengths to fulfill their drive to attain felt consolations. Their search for spiritual highs unleashes the hooks of attachment and catapults them toward whatever promises the uplift they need as a sure sign of God's favor. In the first blush of their enthusiasm, no demand is too difficult: excessive mortifications, self-inflicted penances, physically debilitating fasts that further weaken them—all are condoned as legitimate avenues to consolation.

Like drug users who try to hide their supply or alcoholics who keep emergency bottles in shoe boxes, so people who push against the pace of grace by virtue of their own penitential efforts become adept at concealing what they are doing from their confessors or counselors. Denial is second nature to them. Though they owe obedience to their guides, they prefer to listen only to the urgency they feel to behave independently and to effect the false nirvana that nourishes their pride. It becomes easy after a while to rationalize even masochistic behavior under the rubric of piety and to scoff at anyone who might suggest that such actions are contrary to obedience. The voices of addiction are stronger than the whispers of divine wisdom.

Just as addicts who live in denial listen to no one but themselves, so spiritual gluttons close their ears to messages contrary to what they want to hear. How could what they are doing be wrong when it makes them feel so holy? They argue aloud and to themselves, and they have the evidence to prove it, that they are on the way to perfection. Rather than practice the "penance of reason and discretion" that is "pleasing and acceptable to God" (DN I:6 [2]), such "penitents" prefer following their own will. They take on penances contrary to the rules of a church or a community. They reject the wisdom of experienced spiritual guides and practice what St. John castigates as the "penance of beasts." Their main motivation, whether they know it or not, is not pain but pleasure. The latter drives them to go from one aberrant extreme to the other. It is likely that in his time the saint knew about lay and religious flagellants, who derived perverse pleasure from beating themselves "for Christ's sake."

Gluttonous Addictions and the Demonic

Such extreme asceticism, often done without direction or in defiance of it, is nothing but an expression of willful pride. What portends to promote virtue becomes a vice that is both deceptive and dangerous. Spiritually gluttonous types cannot control their twisted reasonings and bizarre behavior. They become as proud of their accomplishments as would addicts who successfully mask their efforts to stay high. In both cases one shuns the solid wisdom of experienced guides in favor of defending, as virtuous, attitudes and actions that are inherently destructive.

It ought to come as no surprise that the saint finds the devil lurking in wait to deceive and confuse one even more. The Tempter is like a crooked vendor who sells rotten candy in gaily wrapped covers. It looks fresh but if you eat enough of it you're going to be sick.

Spiritual delights, euphoric feelings, and ecstatic consolations are not meant to be lasting. They can, however,
capture one's attention and become ends in themselves.
What more could the Evil One want? Such gluttony compels
one to guard jealously his or her source of supply. One
becomes secretive so as to avoid out- and- out disobedience.
The devil rejoices when initiates who think they know best
are inclined to add more sacrifices, penances, and fastings to
those already specified in their rule of life. To be sure that
they are deriving from their prayers the maximum amount
of inspiration, they may assume what appears to be a more
mortified posture, for instance, prostrating themselves on the
floor rather than kneeling. Such postures soon become more
the focus of their attention than God.

Such disobedience plays into the devil's hands. It compels spiritual adolescents to determine autonomously how
to fulfill their desire for holiness at any price. Any appeal or
command from superiors to normalize their religious fervor
is dismissed as a misunderstanding of what God wants. Soon
the obligation to be obedient seems to be the cause of their
dryness. Unwittingly they become victims of demonic seduction. Now they dismiss themselves from one devotion, now
the next. They flit from this plan of piety to the other like
hapless sparrows seeking crumbs. St. John concludes that the
"only yearning and satisfaction [such self-sufficient types
seek] is to do what they feel inclined to do, whereas it would
be better in all likelihood for them not to do this at all" (DN
I:6 [2]).

Self as the Center for Spiritual Gluttons

The cleverness of addicts, the energy they use to enable
the sickness in mind or body that may destroy them, is
staggering. They will go to any length to prove how right
they are. Similarly, mustering the full force of their self-sufficient pseudo-spirituality, spiritual gluttons will, at first passively, then more aggressively, insist that their spiritual
directors give them free rein to respond to what they call the

promptings of grace. They do not rest until they literally wrest from superiors the permissions they demand. If they do not get the go-ahead they seek, like addicts everywhere, they put on pensive faces expecting others to feel sorry for them. In short order, they become pushy and irritable, so complaining and testy that those in charge will do almost anything to make them go away or be still.

Such types end up as the epicenter of an individual's or a community's attention. Their defenses are such that they manage to convince themselves and others that their eternal salvation is at stake if they do not get their way. When opposition arises, they double their efforts, being at one moment sullen, at another loud. St. John's description of this neurotic style could not be more accurate:

> Since they take gratification and their own will as their support and their god, they become sad, weak, and discouraged when their director takes these from them and desires that they do God's will. They think that gratifying and satisfying themselves is serving and satisfying God (DN I:6 [3]).

Though spiritual gluttons pretend to know more about the life of the spirit than their masters, they are ignorant of their own pushy pride. The taste of sweetness blocks admission of their own need for divine mercy. Respect for the grandeur of God pales in comparison to their gluttony for glory.

A sign of this vice in St. John's time, in which the reception of the host was restricted, was linked to the request to receive holy communion more frequently or to do so without the permission of a priest. Typical of this fault, as in the case of any addiction, was the penchant to be guided solely by one's own opinion. If this meant fabricating a story to get one's way, so be it. As long as one received the sacrament and sought the feelings one wanted to derive from it, one did not attend to whether or not he or she approached the altar with a pure heart.

For one caught in the trap of addiction, the end justifies the means one takes to reach it. Spiritual gluttons learn to tell lies. It is nothing for them to shop around for careless confessors. The discipline of detachment is beyond one at this juncture of the journey. To forego the object of one's gratification, to resist the first urgings of an addiction, is a step yet to be taken—one impossible to accomplish without God's help. Unfortunately, the grip of gluttony is stronger still than the desire for release.

Questions for Reflection

I have put in the form of a "Test Yourself Questionnaire" the signs St. John gives of one who is entrapped in this way. Take time to be still. Place yourself in the presence of God, then ask:

1. When I am engaged in spiritual exercises as common as receiving the eucharist or as special as fasting under the guidance of church law, do I try to derive from these efforts good feelings or secret satisfactions as my first aim?

2. Am I more prone to focus on what these acts are doing for me rather than on the praise and reverence due to God on whose indwelling grace I am wholly dependent?

3. What if I do not get anything out of the exercise, if instead of feeling delightful I feel dry as dust? Am I then inclined to give up or to think I have accomplished nothing?

4. Do I assume that God thinks as poorly of me as I think of myself if I do not receive sensory benefits, for example, every time I receive holy communion?

5. Do I trust in the greater blessings of invisible grace or do I make felt consolations and sensory feelings the gauge of my spiritual growth?

6. Does it ever occur to me that God withdraws such pleasures so that I might focus with eyes of faith on the hidden efficacy of grace more than on my own gains?

7. Do I secretly want to master the Mystery instead of letting the Mystery master me? Do I "desire to feel God and taste him as if he were comprehensible and accessible" (DN I:6 [5])? Do I need to prove myself worthy of being loved or can I accept on faith that God is the God of my life, however undeserving of this grace I may feel?

These same seven questions can be applied to the life of prayer. Beginners of any age are prone to equate a good prayer life with feeling something in the sensory sphere. Dry devotions hardly seem to be avenues to transcendence. Rather than trusting grace to do the leading, one doubles up efforts to make something happen. One comes to believe, wrongly, that some sign of spiritual efficacy is better than none. In fact, appreciative abandonment to nothing but God is the surest way to pull away from the deceptive chambers of sensible comforts as if these were necessary signs of sanctity.

Endless Cravings for Satisfaction

To remain on this immature plane of spirituality is to risk becoming disgruntled and despondent in the very pursuit of divine inspiration. To try so hard is to fail. It is to think and feel that one has done nothing to please God. It is to sink into the low-grade depression that surrounds depreciative people like rancid air. They are full of resentment because things never seem to go their way. Caught in a seemingly endless cycle of elation and despair, it is no wonder that they lose true devotion, lack zest for living, distrust themselves, and cease to persevere in humility and patience.

By trying so tenaciously to please God, one paradoxically drifts farther away from God. A dangerous reversal then occurs: That toward which one once felt delight now becomes repugnant. What used to evoke zeal is now approached with extreme reluctance. As soon as the pleasure

disappears, one is disinclined to stay on the path ordained
by grace. Instead gluttons look for new sources of gratification. Ends become means, and the cycle repeats itself.

Such may occur in the case of someone who has had a
genuine spiritual awakening. Never in her life had Gail felt
so grand. It was as if in a lightning flash all dullness disappeared. She felt drawn heavenward on eagle's wings. The
experience was unforgettable. Instead of being grateful for
its effects, she longed to repeat them. She told others what
happened to her, hoping they would not be envious yet liking
the interest her story aroused and the admiration she saw in
their eyes. She told herself to remain humble while praying
that God would give her another sign that she was a person
favored by the Most High. Rather than allowing grace to lead
her further along the road to spiritual maturity, Gail became
addicted to reading the signs that only mark that one is on
the way. She could not satisfy her gluttony for "otherworld-
ly" nourishment. No sooner had she made one retreat than
she booked another. She felt obliged to follow any program
that promised growth in intimacy with God. To miss her
prayer meeting was unthinkable, even if it meant that her
husband had to do all the cooking and the cleaning. Seldom
if ever did she allow herself a quiet moment for reflection.
She felt unfed by anything less than a whole library of
popular books on spirituality. Like a taste-tester on a fast-
food assembly line, Gail flitted from one topic of meditation
to the next, always in search of the elusive bird of ecstasy.

To stop this dissonance from becoming self-destructive,
to cure the glutton of his or her addiction to "gratification in
the things of God" (DN I:6 [6]), God has to direct one with
love and discretion into the place of grace St. John dubs the
dark night. Here adolescence moves toward adulthood.
Gluttons give up their craving for spiritual sweets. One
learns the wisdom of the cross. Compared to the weakening
effects of egocentric gratification, it is a true joy to tread this
rough road to union with the risen Lord. No one knew this
way better than Francis of Assisi. He understood from ex-

perience the difference between transcendent or perfect joy and pretranscendent or imperfect vital gratification and/or functional satisfaction. Here is one instance of St. Francis' choice of the cross as the royal road to consonance with Christ:

> It was at this spot, on the Feast of the Exaltation of the Holy Cross, September 14, that an extraordinary event took place. Francis, led by the Holy Spirit, prayed these words he had composed in preparation for the feast: "O Lord, I beg of you two graces before I die: to experience personally and in all possible fullness the pains of your bitter passion, and to feel for you the same love that moved you to sacrifice yourself for us."

> And as he prayed, Francis was facing east with his arms stretched out, and there, coming down from heaven, appeared a six-winged seraph. As it neared, Francis saw that it resembled a man with two wings in flight, two wings covering his body, and two wings raised above his head. And with a rush of love and pity, Francis saw that the seraph's features were those of the crucified Lord Jesus Christ, who had spoken to him from the crucifix of San Damiano so many years before and whose image he had kept emblazoned on his heart all these years.

> Love overcame him. And when he awoke, he felt blood running from an open wound in his left side and his hands were pierced with nails, their black heads protruding from his palms and their points bent over as with a hammer on the backs of his hands, so that they looked like little rings close pressed to the skin. And his feet, too, were pierced with nails, only now the heads of the nails were on his insteps and the points bent over on his soles, so that he wondered how he was going to walk. And

indeed from that moment until his death two years later, Francis walked only with the greatest of pain, and most of the time he had to be carried or travel by donkey.

Thus was it that Francis' prayer to the Crucified One was answered. He was forever sealed with the Father's only Son, Jesus Christ. And Francis became in his suffering what he already was in so many other ways, a mirror of our Savior, Jesus Christ.[1]

Graced Release From Spiritual Gluttony

We may now ask what are some signs by which we may recognize a shift taking place from dependency on spiritual delights to finding lasting consolation in the cross. The following are indicative of St. John's promise that transformation is not a distant goal but the result of our willingness to cooperate with grace and to let God do the leading:

1. I cease to feel an aversion for self-denial and trust the truth that I must take up my cross and follow the Lord of glory if I want to experience the liberation of being a son or daughter of God.

2. I know that my own efforts are useless to cure the illness of spiritual gluttony and that I must rely on the cure only the mercy of God can effect in fallen humanity.

3. I begin to understand that the temptations and trials I must undergo, along with the spells of dryness and aridity I must endure, are all part of the process of formation, reformation, and transformation being prompted by grace. I can refuse or accept this call.

4. I learn to make the right choice from watching what happens when I foster the virtues of spiritual sobriety and temperance versus succumbing to the vices of gluttony and self-indulgence.

5. I experience anew the sweet relief of living in obedience to the age-old wisdom of the spiritual

masters. I find myself more submissive to God's will disclosed through such guides and in the challenges posed by everyday life situations.

6. I find that I am better able to recognize my own profile of sinful, inordinate attachments and to practice detachment out of love for God and the desire to serve the Lord with or without the reward of lofty feelings.

7. Most of all, I see as clearly as a pilot on a moonlit night the runway on which I want to land. It is not a cracked pavement strewn with the debris of failed efforts to make myself holy. It is a smooth strip paved by grace. I want to be guided to a safe landing in the arms of God.

To reach this resting point is not the result of human effort. It is a response to a more refined call. As St. John often repeats, the value of our works does not depend on their number or on the satisfaction we might receive from them but on our knowing how to say "no" to our willful self.

Our tendency to push against the pace of grace gives way to the posture of waiting patiently upon God to bring us into the night of faith. This turning within purifies our hearts. It cracks open like eggshells the deceptive veneer of illusory projects of self-salvation. We experience a wonderful sense of relief. We do not have to walk this road to liberation alone. We do not have to expect to feel consoled or confirmed at every turn. We simply need to trust that God is with us and do our task. God is present to us even in times of apparent absence. This is the leap of faith that will guide us to a safe landing.

Other Faults of Beginners

We must still withstand the turbulence effected by two more obstacles: those of spiritual envy and sloth. Before turning to his discussion of the dark night proper and the way in which this grace enables us to grow in spiritual maturity,

St. John has to discuss, admittedly in a cursory fashion, two more imperfections often encountered in beginners.

To cast an envious eye on another is a frequent fault, especially when people are fixated on instant spirituality.[2] Instead of feeling happy for others who seem to be advancing along the way, one is saddened by their being the recipients of spiritual goods. If we detect such a train of thought in ourselves, it is wise to check it by means of the following questions:

1. Does it grieve me to note that another seems to be or is obviously ahead of me on the path to spiritual maturity?

2. Does it bother me to hear others praised? Do I habitually feel inclined to put them in their place?

3. Do I feel especially ambiguous when I hear about the virtuous life others are living? Do I feel a tug inside between admiring them and yet wanting to accuse them of ulterior motives?

4. When others receive a compliment, do I feel obliged to contradict what is said and to undo the praise they deserve?

5. Am I annoyed because I am not the recipient of similar commendations?

6. Do I secretly envy the self I could have been, catching a glimpse of my lost chances in the mirror of their finer style of life?

7. Do I long for and need to be shown preference in my parish, family, or community?

Relation of Envy to Charity

An affirmative response to any or all of these questions may call one to an examination of conscience in the light of the transcendent. What happens to us because of the obstacle of envy is especially problematic because it diminishes our charity. As St. Paul insists, we ought to rejoice in goodness under whatever guise it appears (cf. 1 Cor 13:6).

The only envy the saints condone is that dubbed "holy" because it prompts one to emulate, never to diminish, the gifts of charity beheld in another. We ought to be saddened at not having the virtues of others, says St. John, while rejoicing that they display these Christ-like dispositions so beautifully. We ought to be happy that others are ahead of us in the service of God and reprimand ourselves for still lacking the courage to give our all in the same kind of service (cf. DN I:7 [1]).

Danger of Inertia Due to Spiritual Sloth

The last, but certainly not the least, of the obstacles to discipleship St. John tackles is that of spiritual sloth. It has to do with the inertia, the lukewarmness, that blocks our ability to see a task through to the finish. How many of us start projects and leave them undone? Go down to the basement and take a look. Do you doubt as you survey the piles of work in every corner how tempting it would be to slink back upstairs in slothful bliss?

The way of perfection, as St. Teresa knew so well, takes a combination of joyful labor and utter reliance on God's help. Understandably we grow weary. When the honeymoon of a relationship wanes and the routines of marriage take over, one often wants to run away to greener pastures. Similarly, it is difficult to stick to our spiritual exercises when our efforts seem to be useless and progress slows to a snail's pace. We expect to find the lush grass of new sensory satisfactions when all that awaits us is the dry dust of boring routines. With every diminishment of delight, we may have to resist the temptation to give up. What is the use of trying, we may ask. It seems as if nothing is happening to us either inwardly or outwardly. We question if our desire for union with God could be fulfilled in ten lifetimes.

As this depreciative track of thought accelerates, we may begin to convince ourselves that we are never going to find that for which we have sought for so long. Slowly but surely, the fires of love cool. We feel strangely indifferent to the movements of grace. If we do not reverse this downward spin into sloth, we may be tempted by what a master of the desert experience, John Cassian, names the "demon of dejection." His description of this vice is worth recalling here:

> If our purpose is to fight the spiritual fight and to defeat, with God's help, the demons of malice, we should take every care to guard our heart from the demon of dejection. Just as a moth devours clothing and a worm devours wood, so dejection devours a man's soul. It persuades him to shun every helpful encounter and stops him accepting advice from his true friends or giving them a courteous and peaceful reply. Seizing the entire soul, it fills it with bitterness and listlessness. Then it suggests to the soul that we should go away from other people, since they are the cause of its agitation. It does not allow the soul to understand that its sickness does not come from without, but lies hidden within, only manifesting itself when temptations attack the soul because of our ascetic efforts.[3]

Danger of Turning Away From Our Graced Call

The greatest danger inherent in slothful dispositions is the temptation to "either give up prayer or go to it begrudgingly" (DN I:7 [2]). Not finding the satisfaction one craves due to spiritual gluttony, one now turns away in spiritual sloth from the invitation of grace. Sloth blocks our entrance to the dark night experience. It prompts us to resist the harsh reality of the Golgotha road. To walk with Jesus will ask of us the firmest perseverance. It will call us to deny what we want for the sake of accepting God's providential way.

Commitment to remain true to our founding life form or unique communal call, requires the highest courage.[4] As long as the initial glow of certitude lasts, sloth is not an issue. When we have to keep the faith in times of doubt, when our call leads us to where we would rather not go, then the noonday devil appears. To remain faithful seems too much of an effort. To stay on the ship of obedience amidst such violent storms seems to demand more of us than we are ready to give. Will we muster the courage to stay on board or will we unleash the nearest life raft and float comfortably back to shore?

Rather than risking to will what God wills, we feel sad because things are not the way they used to be. We feel a strange aversion, as Cassian said, to labor day after day without any seeming reward. The center of gravity imperceptibly shifts from remaining faithful to our call to relying on the empty promises of our willful, greedy expectations. It does not take much effort or reflection for us to conclude lazily that if we are feeling complacent with the way things are why should we "rock the boat"? After a full meal it feels good to be a couch potato. Let someone else clean off the table.

Signs of Life-Draining Sloth

Sloth attracts two related obstacles that cling to us like parasites to an unwary host. One is self-satisfaction. This means that slothful spirits "measure God by themselves and not themselves by God" (DN I:7 [3]). The other obstacle is a secret selfishness. So intent is one on self service, that one feels an aversion to doing anything unpleasant for the sake of serving the reign of God on earth.

St. John found in beginners a pattern that goes something like this: a burst of enthusiasm for prayer and good works as long as consolations last, followed by an unwillingness to continue working when one is told to do something unpleasant. It is as if slothful people buy into the popular slogan of secularism that if it feels good it is good and it does not matter whom we disappoint in the process. Sloth is characterized by an aversion to the gospel dictum quoted by St. John: Those who lose their life for Christ's sake will gain it; those who desire to gain it will lose it (cf. Mt 16:25).

Boredom is another prevalent symptom of life-draining sloth. People today seem to need to be entertained all the time. It is as if a penchant for the spectacular renders us incapable of appreciating the ordinary.[5] One of the most common experiences of life is that it is not always pleasant or pleasurable. The sugar canister is empty when I need one more cup to complete a cake. The car runs out of gas because the mechanics forgot to fix the fuel gauge. A flight is canceled due to inclement weather when this is the one meeting I wanted to attend.

To imagine that a spiritual life is much different from the daily ups and downs of ordinary living is to remain sadly naive. Yet beginners are prone to become bored with prayer and the pursuit of deeper intimacy with God because the way can be wounding. We often wait upon God without receiving much spiritual gratification. At such points on the journey, it is tempting to grow lax. Fortitude demands more effort than we can muster. The road to glory is strewn with lots of stones. Things are not as nice as we thought they would be. Sloth says, why bother? Courage replies, whither would we go (cf. Jn 6:68)?

St. John offers an apt comparison to illustrate how slothful types shun the labor contemplative living entails:

> Like those who are reared in luxury, they run sadly from everything rough, and they are scandalized by the cross, in which spiritual delights are found (DN I:7 [4]).

The paradox of the cross is understandably uppermost in St. John's mind. It is the underlying theme of his entire book, articulated in such apparent contradictions as dark-light, sad-glad, suffering-joy. What would be a scandal to nonbelievers is the one true source of hope to which Christ's faithful cling. To be bored by the cross, to flee from temporary hardships that conceal an eternal weight of glory, is to fail to penetrate more deeply into the meaning these paradoxical moments convey.

The truth is, renunciation is the royal road to liberation. Death is an ending that is at once a new beginning. In contrast to faith, hope, and love, boredom breeds indifference and lack of enthusiasm, especially when the going gets tough. This is when people willing to dig deeper feel recharged. They do not expect life to proceed according to their whims. They suspect that what satisfies their will may be contrary to God's will. They are not surprised when the good works they try to do are squelched or hampered by small-minded people, incapable of supporting a vision or work beyond their control.

If one is inclined to be slothful, one is unlikely to want to follow the narrow way of which Christ speaks so convincingly. The hardships this walk often entails are repugnant and depressing to a person who wants his or her own way, period.

Transformation as a Divine Gift

As his analysis of these seven major obstacles, which are treated in the previous three chapters of this book, draws to a close, St. John helps us to see the remarkable way in which God takes the initiative to draw us into the dark night where transformation occurs. Beginners, like butterflies emerging from cocoons, become proficients; fledglings with once weak wings all at once soar free:

> There, through pure dryness and interior darkness, [God] weans them from the breasts of these gratifications and delights, takes away all these trivialities and childish ways, and makes them acquire the virtues by very different means (DN I:7 [5]).

These "means" come not from human efforts but from divine initiatives. The roots of sin are so entangled in our subtle self-centeredness that not even a depth charge could disturb them. Only the sheer grace outpoured from the God who has loved us first and who wills our salvation at a price none but God would be willing to pay can initiate the neces-

sary means to extricate us from the net of sin. This miracle of
liberation occurs only by means of inner purgation. No matter how earnest our actions to attain holiness have been, no
matter how passionately we have practiced self-mortifica-
tion, nothing we do can move us toward our goal. In fact,
such egocentric intensity may only push us farther from it.
The peace and joy found in union with God will continue to
elude us until God accomplishes this transformation in us in
a way and at a time known only to the Mystery.

Awed as he must have been by this dark night of
spirituality and its felt experience in daily reality, St. John
prays that the Word of God will give him, its humble channel,
the light he needs to say something about "a night so dark
and a matter so difficult to treat and expound [that] his
enlightenment is very necessary" (DN I:7 [5]). May the same
prayer be ours as we press onward into the depths of divine
darkness. May God illumine our minds and open our hearts
to whatever it is that we need to both hear and heed.

6

Letting God Do the Leading

(*The Dark Night*, Book One, Chapters 8 and 9)

A young woman feels the first drowsy effect of the sedative administered by her nurse as she is wheeled onto the elevator on the way to the operating room. She thinks of the times she has driven through long, dark tunnels, propelled forward by the knowledge that there is light on the other side. She repeats the psalmist's words, "Be still," and abandons her body to the skill of the surgeons.

A daring rock climber loses his footing and hangs suspended in midair. The only link between him and life itself is his safety rope. He regathers his strength but for a split second absorbs the full impact of feeling utterly out of control.

A mother follows the ambulance carrying her child to the emergency room, stunned because she overheard the paramedics say that her chances of survival were slim: "A head injury of such magnitude involves so many unknowns." She pleads with God to give her baby a chance. Her prayers become more desperate with each labored breath the child draws.

These slices of life could be narrations of our own close encounters with mortality. Such stories are stark reminders of the fragileness of human finitude. They evidence more than any philosophical treatise could our dependence on a Power greater than we are. Illness, accidents, and other forms of loss occasion depths of thoughtfulness. In daily life we drown the question "Where is my heart?" in whirlpools of work. Most of the time we feel in control. We may give God a few quick turns of thought throughout the day, but we do not live customarily in contemplation. Pride and avarice, envy and sloth, erode our bonds with eternal beatitude. We live and act as if we are going to last forever.

The dark night disrupts this delusion. It plunges us into the unknown land of contemplative openness to the "More Than," to the mystery of being and non-being no rational mind can fathom. Only faith can give meaning to this mystery. To believe is to allow the initiative for final decision and action to shift from us to God. The center of gravity then becomes not self-survival but self-surrender.

Entering the Nights of Sense and Spirit

Two coformants affect the changes that occur: one is sensory because as body-subjects we are enfleshed, vulnerable, and temporal; the other is spiritual because as human beings we are more than flesh or function. Our distinctive trait is transcendence.[1] The dark night evokes this deep truth. It does so by darkening or purging our senses so that we can see with clarity the unique persons we are: women and men loved into being by God, creatures distinct from all other living things whose human spirits seek consonance with the Holy Spirit.

This consonance is akin to contemplation. As musical instruments must be tuned to perform with perfection a simple yet daring composition, a feat requiring tedious and at times frustrating rehearsal, so in the experience of the dark night the senses must be purged or realigned or reformed to accommodate the spirit. In the words of Adrian van Kaam, the vital and functional dimensions of the self must become the servants of the transcendent.[2]

The spirit also has to undergo considerable transformation, for clinging to it like barnacles on a ship's hull are the obstacles described in the first seven chapters of *The Dark Night*. St. John has to steer our ship into the fresh waters of spiritual purgation. Only their cleansing powers can restore the dull veneer left by the life-draining parasites of inordinate appetites and prepare our vessel to set sail for the land of union and likeness to God.

It is quite common for beginners to be led into the sensory night. For this reason St. John intends to describe it first. By contrast, those to whom God grants the grace of the night of the spirit are relatively few. They have passed through a number of trials and become disposed, as only proficients can be, to the ways of God that are not our ways. Of such St. John will later speak, for his own story is validation enough of the old adage: Man proposes but God disposes.

Deprivation of the Nights

Recall the taste on your tongue of bitter medicine, the kind that made you wrinkle your nose and beg for water. To be told, "It's going to make you better," did nothing to remove the bitterness. Experiences felt or imagined of sensual deprivation—of being ice cold when we long to be wrapped in a warm wool blanket; of being so thirsty we could spit dust and having nothing to drink—may help us to grasp why the saint says this first purgation, terrible as it is to the senses, makes one hunger and thirst more for God.

Despite the intensity of this sensory night, it is mild compared to the far more terrible awareness of loss characteristic of the night of the spirit. Because one desires to be wholly united with God, one feels doubly distraught when grace leads one to a place of seeming separation. It takes special skill and experience to tell of this occurrence.

Onset of Sensory Testing

A life of intimacy with the Trinity that is obedient, humble, loving, and faithful begins haltingly. It is commingled with the desire for gratification and self-exaltation. One grovels, as it were, in the subsoil of the spiritual life, oblivious to the growth potential inherent in the topsoil. In other words, the love of pleasure replaces the desire to please only God. On the side of the divine, God, like a hound of heaven, hunts us down, takes the initiative, offers the grace, withdraws us from this base, self-centered style of loving, and leads us through the desert of ego-desperation to a higher degree of theocentric adoration. It is God's desire, first of all, to free us from so much reliance on our senses. At the onset of the night they determine how we feel, how we function. Without the grace of the night of the senses, we might be inclined to reduce our faith to what we can feel and understand.

It is God's wish, so to speak, to release us from the methods of discursive meditation that rely mostly on techniques of visualizing images and organizing thoughts. Our way of searching for a more intimate relationship with the Trinity is on this basis alone inadequate and fraught with obstacles. It is through God's gracious initiative that we are being led to a new way of praying, one that will enable us to enjoy a hitherto unknown depth of communion and communication with Christ.

Undoubtedly these advancements do not happen all at once. Grace moves beginners along, but only after we have grown over time in the exercise of virtue. Are we living a good moral life in faithfulness to the gospel and to our unique communal call? Have we shown that we can persevere in both vocal and mental prayer? It is through these practices and the transcendent lights derived from them that we are able to let go of lesser attachments to mere worldly things and direct our lives as a first priority to God.

This intention enables us with the help of grace to place functional ambitions at the disposal of our transcendent aspirations and inspirations.[3] In the light of what has been opened to us through serious, mature prayer and Christian practice, we are less inclined to invest our longing for God in anything less than or other than God.

It is as if our level of trust in the Word is expanding like a wrinkled sponge dipped in water. We seem better able to suffer through times of dryness without growing too discouraged. We are willing to wait patiently until the oppression of not feeling God's presence passes. Though it may seem as if our spiritual growth is on hold, it is not even thinkable that we should leave the road or allow doubts to tempt us to take a detour.

Ironically, when it feels good between us and God, when we have fallen into a rather satisfying and familiar routine, when it seems as if the sun of the sacred is shining on us, it is at this least anticipated of times that God chooses to turn off the light, shut the door, and dry up the well. We were used to quenching our thirst with spiritual spring water. Whenever we lowered our cup, it would come up full. Now it is empty, and our thirst, though greater than ever, is not relieved. The time of sensory testing is upon us.

Signs That Night Is Nigh

God risks to treat his friends this way because in the adolescence of the spiritual life we were given whatever our hearts desired. God knew how weak we were, how inclined to grow discouraged, how tender our feelings, how easily hurt. So our wells were filled. God opened previously closed doors and wiped away our tears. Now that time of splendor in the grass and glory in the flower seems like the memory of a distant refrain. The Mystery leaves us in a room so dark that for a while we think it has no exit. We may try to disentangle from the web of confusion we feel, but to no avail. Discursive imaginings come to a dead end. We cannot move one step forward in meditation. It used to be so easy. Why has it become so difficult? What happened to our inner sensory gifts? No matter where we turn, we are unable to find our way through the thicket. It feels as if we are swimming in quicksand.

So pervasive is the aridity into which we are being led by God that we cease expecting to receive much, if any, consolation from the spiritual disciplines that used to enhance our sense of intimacy with the Divine. These works, once so delightful, are strangely distasteful. These modes of encountering the transcendent, once so sweet, now taste bitter.

God allows this time of testing to take place because we have grown more than we may know in faith, hope, and love. It is fitting that God should wean us from the "sweet breast" of consolations—not to hurt us but to help us. God's aim, like that of a wise mother, is to enable us to walk through difficult times without losing heart. How can children grow if they do not lay aside their swaddling clothes, let go of their parents' hands, and take off on their own two feet? This shift from remaining a child to growing up is a surprise to one walking the way of the spirit. What one expected to happen transpires in reverse. It felt good to be carried by God; it feels odd to be put down. It felt nice to be fed; it feels strange to hold one's own spoon. It felt delightful to be cradled in mother's arms; it feels less secure to be bundled up and sent out in the cold.

All of this happens for a reason, though at the start of this reversal God's mode of teaching is not clear. So-called "recollected beginners" may be confused because they have become almost incapable of enduring the apparent absence of God. When God appears to withdraw from them, they find it hard not to conclude that they are becoming backsliders. It will take time for them to see that the dryness that overtakes them spiritually is for a good purpose: it weans them from the last remnants of excessive attachments to worldly things as ultimate. St. John is emphatic on this point: "A reform of the appetites is the requirement for entering the happy night of the senses" (DN I:8 [4]).

Shortly after one passes beyond the initiatory stages of spiritual deepening, one is led by God into the passive night. Here the word "passive" simply means that it is God who, far more than in the former stage, does the leading, we who do the receiving. The question is: How do I know if I am in the realm of a genuine experience of sensory purgation by God?

Discerning Real Deprivation Initiated by the Divine

Certainly a key sign is spiritual aridity. In perusing the scriptures, especially the psalms and the writings of the prophets, one can find many references to sensory purgation. Examples of such aridity can be found, for instance, in the psalms of lamentation: "How long, O Lord? Will you utterly forget me?" (Ps 13:2). "My God, my God, why have you forsaken me?" (Ps 22:2). "Why, O Lord, do you reject me; why hide from me your face?" (Ps 88:15). So plentiful are such texts that St. John finds it unnecessarily time-consuming to cite them. He will instead trust in life to be our teacher.

Common as experiences of the sensory night may be, it is still necessary to discern if the origin of such deprivation is indeed the work of grace or a result of sin and imperfection. Are aridity and ego-desperation signs of weakness or mediocrity? Are they symptoms of some bodily or emotional sickness? How do we know what is what?

To appraise the direction in which the Spirit is guiding any one person, St. John offers some signs to help us personally or as spiritual directors to discover whether the perceived spiritual dryness is due to a genuine dark night experience or to one of the above defects. It is his conviction that three principal signs must be present simultaneously. Let me focus on each one in turn as well as on the reasons why all three must appear together.

First: Lack of Satisfaction

Think of something delicious: a caesar salad prepared tableside; a foot-long hot dog with mustard and relish at your favorite amusement park; a freshly squeezed lemonade; a barbecued strip steak; a perfectly flavored piece of chocolate mousse pie. Our mouths begin to water in anticipation of the pleasure derived from such delightful food. Who would not feel satisfied after dining on delicacies like these?

Compare this kind of bodily gratification—of necessity fleeting and likely to wane when we become satiated or sick or old—to the uplift of spirit we feel when we receive the gift of a genuine religious experience, the residue of which may edify us for a lifetime. Having enjoyed, so to speak, full health spiritually, it is all the more painful to sense the loss of transcendent vigor, especially during the trials of the dark nights when, humanly speaking, we most need to feel the nearness of God.

Compare what it would be like to have placed before you a steaming bowl of French onion soup, when you have not eaten for two days, only to discover that you are unable to taste anything. You had to consume the soup but you took no satisfaction in it.

So it is with this first sign of sensory purgation. One derives no consolation from the things of God. It is the strangest of experiences. Devotions once elevating are about as spiritually exciting as a mouthful of sawdust to the tongue of an already thirsty person. Whereas to walk in nature and behold the wonders of creation once drew you into a natural state of contemplative awe, now not even the sight of a solitary bird in flight across a blue sky arouses a flicker of wonder.

During this time of sensory deprivation, it seems to be a struggle even to start the day. What faith it takes to accept this dryness as an essential stage on the way to spiritual maturity! God allows this suspension of animation to occur for a number of reasons:

1. Just as the process of drying herbs and fruits preserves their flavor and nutritional value for future use, so the purging of our sensory appetites reserves our heart solely for God. No other delight may take the place of pure adoration, of learning to love and give glory to God with our whole heart and mind, body and soul. Were we to find ultimate satisfaction in anything less than God, we could not offer ourselves wholly to God.

2. Due to the nature of this sudden removal of satisfaction from a person trying to live the good life for God, it is not sufficient to say that this dryness and distaste have to be due to some newly committed sins. St. John does not accept this explanation. He says that if such a withdrawal of delight were due to our human imper-

fections, the propensity would soon arise to seek satisfaction merely in material or mental ways. Again the outer and inner senses, our seeing and imagining, would draw us toward indulgence and instant solutions. This tendency would be in itself an imperfection, indicating how far we are from a genuine sensory experience of the dark night. The inclination, indeed the urgency, to approach the mystery of this movement as if it were merely a problem to be solved would be an indicator that one is still bound, mildly or in great measure, to pretranscendent attachments.

3. Given the above criteria of appraisal, it is still possible that feelings of dissatisfaction or aridity may have little to do with such heavenly or earthly struggles and may only be the result of "some indisposition or melancholic humor" (DN I:9 [2]), which frequently prevents one from being satisfied with anything. For this reason a second sign or condition has to be experienced.

Second: Memory of God's Presence

Think of a widow or widower still mourning the death of a beloved spouse. The person who survives remembers the one who is dead as if he or she were present and alive. Small, seemingly long forgotten events, are more vivid now than when they were first shared with the beloved. For a long time during the mourning process the past becomes more real than the present.

So it is for the lover of God. Once upon a time in the sweet meadows of first encounter, where one grazed on the green grass of abundant consolations, it seemed as if these days of felt nearness to God would never end. Now in the midnight hour one must rely on memory not to despair. Like a person lost at sea whose only hope is to cling to a life raft that points toward a hoped-for shore, so the one engulfed in sensory deprivation finds his or her memory clinging solicitously to God for help.

A relation once taken for granted now evokes painful self-reproach. The spouse left behind cannot help but agonize over moments missed for deeper intimacy because one was too busy or too preoccupied. So the servant of God agonizes over the possibility that this dryness may be due to his or her inadequacy, to a lack of courage to bear the cross, or to some secret distaste for God's ways that poses a threat to union. It is as if one wants continually to replay the tape of what used to be or what could have been if only one had done this or that favor for God. What is really happening here?

1. St. John wants us to understand, even in the midst of inner turmoil, that the dryness we feel is not due to laxity or tepidity. Nor is it due to a secret indifference to God. Were this the case a person could not possibly care so much about the state of his or her spiritual life. Real love means that people struggle continually to improve the relationship, and this requires hard work as any couple committed to staying married can testify.

2. St. John sharply distinguishes between dryness and lukewarmness. The latter type of person is lazy, lacks solicitude for his or her relationship with God, and is will-less when it comes to cultivating a spirit of service. The priority of the transcendent matters, but it does not become a burning commitment, especially where discipline and tough decisions are concerned. By contrast, one who is drawn by God into the crucible of purgative dryness is acutely and continuously concerned. He or she is pained by the thought of falling out of favor with God. Their relationship of intimacy means everything.

3. Along with genuine aridity of spirit one may feel emotionally low or melancholic. This state as such does not prevent purgation on the sensory level from occurring. In this case the dryness is due to more than depression. It is a transcendent experience, depriving one of feeling satisfied by anything or anyone as ultimate.

Were melancholia the entire source of this experience of feeling dissatisfied, its end result would not be an intensified longing for God but a feeling of profound disgust that plunges one into near despair.

Moreover, depression and tepidity as distinct from dryness and aridity do not arouse passionate desires to direct all of one's love and service to God. The main distinguishing factor in summary is this: In the night of purgative dryness the sensory part of the soul feels down and out, low, feeble, and slack, yet because on the spiritual level one is learning to rely more on faith than on feelings, one stands in readiness to do God's will and remain strong.

Elucidating the Dynamics of Spiritual Dryness

Pondering further on this second sign, St. John begins now to elucidate its deeper dynamics. He says that the reason for this dryness involves an alteration, a shift or a transfer by which the life of sense (our pretranscendent social, vital, and functional spheres) is no longer treated as ultimate but rather as a servant of the spirit or of the transcendent sphere of distinctive humanness.[4]

Our senses, earthbound as they are, would not direct us upward to the spirit were it not for this graced experience of deprivation. These experiences are paradoxical openings to the Most High. They help to explain why many the world over, who suffer from material poverty, still retain a deep sense of the sacred, whereas many who are wealthy grow complacent and lose the awareness of their dependency on God. The interesting thing is that while the spirit is enjoying a banquet of choice food (goodness, compassion, trust, charity, and humility) the flesh (anything in us which separates itself from God) tastes nothing and becomes depleted of energy.

By contrast, these times of sensory depletion may be experienced by the spiritually attuned person as immensely liberating. It is as if the spirit receives nourishment from renunciation. Just as the body releases toxins while fasting

and at a certain point feels new surges of energy and well-
being, so the spirit during this time of deprivation may
become more alert about pleasing God and more careful
about failing God.

During the course of the exchange, what at first caused
dryness and distaste will eventually give way to edification
and delight. This does not happen all at once. When the
novelty of the accommodation wears off, it is easy to regress
to the old pattern of seeking spiritual savor in a sensory
mode. One may start to see how much remains to be purged
before our senses are really the servants of our spirit.

The reasons for dryness on this level remain subtle; they
seldom meet one's expectations. Thus to prepare for a life of
deeper harmony with God and the good this entails, God has
to lead one still further into the obscurity and darkness of the
night. At this stage one experiences a renewed concentration
of aridity and distaste. One cannot help but contrast what is
now occurring with the high points of apparent union once
readily enjoyed.

In her autobiography, Thérèse of Lisieux accurately docu-
ments this experience of sensory, if not spiritual, deprivation:

> At this time I was enjoying such a living faith, such
> a clear faith, that the thought of heaven made up
> all my happiness, and I was unable to believe there
> were really impious people who had no faith. I
> believed they were actually speaking against their
> own inner convictions when they denied the exist-
> ence of heaven where God Himself wanted to be
> their Eternal Reward. During those very joyful
> days of the Easter season, Jesus made me feel that
> there were really souls who have no faith, and who,
> through the abuse of grace, lost this precious
> treasure, the source of the only real and pure joys.
> He permitted my soul to be invaded by the thickest
> darkness, and that the thought of heaven, up until
> then so sweet to me, be no longer anything but the
> cause of struggle and torment. This trial was to last

not a few days or a few weeks, it was not to be
extinguished until the hour set by God Himself
and this hour has not yet come. I would like to be
able to express what I feel, but alas! I believe this is
impossible. One would have to travel through this
dark tunnel to understand its darkness.[5]

Transformative Implications of the Second Sign

St. John compares the transformation wrought by God in
us to what happened to the chosen people in the desert. To
them God gave heavenly food, so nourishing that no one had
to endure hunger (cf. Wis 16:20-21). Even so the Israelites
continued to crave the kinds of food they once ate in Egypt
(cf. Ex 16:2-3). Their palates were used to this fleshmeat. What
had sensory appeal in this alien country seemed more attractive to them than the manna delivered by angels (cf. Nm
11:7-9). In the memorable words of the master:

> The baseness of our appetite is such that it makes
> us long for our own miserable goods and feel
> aversion for the incommunicable heavenly good
> (DN I:9 [5]).

Once more we are tempted to settle for less rather than
to heed the invitation to seek and find much more. No
wonder St. John thanks God for this night of sensory reformation and redirection. This aridity is the result of a genuine
purgation of the appetite for lesser delights as if they were
ultimate. Thus freed, one feels strengthened and energized
to cooperate with forthcoming contemplative graces that are
transformative.

This surge of energy is spirit-filled. Its wellspring is the
Holy Spirit, who offers substantial, interior food. While it
may be as seemingly tasteless as manna in the desert, this
food provides nourishment that transcends sensory savor. It
feeds the spirit contemplatively and thus in the beginning it
is "dark and dry to the senses" (DN I:9 [6]). Here human
expectations of ecstasy are bound to be thwarted. The soul

food God now gives remains secret and mysterious even to the person who receives it.

God serves this food directly to the spirit. Because it bypasses the senses, they are left in dryness. Our physical taste buds have little to brag about; we have few stories to tell of being touched ecstatically by God. Our mental faculties, too, bog down. Who can explain something so wordless? Yet the emptiness experienced vitally and functionally becomes a kind of fullness on a higher plane. It draws us, says St. John, to remain alone and in quietude. We are strangely unable to concentrate on one or the other thought. As impossible as it would be to hold a rainbow in one's hand, so is it impossible to capture or compel the sheer grace of infused contemplation.

The second sign of the sensory night that comes to us as pure gift thus results in our inclination to dwell in solitude, to remain reverentially still, in quiet awe, without investing our total care and solicitude in any outer or inner work. Now is the time to let go and let God take the lead. In such a stance of gentleness and humility, of carefreeness and relaxation, one opens inwardly to receive this heavenly food. Functional tasks get done efficiently. We eat, dress, minister to others, do daily chores, and go to bed. Life is not neglected. All the while something is happening to us inwardly. A delicate feeding is occurring without any effort on our part. As St. John says:

> … this contemplation is active while the soul is in idleness and unconcern. It is like air that escapes when one tries to grasp it in one's hand (DN I:9 [6]).

Scriptural Validation of Transformation

Into the mind of the master come the words of the Lover to the bride in the Song of Songs (cf. Sg 6:1-4) to show how God is leading the soul along another path. The beams of love are so intense that the senses cannot bear them and so the bride begs the Beloved to turn his eyes away from her. These looks would hinder, not help his work. One can see, but only with the inner eyes of the heart.

As grace draws one into this divinely directed secret place of contemplation, the receiver enters a new space. In this hitherto unknown land the old ways of discursive meditation no longer produce fruit. In this new state it is not we but God who is in charge, more so than in the former state. For proficients it is no surprise that God has to bind up and hold captive the interior faculties. Similarly God pulls the pins out from under the intellect, empties from the will its normal expectations of choice and decision, and removes from the memory categories that used to give one a feeling of control. Humiliating as it might be, at this time a person's own efforts are useless. Pushing toward a solution would only be an obstacle to inner peace and the pace of grace. Powerlessness on our part enables the Mystery to release a deeper spiritual power in us—the power of the Cross.

The Cross enabled the saving event of redemption to happen at the moment when, humanly speaking, Jesus was so dry physically that he said, "I thirst" (Jn 19:28) and so empty spiritually that he repeated the ancient lament, "My God, my God, why have you forsaken me?" (Mk 15:34). At this paradoxical moment of weakness and strength, of powerlessness and true power, our salvation was at hand.

One may at such moments be overtaken in the midst of pain by a wave of peace that is as gentle as it is quieting, as inexplicable and solitary as it is satisfying and healing for self and others. Such inner tranquility amidst turmoil transcends any sort of gratification registered in the senses. While this peace may not be palpable, it has about it a perennial quality. This, St. John might say, is the "real thing." It is the peace that is Jesus' farewell gift to his disciples (cf. Jn 14:27), the peace of God that passes beyond all understanding (cf. Phil 4:7), the peace that transforms recalcitrant laborers into imitators of Christ and ambassadors of the Good News. Definitive as this second sign is, as sure as it signals that one has entered the passive night of the senses, one more indicator is needed.

Third: Powerlessness as Openness to Pure Spirit

This sign is unusual and unnerving, especially for a person accustomed to accomplishment in work and prayer. The tools of the latter trade are meditation and imagination, two perfectly good interior operations; the problem is, they do not function as expected despite one's best efforts. One feels powerless to overcome this apparent obstacle. While by human standards everything seems out of order, by divine standards all is well, for our powerlessness clears the channels for God to communicate with us in new ways.

Previously our senses served as access points to the transcendent dimension. For example, we could read a passage from scripture, like the story of the Good Samaritan (cf. Lk 10:29-37), or say a prayer like the "Our Father" (cf. Mt 6:9-13), and analyze it discursively or synthesize the ideas derived from it. Such exercises often led to encounters with the Divine, some fleeting, others more lasting. Now all we feel is dryness. God uses this precise moment of powerlessness to communicate with us in a purely spiritual way by means of simple communion or contemplation. It happens as naturally as the inhaling and exhaling of fresh air with no step-by-step process, no succession of ideas, no particular thoughts.

St. John came to see through his own life experience and that of others who came to him for spiritual direction that neither our exterior nor our interior senses, neither our seeing nor our imagining, can attain this level of infused contemplation. It is truly given unto us in God's own time by the power of the Holy Spirit. This experience so transcends human efforts that our powers of imagination, which were previously so helpful, feel like poor swimmers in a stormy sea, unable to rely on the usual supports of this or that conclusion or consideration. It is as if God is tuning in on a wavelength that our inner radar was not tuned to receive, yet the signal is loud and clear.

Because of the nature of this third sign, one can deduce that the dissatisfaction felt in the senses is not the result of being in what the saint dubs a "bad humor." It is not caused by moodiness or laziness. Were that the case, one could return with relative ease to the fervor once produced by formerly effective spiritual exercises. When the mood passed or more energy emerged, one could redirect his or her faculties along now familiar lines. Since this purgation is genuine, not self-induced but Spirit-inspired, such a return to one's old ways is not possible as long as one is in this state.

Entrance to the dark night means that the powerlessness to meditate in a mainly discursive fashion will now be more or less continuous. Such a state is relatively lasting. However, St. John has to admit, that at the onset of these spiritual nights God usually does go slowly. He does not deprive us completely of sensory satisfaction or of the ability to meditate. The Spirit seems to know who is ready to be weaned all at once and who needs more time. Advancement means that one has to be led in due course ever further into the purgative way, leaving behind the work of the senses and the human efforts they imply. To let go and let God take the initiative may sound easy, but for many it is the hardest and the longest leap to make.

One who is at least at the entrance of the road to contemplation will inevitably be and act differently. Three indicators of the limits of progress are:

1. The night of aridity is not yet as continuous as one suspects it may soon become.

2. At times one is overcome by bouts of dryness; at other times all seems "normal."

3. On occasion one can engage in step-by-step meditations while at other moments these efforts seem to fade away like fog lights in a thickening mist.

For people so good and well-meaning, it seems difficult to accept that God places them in this darkness of not feeling, of not knowing, solely for the sake of reforming and humbling them. The aim of this divine initiative is to reshape an appetite misshapen by habitual and harmful attractions to consolations. Such attachments despoil the real goal of the life of the spirit: to love and serve God wholly and to become self-giving for others' sake.

Having led a person thus far, God may also decide to lead one no further. That may come as a surprise unless we accept, as St. John does, that not everyone is destined by the Mystery to live a strict contemplative life of union with God.

All are called by virtue of the gift of faith to exercise the highest degree of charity, but in truth "God does not bring to contemplation all those who purposely exercise themselves in the way of the spirit, nor even half. Why? He best knows" (DN I:9 [9]).

On this sober note, St. John concludes his discussion of the "signs." He challenges anyone engaged in the arduous and awesome task of spiritual direction to know exactly what is what. Such knowledge cannot be derived from a crash course, a personality inventory, or a summer program. This art and discipline entails a lifetime of learning, wisdom, and experience. One must also realize that for nearly "half" of the people God "never completely weans their senses from the breasts of considerations and discursive meditations, except for some short periods and at certain seasons" (DN I:9 [9]). This being the case, we need next to know how one is supposed to respond and act during these continuous or brief episodes of transformation, as the case may be. How ought one to behave in a night that is as dark as a tomb for the senses yet as bright as the dawning day for the spirit?

7

Proper Dispositions for the Journey Into Darkness

(*The Dark Night*, Book One, Chapters 10 and 11)

When we have to face a particularly trying time in life, what helps us to see it through is the conviction that cloudy days do pass, that the temptation to give up is temporary. We trust when sunshine is in the forecast that storms will soon subside.

My niece was shocked to learn after a checkup that she had to undergo serious brain surgery. The news sent more shock waves through our family. The hardest thing to endure, she said, was the six weeks of anticipation prior to her operation. On the day the surgery took place, she felt strangely at peace. She looked happier than she had during the endless ordeal of waiting. We were convinced that she would make it, and she did, though not without suffering permanent hearing loss in one ear.

An experience as frightening and disrupting as this cannot help but be life changing. An alteration, a transformation, affects us both physically and spiritually. What matters most and what matters least are no longer up for grabs. Who one's true friends are is not in question. That prayer means more in the obscurity of not knowing where one is being led than at times of certainty comes as no surprise.

Whenever we describe or recall an event that propels us in a new direction, we may get an inkling of what a desert experience means in religious terms. There is a strong bond between the dryness and aridity of the desert and the night of the senses. One without the other is inconceivable.

Exchanges in the Night

The desert comes upon us at a time we cannot exactly foresee. It ends on an hour not scheduled on our calendar. It does pass, but not without leaving in its wake a changed person. To endure our own deserts in a disposition of appreciative abandonment to the Mystery is as difficult as trying to climb a mountain without a rope. We believe that what is happening does have a purpose, though we do not see it yet.

The main reason we are being thus led is captured in the word "exchange." When a friend buys us a gift that is not right we are not ashamed to exchange it for something better. God gives us the gift of our senses. There is no greater package full of presents than those of seeing, hearing, touching, tasting, smelling, feeling, and imagining. At desert moments, when we are physically drained and emotionally spent, we are also slowly being made ready to exchange these gifts of sensual pleasures for something more substantial.

The original giver now becomes the exchange teller. God, so to speak, does the work of organizing the particulars for us. God exacts no surcharge for the gift of sensory purgation save our trust and self surrender. What happens is that our distinctively human gifts of awareness and felt transcendence are withdrawn from their lower dimensional dependency on the senses. We are being drawn to the higher regions of the spirit. Once we reach this vista, we are able to comprehend more of who we are and who God is for us. In the end God exchanges another former gift, that of discursive meditation, for his new offering of infused contemplation.

We may in the beginning be uncomfortable with this. It is like being lost in an unfamiliar neighborhood. From the spiritual point of view, we have to accept the fact that we have no power to meditate on the basis of sense knowledge alone nor with the help of our lower reason and imagination only.

The things of God remain our deepest concern; we simply cannot pursue them as we once did. At first we worry. Are we doing the right thing by waiting? Should we let go of our tendency to take the bull by the horns? Have we gone astray? Is this why we are feeling few aspirations to cling to the Mystery in faith?

No doubt the afflictions of the night make us wonder if a greater good is really being exchanged for a lesser one. We feel so little support or satisfaction in anything. It would be easy to dismiss as a bad joke St. John's conviction that we are undergoing necessary changes that will ready us to receive an abundance of spiritual blessings. As far as we are concerned, it feels for now as if we have been abandoned by God.

"I had to nurse my husband for five agonizing years before the Lord took him," a woman told me. "All I felt for the longest time was anger and self-pity. I say *felt* because that was the strange part. It was as if I became two persons, especially at the start of his illness: One part of me drifted toward low-grade depression; the other watched this stripping occur while understanding that God was leading me to new depths of surrender and peace. An exchange was taking place spiritually, but I did not *feel* anything but emptiness emotionally. Only later did I come to appreciate the enormous wealth of wisdom and experience I had received."

A similar tension may arise in our own life of prayer. In an effort to ward off aridity, we may tend to wear ourselves out in futile attempts to return to our old ways. Then it was possible to concentrate on a selected subject of meditation and derive at least some satisfaction and inspiration from it. As my friend related to me, "I doubled the number of prayers I said since I secretly wanted to control the outcome. I thought that if I ceased asking God to help me and my husband something horrible would happen. I started to make secret bargains with God, thinking that if I did not do so, that if I suspended this frenetic prayer activity and became more contemplative, God would accuse me of doing nothing and my husband's condition would get worse. Only in time did I accept the call to stillness as the key to serving my own and his best interests."

According to St. John, one side of us wants to persist in meditation; it has to draw upon all the sensory supports available. Resistance arises from the other side of us; it is reluctant to let us once again take over the reins of control of our prayer life. We ought to be repelled not by lack of a zealous do-it-yourself mentality but by our inability to relax and trust God to lead us. There is that of God in us that wants us to be still. We are being invited to exchange our typical performance demands, as these also apply to prayer, for doing nothing, in short, for the idleness of trusting abandonment. Such *idleness* (resting in God) may be the only way we can overcome the *idolatry* (testing of God) that stands behind our inner and outer efforts to produce a felt prayer life by means of our own take-charge tendencies.

Such activity may appear to counter aridity, but it despoils the exchange God wants to effect in us. It impairs God's work. It is in the long run of no profit to us. It makes us miss the divine direction beckoning us to a deeper spiritual life through a desert experience. St. John laments our lack of understanding: "In searching for spirit, they lose the spirit which was the source of their tranquility and peace" (DN I:10 [1]). He adds:

> They are like someone who turns from what has already been done in order to do it again, or one who leaves a city only to re-enter it, or they are like the hunter who abandons his prey in order to go hunting again (DN I:10 [1]).

Detours, Traps, and Snares Encountered in the Sensory Night

Common wisdom tells us at this point that it makes no sense to strive so hard to meditate when it is useless. Why not attend to the indicators given by grace and explained by the classical spiritual masters that mere mental exercises produce little or no profit at this time? It is futile for us to push against either the pace or the strategy of grace. All we succeed in doing is losing our peace because we are being led by the Spirit along a different road. What St. John regrets is that there may be no one to whom we can turn to help us undergo this alteration.[1] Teresa of Avila was fortunate enough to find an excellent master in him, but she had to learn the hard way that learned, wise, and experienced directors are few and far between. She describes what it is like when one in search of spiritual guidance is instead misdirected:

> At this point the devil began to upset my soul, although God drew out very much good from this. There was a cleric of excellent intelligence and social status who lived in that place where I went to be cured. He was learned, although not greatly so. I began to confess to him, for I was always fond of learning. Half-learned confessors have done my soul great harm when I have been unable to find a confessor with as much learning as I like. I have come to see by experience that it is better, if they are virtuous and observant of holy customs, that they have little learning. For then they do not trust themselves without asking someone who knows, nor do I trust them; and a truly learned man has never misguided me. Those others certainly could not have wanted to mislead me, but they didn't know any better. I thought that they really knew and that I was obliged to do no more than to believe them, especially since what they told me was liberal and permissive. If it had been rigid, I am so wretched that I would have sought out others. What was venial sin they said was no sin at all, and what was serious mortal sin they said was venial. This did me so much harm that it should not surprise anyone that I speak of it here in order to warn others against so great an evil. I see clearly that in God's eyes there is no excuse for me, for that

the things by their nature were wrong should have been enough for me to have been on guard against them. It was on account of my sins, I believe, that God permitted these confessors to be mistaken themselves and to misguide me. And I misled many others by telling them what these confessors told me.[2]

Guided by grace, St. Teresa managed to avoid the two traps that ensnare most people: either they make an about face and abandon the road or else, while walking along the way, they fall to pieces and lose courage. At the very least, they build roadblocks to their own progress by doubling their efforts to do discursive meditation, either because this is the only style of prayer they know or because an unwise and inexperienced director has pointed them away from the lines of direction being drawn by the Holy Spirit and guided them instead on an unnecessary detour. Should they find themselves on this obscure byway instead of on the highway paved by grace, they are likely to overwork themselves trying to avoid potholes and roadblocks. So fatigued are they by these useless meanderings that they lose track of where to go. They begin to think that perhaps they are failing to find relief because they are negligent or sinful or because they are not doing enough. They forget that transformation is not a plan to execute; it is a gift to receive in trusting abandonment.[3]

Guidance From Good Counsels

Grace signals to persons in the sensory night that it is useless during its duration to return to discursive meditation. God is beckoning them to follow the way of contemplation, a way beyond the range where imagination and meditative reflection once worked best for them. What is a person to do? How ought one to conduct himself or herself? St. John offers wise counsel in this regard:

1.   Rather than feeling confused, one ought to feel comforted. It is as if we are children once more clasping the hand of our parents in a swirling crowd. We are certain that as long as we hold tight we cannot get lost.

2.   Rather than succumbing to the temptation to return to more comfortable quarters, it is best to persevere patiently, to wait upon the Lord, to see in discomfort and affliction crosses that are blessings.

3.   Instead of trusting our own urgings to regain control, we must resist these and place our trust in God as a sick child trusts his or her parents to administer proper medicine. A God of love will meet the needs of sincere seekers who follow the call with simplicity of heart and uprightness of life.

The Beloved will anticipate our needs and answer them in ways beyond our childish expectations. We are destined to be brought out of the thicket of doubt into the bright light of pure love. This light will shine on us even more radiantly after we pass through the other night of which St. John will later speak, the night of the spirit. We may or may not be among the few on whom God may bestow this favor without our deserving it in any way. However simple or profound our prayer life may be, God will honor the promise not to leave us orphaned (cf. Jn 14:18). The degree of holiness God grants to us is not dependent on the gift of dark contemplation. Who knows how many known and unknown saints there are who attained the highest degree of sanctity but were not the recipients of this gift?

In the meantime, in the night of sense, the key attitude to which St. John returns is that of paying no attention to discursive meditation "since this is not the time for it" (DN I:10 [4]). For what, then, is it time? The saint's answer sounds almost too simple. We would expect his counsel to be more complex. He says that now is the time for us to remain at rest and in peace, to simply be still. We are so accustomed to doing something, whether in the realm of work or prayer, that it is odd to be advised to direct ourselves as well as others to relax, to let go, not to feel guilty about seemingly doing nothing or wasting time. Our old habits tempt us to believe that this disinclination to process anything mentally is either a mistake or an outgrowth of laxity. It is difficult to quiet the prodding voice and the false guilt such idleness evokes.

Our best defense, according to St. John, is the patient, persevering prayer of naked unfelt faith. This is the only activity in which we ought to engage. The prayer of trust and surrender, when we really believe in its efficacy, calms and quiets us like a child on its mother's lap (cf. Ps 131:2). Our only task is to let God lead us from infidelity to fidelity to our deepest call. As we read in Psalm 68:7, God gives the lowly (because of sense deprivation) a home in which to live; he leads the prisoners (of the senses and lower reason) forth into [the] freedom (of infused contemplation); but rebels (against the dark night) must dwell in a parched land. To be led out of the parched land means letting go of "the impediment and fatigue of ideas and thoughts" because "All these desires disquiet the soul and distract it from the peaceful, quiet, and sweet idleness of the contemplation that is being communicated to it" (DN I:10 [4]).

Listening to the rhythms of grace enables us to see that this contemplative work is not our doing. Frowning foreheads and pounding heads signify too much care on our part, too much thinking and meditation, too many attempts to master the mystery. Could anything be more consoling than the following advice to one accustomed to sweating for sanctity?

1. Be content simply to abide in loving and peaceful attentiveness to God.

2. Live without concern, relax your fretful efforts, let Jesus be your all in all.

3. Taste and savor the goodness of divine love. Recall that the initiative for union belongs solely to God.

Hardest to endure, the saint warns, will be the scruples that surge up like stormy waves smashing into a usually sunny shore. The spiteful voices of self-exertion start their nagging refrain: "You are wasting your time, you fool ... you could be doing something useful ... who do you think you are pursuing such quiet in prayer ... you better do something soon or else you may lose whatever you've gained ... ."

St. John does not dignify these pesty yappings by trying to deal with them directly. Rather we are told in the most matter-of-fact way to endure them peacefully. To be lifted up to a higher state of prayer has nothing to do with hardships and scruples; it means remaining at ease with God and enjoying great freedom of spirit.

Responding to the Transcendence Dynamic

Accustomed as we are to being in charge, it ought not to surprise us that St. John wants to help us reverse this tendency by fostering in a radical way our sense of dependence on God. Were we to make pushy moves at this point, were we even to desire to do so, we might hinder or lose altogether the goods God is bestowing on us. All God asks, so to speak, is that we send our senses and lower reason on vacation when we are praying and accept in peace and effortlessness what God is doing in and for us.

The analogy with a work of art in progress, given by St. John, is clarifying. He notes that were a model posing for a painting or for the retouching of her portrait to move or to arise to take care of something else, the artist's concentration would be broken. He would be unable to complete his commission. By the same token, one whom God is leading into the calm waters of inner peace and contemplative rest must not carry on other operations or become ensnared by lesser affections or interests in times of prayer. The distractions stirred up in this way would disrupt the quiet God wants to initiate in us. The result would be not greater delight but starker dryness, not fullness but emptiness. The support, knowledge, and love we seek cannot be supplied by sensory means or lower reason. A shift to the Spirit, an upward movement of transcendence, has to occur or we will feel the lack of peace even more acutely. Therefore:

1. We must pay no mind to the fact that we seem to have lost the ability to meditate discursively.

2. If anything, as servants of the transcendent, we ought to desire this repositioning of our lives as swiftly as grace allows.

3. We must attend mainly to putting no obstacles in the way of the infused contemplation God may grant the person readied by grace to receive this pure gift.

4. To accept such a gift peacefully and with gratitude, we must allow the Holy Spirit to widen the space for grace already in our hearts.

5. Our human spirit has to be enkindled by the fire of the Holy Spirit if we are to receive the dark and secret self-communication of God that is infused contemplation. According to St. John, "... contemplation is nothing else than a secret and peaceful and loving inflow of God, which, if not hampered, fires the soul in the spirit of love ..." (DN I:10 [6]).

6. At this moment of peaceful letting go, of calm solicitude for pleasing God, one's inmost being like dry wood struck by a torch is "Fired with love's urgent longings" (DN I:10 [6]).

Enflamed by Love's Forming Energy

To try to describe the fire of love is a formidable responsibility. This experience is subtle, especially at the start of the transformation process. Our pretranscendent senses are still too impure and impervious to resonate with our transcendent spirit. The fire may also weaken and die out because we have not cleared a space in which it can burn. Due to our own misunderstanding of what is happening, we fail to create a welcome room within our hearts for this divine visitation. Still, even if the main conditions for contemplation are met, we may begin to feel an inexplicable longing, an unquench-able hunger and thirst for God.

As the initiatory fire of love continues to draw us into its circle of warmth and light, we are unable to deny our attrac-tion to it. We are convinced that nothing less than this enkin-dling can satisfy us. All this happens without our knowing in any precise way what grace is doing. The only thing we know is that we want to be united with the source out of which this love and our attraction to it is flowing forth. This explains why St. John was willing to give up everything for the sake of being at one with "I-don't-know-what/ which is so gladly found." At such turning points on the road to union, poetry more than prose becomes the favored expres-sion of the inexpressible. What is it like to be enflamed with love, to desire God with urgent longings? John replies:

> The generous heart
> never delays with easy things
> but eagerly goes on
> to things more difficult.
> Nothing satisfies it,
> and its faith ascends so high
> *that it tastes I-don't-know-what*
> *which is so gladly found.*
>
> He who is sick with love,
> whom God himself has touched,
> finds his tastes so changed
> that they fall away
> like a fevered man's
> who loathes any food he sees
> *and desires I-don't know-what*
> *which is so gladly found.*[4]

The poet finds in the words of the Psalmist (cf. Ps 73:23-26) something of the same intensity. When contemplative love enflames the heart, it changes the entire course of one's life. The senses now serve the spirit. According to Adrian van Kaam, our life ceases to be dominated by our pretranscendent vital and functional dimensions. They are transformed into servants of our Christ-centered spirit. The center of gravity, in short, shifts to the transcendent dimension. Sensible affections become pointers to the "More Than" rather than ends in themselves. Nothing of sensory apprehension and appreciation is lost; it simply ceases to attach itself exclusively to one or the other object, person, or place. One sees all as coming from God and returning to God. During this alteration, one comes to expect dryness and a cessation of the past dominance of former desires. When these "little beyonds" prove to be unsatisfactory, our longing for the "Great Beyond," who is God, increases.

Thirsting for the Transcendent

Something in us, as the psalms of David attest, is being annihilated. Exactly what is being recrafted and to what degree change is occurring remains unclear. All we know in unknowing is that we can neither turn around nor turn away. We must continue to move toward a destination for which we have few, if any, descriptive or informational categories. We know only that nothing in heaven or on earth that used to give us satisfaction can do so now. We are caught in the Beloved's snare. We are being led we know not where, yet nothing can persuade us to choose another path. Perhaps no one has described this compelling force of love more poignantly than St. Augustine:

> Too late have I loved you, O Beauty so ancient and so new, too late have I loved you! Behold, you were within me, while I was outside: it was there that I sought you, and, a deformed creature, rushed headlong upon these things of beauty which you have made. You were with me, but I was not with you. They kept me far from you, those fair things which, if they were not in you, would not exist at all. You have called to me, and have cried out, and have shattered my deafness. You have blazed forth with light, and have shone upon me, and you have

> put my blindness to flight! You have sent forth
> fragrance, and I have drawn in my breath, and I
> pant after you. I have tasted you, and I hunger and
> thirst after you. You have touched me, and I have
> burned for you.[5]

A young woman who felt the same enkindling of love's flame in the depths of her being was Thérèse of Lisieux. *The Story of a Soul*, like *The Confessions of St. Augustine*, verifies St. John's conviction that the yearning for God does not wane as do dying embers. Once enflamed, its intensity increases. The desire for union with the Divine can be so overwhelming that it feels as if one's bones are drying up like fossils in the desert. This kind of thirst cannot be slaked. It is so intense, so alive, that it drains one's strength and zaps momentarily one's zeal. Only God matters at such a moment. This is the living thirst of which David speaks in Psalm 42:

> As the hind longs for running waters,
>   so my soul longs for you, O God.
> Athirst is my soul for God, the living God.
>   When shall I go and behold the face of
>   God? (Ps 42:2-3).

Such a thirst could kill one if it lasted. Thanks be to God, "its vehemence is not continual, but only experienced from time to time, although usually some thirst is felt" (DN I:11 [1]).

To be accurate in his description of this transforming event, St. John feels obliged to explain that at the onset of the dark night of the senses one does not grasp that this thirst is about transcendent love. One feels only the dryness and the void. Because these episodes of sensory deprivation cannot yet be comprehended as avenues to love and liberation of spirit, one assumes that such feelings of aridity and emptiness demand a response other than that of waiting upon God and remaining at rest. They evoke in one anxiety about not serving God with habitual dispositions of care and concern, or grief over possibly losing the ground one has gained with

the help of grace. It requires repeated acts of trust and surrender to become, in the midst of living with one's pain, a
sacrifice pleasing to God. One has to be content to remain
both a spirit in distress and a disciple at peace, a witness to
Jesus' agony in the garden as well as to his risen glory.

From the counsels of St. John we can thus derive the
following description of purgative contemplation:

1. It arouses in one a gentle yet firm sense of solicitude
and concern for God.

2. It purges the sensory or pretranscendent dimensions
of our human life form, including our vital need for
gratification and our functional need for satisfaction. In
other words, it recrafts the meaning we give to what we
see, hear, touch, taste, and smell.

3. At first slowly, then more and more powerfully, it
enkindles longings for God in our spirit, thus enabling
the transcendent dimension to take precedence over
and to transform our lesser concerns.

While this reformation is occurring, it may feel as if one
is undergoing a strange cure for an unknown ailment. One
remains faithful to trustworthy prescriptions, though the
promised positive outcome of the operation recedes in the
face of the immediacy of suffering. Purgation of the inordinate appetites and attachments that have held us in
bondage for so long makes us feel as parched as once lush
grapes drying in the sun. Darkness surrounds us. Our only
light is faith and the brave hope that dawn will illumine this
starless night.

At times the seemingly endless night of contemplative
reformation partially lifts, but soon again clouds veil its
resplendent light. All we can do is to trust that God is
granting us many virtues while relieving us of many more
vices. To experience such faith, hope, and love is not, as St.
John says, the result of human effort; it is the effect of "ah, the
sheer grace!"

At some point all of us are confronted by the harshness of reality whose disturbances of our heart only grace can heal. Businesses fail. Friendships are betrayed. Loved ones die prematurely. Illness strikes. People are plunged—like it or not—into prisons of public or private pain. To back away fearfully from what at first glance may appear to be relentless trials is a natural reaction. Our senses may seek pleasure, but our spirit cannot be content unless we are striving to please God. The tension within us between sense and spirit challenges us to find meaning in suffering. Is there a perspective from which we can comprehend how such experiences can also express something beneficial and providential?

Deprivation as an Opportunity for Formation

Faith alone enables us to live in the conviction that what is happening has infinite significance. It is the Lord who takes the lead. Christ draws us gently yet firmly into the night, cleansing us as rain does a muddy road from the dross of worldly delusions that claim to defy disappointment and death. This purging has a purpose in the divine plan. God has to accommodate our senses to our spirit to enable union to occur. We cannot effect this transformation by our own power. Thus our lower, pretranscendent "I" has to be reshaped in the night of the senses. The meditations of a busy mind have to be stilled now so that later in the night our human spirit will be ready to undergo accommodation to the Holy Spirit.

To see sensory deprivation as a formation opportunity requires a leap of faith. Suffering may seem meaningless to the one who has to endure it unless a supportive master like St. John continues to reassure us that there is a method to the divine madness. For the moment we can do nothing but trust in the promise that this "departure from the fetters and straits of the senses [is] a sheer grace" (DN I:11 [3]) and that many benefits will be forthcoming. Often it is only in retrospect that God's silent yet steady nearness to us becomes a source of wonder. All we felt for the longest time was God's absence.

When the light finally dawns and we behold in awe the transformation grace has enabled, we feel utterly humbled. How could we have doubted the goodness of God? Knowing what we now know, we would gladly pass through the night again, were God to ask this of us.

Renunciation Leads to Liberation

What does it mean to say that "I went out unseen?" St. John says that this phrase refers to the sense of liberation one feels when one's senses, so to speak, fall asleep. One escapes unnoticed by these guards from the bondage of their feeble, limited attempts to know and love God. Our senses easily succumb to the lure of false gods. The danger of their exposing us to error is great. Detours from the narrow path will happen if we rely mainly on sense data and on lower reason to sustain us. If our lower, pretranscendent "I" takes the lead, if the vital-functional dimension tends to master rather than serve the transcendent, we are bound to get into trouble. Hard as we try to attain spiritual maturity, we stumble at every step into potholes of imperfection.

Formation ignorance, defined by Adrian van Kaam as ignorance of our true transcendent calling by Christ, is fueled by the false flights of fancy prompted by the pride form and its coalition of capital vices.[6] The wonder of the sensory night resides in its liberating quality. This night releases us from binding attachments to impermanent earthly and even heavenly sensations of pleasure and delight as if these were ultimate. The night casts a cooling shadow over the presumptions of holiness produced at times by analytical or psychological musings that claim to master the Mystery. Finally, the night produces many goods that are lasting. Among these is the graced acquisition of virtues like patience, peace, and prudence.

I am reminded here of the stories older people like to tell of hard times remembered as if they happened yesterday. As the details of an event unfold, one senses that no matter how tough they were one would not trade them for the world. St.

John himself is like a wise elder looking back on trying times and able to say that they were splendid, not because of human cleverness but because of what God allowed him to learn through them. The way that then seemed bedeviled by hardship now evokes a benign chuckle. Adversity becomes an avenue to the stars. Affliction yields to the deeper truth of benediction. What seemed to hamper spiritual growth now proves to have been not an obstacle but a blessing in disguise. The path that stretched one almost to the breaking point of physical or emotional or spiritual pain becomes from this perspective not a source of arbitrary punishment but of formation wisdom.

How renunciation can lead to liberation is and remains a mystery. Part of the story of this turning can be told by great dramatists, poets, and spiritual masters, by grandparents fingering old photos and trying to explain to children why suffering has been a good teacher. When one feels challenged to reclaim life in the face of affliction, one has come to a kind of second conversion. Letting go of the controls, we allow God to take the initiative. We gladly leave behind the baggage of illusory fulfillment to enter the purifying fires of the transcendent night that lead us resolutely to oneness with the Eternal. The results, says the saint, are "great happiness and grace" (DN I:11 [4]). The reasons for this audacious claim ought by now to be clear:

1. The sensory night reveals with stark clarity that deprivation is the only sure road to divinization. To put to rest our carping appetites and nagging affections for things as substitutes for the transcendent is unspeakably beneficial to one who would be raised by God to spiritual maturity.

2. To endure this night in a spirit of fidelity and courage is to be in good company. It is to join the ranks of those called and chosen to enter into the reign of God by passing through the narrow gate. The road on which one walks leads to new life in the Lord (cf. Mt 7:14).

Pure Faith—A Sure Gate to God

For St. John the "narrow gate" of which Jesus speaks is the dark night of the senses. There the Divine Forming Mystery despoils our futile attempts to displace the transcendent dimension by illusory substitutes. The only ticket that enables us to pass through this gate is pure faith. Such strong conviction in the ultimate benevolence of love divine is a sure sign of spiritual maturity. The nets of selfishness that would strangle the spirit are disentangled in the night. Our lower senses are lifted up by grace and led into a land of peace and joy hitherto unknown. The road narrows before it widens. Still awaiting us is the night of the spirit.

One who would journey to God in pure faith has to do so along this road. There is no other way. It is only by means of pure faith that we can be united to God. This is the most recurrent theme in *The Collected Works of St. John of the Cross*. If few are willing or called to walk all the stages of this way with the Lord, then so be it. The first passage through the narrow gate leads us into the night of sense. Fewer still seem willing or called to walk farther along this road into the night of spirit. This way is even more narrow, dark, and terrible than that which preceded it. The reformations of the sensory night, the trials these occasion, cannot be compared to this next phase of transformation, but then neither can its exquisite benefits. These will be explained by St. John in due course. For now he turns his attention more explicitly to the benefits yet to be granted in the night of sense.

8

The Blessings Darkness Bestows

(*The Dark Night*, Book One, Chapters 12 and 13)

"This old neighborhood never changes." Yet the people moving into it are more diverse in race, color, and religion than ever before. You know you are deceiving yourself by ignoring their presence.

"I feel fine." Yet blood tests show you are anemic. You have to change your lifestyle, exercise, rest, and eat regularly, or the tiredness you feel occasionally will become permanent fatigue. There is no excuse to persist in your stubborn denial of the aging process.

"You're perfect for this partnership." Yet the next day you learn you are no longer the candidate the firm wants to hire for this position. You keep your chin up and try not to show your disappointment.

"I pray every day, but God mustn't be listening." Yet you hear in a sermon that you ought to be more trusting. You feel a mixture of guilt and resentment and don't know why. You are ashamed of feeling angry at God while wondering why you are being treated so harshly.

These examples remind us that life does not place itself on hold like a garment in layaway. It moves inexorably on. It offers for our consideration a myriad of choices. The dreamer in us longs for that day when the world will stop or the train of change will grind to a halt. The realist knows that for every peak there is a valley, for every road a fork.

No Pain—No Gain

Coping with these ups and downs takes candor and courage. We have to choose with as much clarity as possible one or the other path. This can only be done to the degree that we are confident that God's will for us is good. There is no other way to survive as distinctively human than to believe in the ultimately benevolent meaning of an event that demands of us as many changes as does the night of the senses.

To comprehend not only after the fact but in advance that this experience of deprivation is meant to be a reason for rejoicing is a feat of convinced faith. To say that purgation is beneficial is not the pious raving of a religious fanatic. Such a conviction is the end result of a mature faith, one that has been tested in fire. Such a believer is qualified to lead and to teach others who are also seeking answers to some of life's most difficult questions. Only a person of wisdom, learning, and experience like St. John would dare to say in so many words: "Listen, my friend, your sense of loss is deeply felt, but it is not the end of the line. There is meaning to the Mystery's madness that does not immediately meet the eye. Wait and see what God has in store for your spirit. No storage facility could contain a fraction of the treasure that is to be yours."

St. John turns to scripture to illustrate the truth that gain without pain is seldom if ever possible for humankind. He recalls the story of Abraham, who prepared a great feast on the occasion of his son Isaac's weaning (cf. Gn 21:8). Little could he have foreseen the painful test God would ask him to endure to verify his obedience. Was he willing or not to sacrifice his own son (Gn 22:1-14)? In passing the test, it is as if Abraham himself is weaned by God from the infancy of the spiritual life and readied for his adult journey in faith. God like a wise mother initiates this growth process. Neither psychological nor spiritual maturity can occur if parents are overly protective. A smothering version of maternal love is a dubious form of affection. Good mothers and fathers know when it is time to let us make our own way along the road of life. It would be debilitating to dress us in swaddling clothes when we're entering young adulthood. True nurturing encourages us to take off our baby garb and don more durable clothing. God's will is not that we remain passive and helpless. Jesus himself had to leave the safety net of Nazareth and risk the insecurity of the unknown on his journey to Jerusalem. The Father had to let Jesus walk his way, and so must we.

In these nighttime adventures, our spirit matures. God sets this painful weaning process in motion not to punish us but to empower us. An aging person cannot continue to eat pablum. The sweet mush infants consume cannot nourish a man or woman in need of meat and potatoes. One has to eat a whole chunk of bread, crust and all, to grow. That is why St. John, at first secretly, then openly, celebrates these nights of sensory deprivation. In them people get a chance to taste "the food of the strong," another of his expressions for "infused contemplation" (DN I:12 [1]).

The condition for such wholly satisfying spiritual nourishment has to be dissatisfaction on the level of sense. Looked at from this perspective, one does not regret aridity or shun darkness. One suspects that only when the ground is dry does the rain cease to be taken for granted. Only when the stomach is empty does one feel intense appreciation for every morsel of food. From such a vantage point, it is easy to see why Jesus felt so at home with the poor. They, more than the rich, were ready to rejoice in the benefits of the night. Let us look at each of these in turn.

Growth in Self-Knowledge

"Know thyself" is a dictum of perennial philosophy. The quest for such knowledge permeates every page of scripture. It is, as great teachers and writers tell us, wrought in the crucible of suffering and in the search for its meaning.

According to John of the Cross, the chief benefit of the night is knowledge of self. This implies knowledge of one's own misery; that is to say, of one's inability to make it through this experience without the help of a Higher Power. St. John is bold in his claim that not *some* but literally *all* the favors God imparts to us come wrapped, not as an *exception* but as a *rule*, in this kind of knowledge. Suffering, whatever else it may be about, is a great teacher.

One does not have to be a mystic or a mathematician to know that chaos produces an abundance of creativity. Listen to the music composed by Beethoven when he was deaf or read the poetry of John Milton written when he was blind. Ponder the underground tales of Dostoyevsky or view the paintings of Christ in agony by masters of the Renaissance. Study the life of Corrie ten Boom or consider the charitable works of Mother Teresa of Calcutta. Read the diary of Anne Frank or see films depicting the survival of other holocaust victims. Who could doubt the link between misery and mindfulness, between suffering and self-knowledge? Being stripped of the illusion of self-sufficiency by means of material or spiritual agony can become the avenue by which one is able to find beauty and to love more abundantly.

That misery can be the fount of mercy is a profound revelation. Former Secretary-General of the United Nations Dag Hammarskjöld made clear in his diary, *Markings*, the different ways that the blessings we seek are often to be found not in prosperity but in adversity. He once wrote:

> Let everything be consumed by the fire in the hope that something of value may be left which can be riddled out of the ashes.[1]

St. John offers a parallel example of this paradoxical truth from the book of Exodus 33:5. The passage on which he dwells focuses on the connection between humility and self-knowledge. When a way had to be found to make the people of the Covenant knowledgeable about themselves and God's plan for their salvation, they were instructed to remove their festive clothing and the other adornments with which they were familiar. Awaiting them was no ordinary crossing. They were not to make the passage as victors or warriors but as workers whom God would treat not as royalty but as servants bound to obey the law he had set forth.

The customary clothing they were to leave behind is comparable to the sensory stripping that occurs in a dark night experience. For the moment mirth gives way to misery, festivity to the stark fact of human weakness and dependency on God. When we feel as low as this, we have no illusions left. We come to know ourselves as we are. We learn by trial and error to accept the wisdom of God's plan to lead us into deserts of deprivation. This has to happen if we are to be made ready and worthy to cross over into the promised land of liberation.

When life proceeds according to our plans, when misery is as remote to us as the moon, we may remain ignorant of who we are as children of God. We pass blissfully from one experience to the next as if the party will never end. Our spiritual life is like being at a banquet where we enjoy a smorgasbord of delightful treats: consolations, sensations, feelings of gratification, inspirations, all in abundance. We grow more and more complacent. We are content. We believe all this is proof positive that we have been chosen to serve God in a special way. Perhaps in false humility we do not explicitly formulate this thought; we are too modest for that! Chances are we at least harbor the notion of being someone special. How could we not feel pleased with ourselves since, owing to the satisfaction we derive from living a disciplined spiritual life, it appears as if we are almost at the top of the mount.

Then comes an awakening that shakes our complacency to the core. God clothes us in other garments. What previously required little effort on our part, like prayer, now demands tiring labor. Delight is displaced by dryness and desolation. Inner lights once bright as day are now as dark as a moonless night. What is happening can confuse us, even depress us, unless we realize that this experience offers us an authentic chance to grow in the virtue of self-knowledge.

Now we see as if for the first time the reality of our human condition. These limits paradoxically light our way to God. Overwhelmed by our nothingness, we are able to acknowledge the full depth of our dependency on God. We find no ultimate satisfaction in our own plans and projects because it is clear that without God's help we can do nothing. From the point of view of transcendence this place of *no-where* is the privileged arena of our at last being *now-here*.[2] We are where God wants us to be. Our lack of self-satisfaction pleases God. With this lowering of the shield of complacency, we can appraise anew whether or not we really mean it when we say, "Thy will be done."

As far as St. John is concerned, the dejection we feel about possibly displeasing God or about not serving our Divine Master is from a transcendent perspective like incense rising. Our former deeds and delights, however worthy of note they may have been, placed us at the risk of remaining oblivious to our many imperfections. Self-knowledge is thus the wellspring from which many other blessings flow. If this well runs dry, we are in grave danger of never discovering what God has in store for those who, through suffering much, have learned to love more.

Growth in the Knowledge of God

When another's suffering arouses our compassion, we are more likely to adjust our style of communication to meet their readiness to receive a consoling word or some sympathetic silence. In the face of an experience of our own nothingness, any haughty or presumptuous tone is laughable. We tend to communicate with God in a more respectful way. Awed by the immensity of the Almighty, we are more courteous in our prayerful conversations. When we were proud of our prosperity, seeing this as a sign of spiritual success, we were less humble. When we had more consolations than we could remember, we acted with less deference to God. Satisfactions and stirrings, typical of beginners, were interpreted as proof positive of great holiness. This attention made us more daring with God than was proper. We risked becoming downright discourteous, as inconsiderate toward God as we might be toward old friends whose feelings we seldom bother to consider.

Referring to the book of Exodus once again, St. John says this change in modes of converse happened to Moses. When God spoke to him on Mount Sinai he was overwhelmed by gratitude and gratification. This initial consolation was so powerful that he would have flung himself into God's arms with a boldness belying proper deference to the Divine. Just in time he was ordered to stop and take off his shoes (cf. Ex 3:4-5).

Moses momentarily forgot his place. He was about to behave in a disrespectful manner, lacking discretion and detachment from his potentially selfish desire to defy the barrier between creature and Creator. Moses had to be taught the proper way to converse with God. He had to cease being so presumptuous and obey the command not to approach God in a functional manner. So well did he learn this lesson that caution and discretion led him not to dare to look upon God face to face (cf. Ex 3:6 and Acts 7:32).

St. John interprets this incident analogously, saying that as Moses left aside the shoes of his appetites and gratifications (meaning his lesser, more vitalistic ways of relating to God), he was suddenly aware of his poverty, his nothingness, his miserable condition in the sight of God. Only when this posture of creatureliness became as natural to him as his gift for leadership was Moses fit to receive God's word and to become a God-molded prophet.

The same story repeats itself in another biblical figure, the man Job. When life was good for Job, when he was the recipient of every delight and glory imaginable, he thought that he and God were the best of friends. It was his custom to converse with God by rehearsing his many blessings, as one would do in a person-to-person exchange. Job, like

Moses, thought that he had reached the graduation class of intimacy with God when, in fact, he was only in the elementary school of the spiritual life. God had to prepare him for a more mystical mode of encounter by means of events Job least expected or desired, including, among others, those dreadful occurrences cited by St. John: Job's lying naked on a dunghill; being abandoned and persecuted by his friends; feeling anguish and bitterness for a seemingly endless period of time; seeing the earth upon which he had toiled diligently parched like a wasteland (cf. Jb 2:7-8; 30:3-11). At the moment Job was depleted vitally and dubbed by himself and others an abject failure functionally, he became really pleasing in the sight of God.

Neither theological arguments nor personal lamentations could restore the flow of conversation between Job and God. The mystery of a presence more awesome than Job could analyze in his mind overtook him and alleviated his doubts. The Most High came to Job gratuitously and raised him from the heap of ashes where he had consigned himself to stay (cf. Jb 42:10-17). God came when the time was right and revealed to Job deep truths. Job came to know more of God in his adversity than in all of his prosperity put together (cf. Jb 38:1 ff.).

Illumination of Divine Wisdom

Not only does this time of dryness—where the sensory appetite has no satisfying object—confer the gift of self-knowledge and the way to converse with God, it also gives us a new view of God's grandeur and majesty. In a special way the night of the senses fulfills the prophecy given in Isaiah 58:10 that light will illumine the darkness. This means that grace bestows upon the seeker both self-understanding and some understanding of God. To acknowledge how lowly and miserable one feels without God is to really know how much one longs for God.

The night snuffs out the lesser lights associated with sensory supports. In this dimness the intellect is freed to seek a higher truth. The mind can move like a bird in flight from limited, earth-bound explanations to spiritual revelations. Even when one's desire is drawn effortlessly to God, as was that of Moses and Job, it is still not pure. One's motives are likely to be mixed. Hence gratuitously aroused consolations can impede the elevation of spirit to which the Mystery may draw us when we least expect it. Cut off from consolation, we feel lost and alone. Anguish can spark the urgency to find the reason for such a feeling of loneliness. Dryness on the sensory level of stimulation can quicken the pace of transcendent aspiration.

Scripture suggests that the more wisdom we seek, the more sorrow we can expect; the more knowledge we have, the greater our grief will be (cf. Eccl 1:18). This thought supports St. John's conviction that by means of the dark night of contemplation, naturally a source of profound lamentation, God supernaturally instills divine wisdom. This can happen only in a person whose spirit is "empty and unhindered" (DN I:12 [4]). The divine inflow of grace necessitates that obstacles be cleared away. The timbers and boulders that impede the waters of life are the vital pleasures and functional satisfactions with which we were inclined to equate the height of spiritual maturity.

In the words of the prophet Isaiah, St. John finds the answer to this dilemma. Quoting Isaiah 28:9, he explains that God teaches this knowledge of contemplation, this message of maturation, to persons weaned from the milk of spiritual sweetness and from the honey of discursive meditation. The senses in their corporeal dependency cannot contain the influx of divine wisdom; hence the deprivation of the dark night is compared to a cleansing process. Neither can the wisdom of transcendent presence be confined to the operations of the mind; hence the withdrawal of the intellect from formerly satisfying ruminations is compared to the maternal decision to let the child go forth alone on the long road to adult living.

The benefit of darkness is that it can heighten our powers of hearing, a fact well documented in studies of people whose power to see is even slightly impaired. I remember going down to the beach late one evening with only a flashlight. When I reached the shoreline I shut it off and heard with awed intensity the sounds of the night. Every one was clearer: the lap of the waves, the whirling of insect wings, the rise and fall of voices from a nearby porch. It was wonderful the way darkness heightened perception. My eyes soon accommodated the shapes and shadows cast by clouds and the occasional flickering of lights from a fishing boat. The deprivation was at first disconcerting, but once I stood still and listened I saw and heard more that I could have during the day with its incessant distractions.

St. John associates such deeper listening with detaching oneself from sensate, vitalistic channels of perception and affection as if these were the only passageways to self-knowledge in God. Citing Hebrews 2:1-3, he compares standing watch with appetitive detachment, which is for him the first step toward spiritual maturity. "Fixing one's foot," his rendition of firmness in fidelity, supports the awareness that, try as one might, one can no longer meditate with the sensory faculties—that is to say, discursively. Contemplating what God says means coming to a plane of transcendent understanding that brings with it new found peace and joy. In St. Augustine's memorable phrase from the *Soliloquies*, "Let me know myself, Lord, and I will know you," St. John finds confirmation of the connection he found between self-knowledge and knowledge of our Divine Source (cf. DN I:12 [5]).

Psalm 63 offers further proof of the paradox that in the night there is light:

> O God, you are my God whom I seek;
> > for you my flesh pines and my soul thirsts
> > like the earth, parched, lifeless and
> > > without water.

I will remember you upon my couch,
   and through the night-watches I will
      meditate on you:
That you are my help,
   and in the shadow of your wings I shout
      for joy.
My soul clings fast to you;
   your right hand upholds me (Ps 63:2, 7-9).

In this affirmation of David's, it is clear that sensory deprivation is efficacious. Aridity is like a dry wind in the desert leading one to seek with renewed vigor an oasis of spiritual nourishment. Lofty knowledge of the Godhead is more likely to happen when our intellect is darkened and love lifts us into the cloud of unknowing. There the Mystery reveals itself on a plane of knowing beyond any words or images the mind can master. The psalmist proclaims that this epiphany of God breaks through human interpretations. There in a desert land, in a place parched and without water, amidst dry blowing sand blocking sight and covering customary routes, God appears to David and reveals the power and glory of the Most High. "God is our refuge!" (Ps 62:9). St. John summarizes what occurs as follows:

> … The means to the knowledge of the glory of God were not the many spiritual delights and gratifications [David] had received, but the sensory aridities and detachments referred to by the dry and desert land … the way to the experience and vision of the power of God did not consist in ideas and meditations about God, of which he had made extensive use. But it consisted in not being able either to grasp God with ideas and walk by means of discursive, imaginative meditation … (DN I:12 [6]).

To enter this land with all its uncertainty is to find a solid road to infused contemplation paved by grace. To accept as a blessing the apparent adversity of the dark night, its aridity and inner void, is to find oneself closer to God than one might be in the bright light of day. To know God rather than merely knowing about God is to be open to the depth dimension of divine self-communication. The knowledge given in the night of the senses may not be nearly as plentiful or as abundant as that to be bestowed in the more profound night of the spirit, but it produces a veritable gold mine of benefits. Among the best of these is its healing of the ill effects of the seven capital sins.

Humility versus Pride

When our life falls apart, when our plans fail to materialize, when we know we have lost control, when our hearts are empty, of what have we to be proud? This downsizing of the myth of self-sufficiency is perhaps the foremost benefit of the passive night of the senses. The grace of this experience decreases pride to the degree that it increases humility. Teresa of Avila says in *The Interior Castle* (Mansions 10, Chapter 6) that humility enables us to stop lying to ourselves and to walk in the truth of who we are.[3] Spiritual pride under the shadow of a multitude of sins cannot withstand the white light of humility. This essential disposition of the heart is acquired often in the school of hard knocks. The acquisition over time of the virtue of humility, however, cannot reach its climax unless we see into the flaws and falsehoods that have thus far sustained the vice of pride.

In times of prosperity, when the I-can-do-it-without-the-help-of-God mentality seems triumphant, it is easy to push humility onto the back burner. Now, having fallen from the pedestal of illusory independence, we feel wretched and forlorn. Any thought of being able to make it on our own is laughable. It is the farthest thing from our minds. Even the tendency to assume that we are better or more advanced than others is at a standstill. The opposite appears more true. Others seem better than we are.

St. John concludes from this that humility is like the sturdy trunk of a tree from which stems other virtues like charity. Once pride has been pulverized by the purgative night, it is possible to behold not only self but others in a new light. If "I" need so much love and understanding, then so do "you." The humble person is by definition inclined to esteem others more than themselves. Prior to this experience of dryness in relation to the Divine, what prevailed was a holier-than-thou posture of judgmentalism toward those who seemingly had less than we. This proud stance crumbles in the face of our current misery. Because the danger of a pending downfall occupies all of our attention, there is no time to scrutinize another's conduct.

In the psalms St. John finds an example of what happens. While he was in this night David lamented in Psalm 39:3: *"I became dumb, and was humbled, and I kept silent in good things, and my sorrow was renewed"* (quoted in DN I:12 [8]). For David, as for Job in another book of the Bible, if blessings are seeds, then a drought has prevented their growth. This year there will be no harvest. The good times have ground to a halt. Words of self-praise are sealed inside one's lips. Silenced are the put-downs once directed at other people.

Knowledge of one's fallen condition makes it almost impossible not to feel compassion for another's plight. He who was once proud of being utterly self-sufficient becomes submissive. She who insisted on having her way is suddenly obedient. The spiritual journey can now begin in earnest. Aware as these persons are of their own wretchedness, they are ready and willing to listen to the teachings of a wise master. Whereas previously they thought they had all the answers, they are now eager to receive spiritual direction and help from almost any respected quarter.

Gone like leaves from trees devoured by locusts are traces of the affective presumptions of holiness they harbored when they took for granted God's favors. Now humbled, they can proceed as pilgrims. So intense is their longing for God that they do not realize that all the other imperfections of the capital vice of pride are being swept away simultaneously. They are the recipients of powerful graces, but for now all that matters is the importance of their relationship to God. In this posture of receptivity the floodgates of other benefits of the dark night open and benevolent help comes swiftly to their aid.

Reformation of Avarice, Lust, and Gluttony

One by one the night of the senses deflates and reforms the imperfections or obstacles that block our journey to God. Avarice cannot withstand the cleansing power of aridity. At one time or another we will find ourselves at the "so what?" moment when all the possessions in the world cannot make us or anyone happy. The night assures us that we are more than what we have. Neither material goods nor spiritual, neither pious objects nor a proliferation of devotional exercises offer us lasting contentment.

Overlooked is the goal such practices are supposed to help us reach. In the night we cannot count on the gratification we once took as a sure sign of progress. Forms of prayer, once pursued with alacrity, now leave us at a loss. They are no longer delightful or easy to do but tedious and laborious. We use these means so moderately now that a new danger looms: not that of zealous excess but of bored indifference.

Despite the confusion we feel, divine guidance is at work. As we have seen, the night imparts the disposition of humility. This readies us to do whatever God asks, even if we feel more displeasure than pleasure. Lack of gratification frees us to follow the lead of grace. Detached from many things, we are open to the ones that really count.

A similar reform happens to the vice of spiritual lust. This obstacle like a weed in the desert cannot withstand the heat of sensory dryness. The distaste felt in the face of formerly gratifying devotions informs us that these were often done more to please ourselves than to honor God. Detachment from ulterior motives washes clean the smudges and stains of such impurity and enables us to proceed beyond the fickle give-and-take of spiritual lust to resonance with the purer notes of transcendent love.

Eager as he is to move on to his analysis of the dark night of the spirit, St. John does not dwell at length on the relief from spiritual gluttony the sensory night enables. He does assure us that the imperfections associated with this capital vice also lose their power. Countless benefits are accrued by means of the liberating effects of the night. It both deflates and reforms one's dependence on and desire for spiritual sweetness. As gluttons must get in touch with and give up their passion for food, so must people curb their appetite for sensory delights as ultimate, whether their source is as earthy as dinner and a drink or as heavenly as an ecstatic uplift in prayer. All such sensations are curbed and bridled like wild horses in the desert in this arid and dark night.

Nothing on which body or soul feeds can satisfy us fully. God allows this purgation to last as long as it takes to bring our passions and desires for "lesser beyonds" to the point of illumination or reformation. An awakening that goes this deep cannot occur without mortification. In other words, something in us has to die if something better is to be born. When misdirected, passions lose their strength; when they become sterile because they are not being satisfied as before, they go into a kind of incubation period where resculpting occurs, often without our realizing what is happening.

St. John compares this experience to the way the udder of a cow desiccates when her milk is not drawn daily. She will produce again under the proper circumstances but not now. Similarly, withered desires and spiritual sobriety seem worlds apart from felt consolations and near intoxication where the sacred is concerned. Yet to wither is not to kill entirely. With proper sun and water a plant can be restored. This is a waiting period one ought not to rush. Good things that are not readily clear are taking place according to the urging of grace. Admirable benefits will result.

When lesser desires and passions are stilled and we begin to taste something of transcendent peace and tranquility, we have no choice but to let go and to be led by God. St. John says in a sparsely worded but weighted line: "Where neither the appetites nor concupiscence reign, there is no disturbance but only God's peace and consolation" (DN I:13 [3]). In truth, God never takes something from us without returning something to us a hundredfold.

Remembrance of God and Growth in Virtuous Living

If fear of the Lord is the beginning of wisdom, then the only real dread one ought to have is that of not retaining a habitual remembrance of God. This remembrance is best cultivated during the dark night. Like an industrial size sweeper removes the day's debris from a hotel conference room, so sensory purgation cleanses our souls of the illusions, imperfections, and obstacles that dull perception and darken the transcendence dynamic. Instead of clinging in craven fear to the tangible appetites and affections we used to trust, we find our minds and hearts turning to God.

What St. John dubs a truly great benefit of the night is that we learn to overcome compartmentalization and to practice all the virtues together. We have to be at the same time patient and persevering, committed to pursuing the life of the spirit whether or not we feel much satisfaction. We have to abandon ourselves appreciatively to the Mystery, whatever the circumstances in which we find ourselves.

In the aridity of the night, we can no longer rely on being motivated to grow solely because of the consoling signs of progress we receive. There are none. We do what can and must be done to please God. That's all. Thus do we gain the virtue of fortitude, drawing strength from our weakness, seeing challenges in setbacks, detecting pockets of indifference and grids of defensiveness that previously eluded us.

Slowly but surely we begin to grow in spiritual maturity. We become more conscious of the importance of practicing the corporal and spiritual works of mercy. We try to live the cardinal and moral virtues as if they were second nature. Such wholeness is another benefit of the night. As when several pieces of a puzzle come together and we know we will not be defeated, so now we enjoy: "the delight of peace; a habitual remembrance of God, and a solicitude concerning him; cleanness and purity of soul; and the practice of virtue" (DN I:13 [6]).

In Psalm 77, St. John finds scriptural confirmation of this experience. In the night, David says, his only remembrance was of God. In this state, with no other consolation to sustain him, he still found comfort, exercised virtue, and was, in effect, transported by the Transcendent. In the psalmist's words:

Aloud to God I cry;
    aloud to God, to hear me;
    on the day of my distress I seek the Lord.
By night my hands are stretched out without
      flagging;
    my soul refuses comfort.
When I remember God, I moan;
    when I ponder, my spirit grows faint.

O God, your way is holy;
    what great god is there like our God?
You are the God who works wonders;
    among the peoples you have made known
      your power (Ps 77:2-4, 14-15).

Reformation of Anger, Envy, and Sloth

In this blessed night, the agitating voices of three more vices fall silent. Purgation of appetitive desires to lord it over others, or to make fun of their gifts, or to feign indifference leads to the acquisition of the virtues or dispositions to which these imperfections are opposed. The result is a reformation of anger by meekness, of envy by charity, and of sloth by perseverance.

The effect of aridity is to soften and humble the hard of heart, to make us see how difficult it is to resist temptations and to persist in obedience through trials. God does not let us go during the course of the night. We are, so to speak, backed into a corner by the Mystery. It is impossible to escape our call. Of what use is it to hold on to our anger when we can give it up and become God-molded persons? To be meek is not to be weak. It is to go out of ourselves in care for God and neighbor.

The result of living in such Christ-likeness is seen in the slow but sure cessation of anger at ourselves. We feel less and less impatient with our imperfections. We do not expect to overcome either our own or our neighbor's faults overnight. We let go of the myth of becoming saints in a moment. We are neither displeased nor disrespectfully angry with God for not making us perfect according to our timetable.

Envy also undergoes a spiritual face-lift. The suffering caused by the sensory night inclines us to be more charitable toward others. The truth is, we know we are capable of planning and executing some vicious though subtle forms of revenge. When people prefer others to us or when they themselves seem to be more advanced than we in the spiritual life, we may feel envious. Sly words of condescension or condemnation come from our lips more readily than praise. In the misery of this dark night experience we are more inclined to concede that God has the upper hand. Who are we to complain or to judge? If any envy remains in us, it is a "holy envy" of those who, though formerly condemned by us, now seem to be the persons we are called to emulate. This shift, St. John says, is a sure sign of growth in virtue.

The tedium we felt about spiritual things lingers, but it is less persistent. We became slothful when spiritual consolations were on the wane. As long as we enjoyed gratification, we were willing to persevere. When we did not experience what we either tried to attain or felt we deserved, our enthusiasm dampened like hot coals under a dripping hose.

Such fickleness in regard to faith is turned around in the night. We see that the weariness that began to overtake us had to do with our excessive reliance on spiritual feelings. Now that God has taken this satisfaction away from us we do not have to preserve the false equation we made between gratification and growth. We know we can grow in spiritual maturity even, and perhaps only, in the absence of reliance on certain feelings. These do not translate into the certitude of sanctity.

Blessings of the Night

It would seem as if St. John cannot stop naming the benefits that flow from "dry contemplation" (DN I:13 [10]). The last thing we would assume contemplation to be is dry. What could be ordinary about the surprises of God? Yet what can we mortals say of the desert spaces in which the self-communication of the Divine is disclosed? When we least expect it, when we feel utterly helpless and unworthy, we may receive a delicate touch of pure love. God grants us an awareness of what really matters. If only for a moment we are lifted into another order of reality. Evelyn Underhill describes this paradoxical blend of dryness and sweetness in her book, *Practical Mysticism*. She writes with characteristic candor:

> This life shall not be abstract and dreamy, made up, as some imagine, of negations. It shall be violently practical and affirmative; giving scope for a limitless activity of will, heart, and mind working within the rhythms of the Divine idea. It shall cost much, making perpetual demands on your loyalty, trust, and self-sacrifice: proving now the need and the worth of that training in renunciation which

was forced on you at the beginning of your interior
life. It shall be both deep and wide, embracing in
its span all those aspects of Reality which the
gradual extension of your contemplative powers
has disclosed to you: making "the inner and outer
worlds to be indivisibly One."[4]

Underhill would agree with St. John's conclusion that
"Each of these communications is more valuable than all that
the soul previously sought" (DN I:13 [10]). At first one doubts
that this could be so. Common sense would seem to indicate
that contemplation is not or cannot be dry. Surely it has to be
more showy or ecstatic.

The "real thing," according to the master, is "very delicate," so much so that the senses do not grasp or comprehend
it. The more one follows the leadings of grace and undergoes
the purgation of his or her sensory affections and impulses,
the more one obtains the truly sublime gift of liberty of spirit,
a posture of freedom to follow God wholly and to be open to
receive as a further benefit of the sensory night the twelve
fruits of the Holy Spirit. These are: charity, joy, peace,
patience, benignity, goodness, long-suffering, mildness,
faith, modesty, continency, and chastity (cf. Gal 5:22-23).[5]

The equation of renunciation and liberation recurs in the
writings of St. John. Imagine the feeling a prisoner has on the
day of her release. It is as if she has been given a new lease
on life. So it is when one is freed from the clutches of three
powerful enemies: the *world* in its worldliness, with its
deceptive promise that having things can guarantee happiness; the *flesh* in its attempt to sever itself from the spirit; and
the *devil* in his seductive ploys to keep us bound to
pretranscendent realms of pleasure and satisfaction as if
these were ultimate.

The beauty of the night is that it almost effortlessly breaks
through these falsehoods by showing us the inevitable limits
of sensory delights. Once these desires are put to rest, we are
released from the prison of empty promises. Then neither the
devil, nor the world, nor sensuality can fool us. None of these

enemies has the power to overcome the transcendent thrust of our fully human spirit.

The desert of aridity becomes like a secret garden where we walk hand in hand with God. We follow our Divine Friend where we are led whether or not we reap the reward of recordable feelings. We are beyond being moved to act only because of the satisfactions we derive from divine direction or from our deeds. All we dare to focus on is whatever will please God. No matter how many times we fail, what we most want to do is the will of the Father. While self-satisfaction may have been prevalent in times of prosperity, we now see life from another perspective. We are more attentive to the movements within us that still need reformation.

The fear we feel is not of an avenging God; it is more a "holy fear" reflected in our feeling disquieted about how much in us needs to be liberated if we are to love God alone. We feel dissatisfied with ourselves because we know there is always more room to grow. Our capacity for ongoing self-examination is neither scrupulous nor introspective. Gently yet firmly we strive to live in the presence of the Most High. From this posture of faithful encounter with a loving God, we pray to preserve and increase the virtues associated with Christ-like living.

Sensory aridity helps us also to overcome the domination of our life by unpurified, pretranscendent drives and desires. It opens us to receive infused graces. We know these are not in any way the products of our own diligence. They are pure gifts of God. We learn to treat lightly whatever sensible consolations we derive from the continuation of certain spiritual practices. These graces are God's to give and God's to retain. Either way our faith increases. What matters is to move in the direction God wants us to go.

Any awe-filled fear we may feel is not due to aridity as such but to another concern that will not go away. Are we showing enough solicitude for God? Does our care for Christ match in any way Christ's care for us? Does the Lord know how much we yearn to serve him? We are not asking for sensory proof; that need has disappeared. Our attention centers on fulfilling our divine life call, whatever the cost. We want to cling to our faith in the darkness of not knowing where we may be led. We want to be God's servant, as David was, even when we give in to our human weaknesses. In fact, we can proclaim with the psalmist that our spirit in its affliction is itself a pleasing sacrifice to God:

> O Lord, open my lips,
>   and my mouth shall proclaim your praise.
> For you are not pleased with sacrifices;
>   should I offer a holocaust, you would not
>   accept it.
> My sacrifice, O God, is a contrite spirit;
>   a heart contrite and humbled, O God, you
>   will not spurn (Ps 51:17-19).

Called to Go Where God Leads

Precious indeed are the benefits of this desert dryness. We feel like persons with chest ailments who go to the Southwest for a cure. The prescription for treating our condition may be painful, but the results are worth it. No wonder St. John mouths without exaggeration one long "ah!"—"ah, the sheer grace!" How freeing it is to go out unseen, that is, to be released from subjection to the sensory appetites and affections as if these were the be-all and end-all of the spiritual life. No longer can this lie entrap the saint's soul. No longer do the clinging vines of mindless gratification hold the master in their grip.

One so awakened by the purgation of the night can now go forth, spurred on by the freedom one in love with God feels. Once these wayward satisfactions are tamed and subdued, the initial battle fought to bring pretranscendent pulsations and ambitions in tune with transcendent aspirations and inspirations draws to a close. We can move like new persons at a new pace.

Calmed are the erratic rhythms of excessive joy and sorrow, of pleasure and displeasure. Stilled are idle expectations and nerve-wracking anxiety, the staccato upswing of hope followed by the cringing reflex of fear. The newfound equilibrium we experience is the fruit of dying to delusion. We put to rest or put in their proper place our sensory desires. Our entire social-vital-functional-transcendent self feels as in tune outwardly and inwardly as a fine symphony. The body serves the spirit; the spirit appreciates the body's exquisite instrumentality. One catches a contemplative glimpse of life when the intricate ruminations of discursive meditation are held in suspension. Now that the household of the lower regions of our life is at rest, we are ready to proceed on the adventure of deeper intimacy with God that awaits us in the dark night of the spirit.

9

Moving Into the Night of the Spirit

(*The Dark Night*, Book One, Chapter 14)

After a noisy day of important meetings, casual conversations, incoming and outgoing calls, counseling sessions, media bombardment, and telephone messages, it is a relief to walk through my house late at night and listen to the stillness. I treasure these times of silence. I want them to last and last. When sleep comes, my senses shut down like a factory assembly line between shifts. On a good night I am drawn effortlessly into the restorative rhythms that result in deep rest.

St. John compares sleep to the little deaths or detachments that occur when we are led by grace into the dark night of the senses. Inordinate passions rushing hither and yon like a river of white water flow at last toward a calm lagoon. Appetites once as voracious as a den of unfed dogs have been satisfied with food that provides nourishment long after the meal ends. With senses stilled, with passions quelled, with appetites calmed, one's bodily house is at peace, ready to receive visitations of the Holy Spirit. When our senses are asleep, our spirit stands alert in attentive presence to the Transcendent.

The Night Invites Divine Initiative

It is right to refer to the night of purgation as a happy event. When our house is still and we feel safe and secure, it is lovely to walk through the door into the fresh air under the starry sky. So, too, the person fired with longings for God can now begin the next phase of the journey, setting a new pace on the path of purgation, illumination, and union. This is, in St. John's words, the way of proficients. It is the "illuminative way" or the "way of infused contemplation" (DN I:14 [1]).

The sign that distinguishes this way from all that has preceded it is that God now takes over totally as our guide. God is the Good Shepherd, who pastures us over field and dale to a secret place where the grass is sweet for grazing; God is the vendor who offers a cool drink to travelers in the desert. The water is free. It refreshes bone and marrow. It relieves our thirst for the Holy immediately without any intervening meditations, inner discourses, or active efforts. The entire people of God benefit from the graces bestowed on us or any person in this state, for all of us are members of the one Body of Christ.

This tranquil scene is like the calm after the storm. The sensory night does not destroy, it reforms, the senses. We seek God's temple and hear more sharply God's call. In this period of reformation, we are being prepared, should this be the will of the Father, to be led into another, more oppressive night of the spirit. Yet this oppression will also prove to be progressive. For through this still more narrow door we will reach a land as yet unknown, the land of the union of love.

It is a fact that not many on earth are destined to be led along this path. St. John says that only a few usually reach the unitive way. This is because the night of the spirit is as a rule accompanied by heavy trials and sensory temptations that can last a long time, depending on what God asks of a person. There is nothing easy about dealing with the following degenerative "spirits":

Fornication

Citing 2 Corinthians 12:7, St. John predicts the appearance of an "angel of Satan," named by him the "spirit of fornication." Like a violent hurricane batters a fragile shore, so this spirit buffets the senses of the Spirit-filled with strong temptations. Illicit images afflict one's memory, imagination, and anticipation. To resist such thoughts and the actions they imply can be a veritable hell for one trying to heed God's voice. In fact, St. John says that to meet this bad spirit head on, to say no to its sly insinuations, is to endure a struggle so powerful that it feels worse than death (cf. DN 1:14 [1]).

Blasphemy

Added to this kind of raging in the night may be the "spirit of blasphemy." Like smoke from a clogged fireplace, it backfires into one's mind and heart, clogging the channels of obedience and commingling with a slew of doubts, despairing thoughts, and weird ideas moving one away from God and toward the popular pulsations of a selfish world. The impact of such blasphemy can be so great, the suggestions to curse God so strong, that in one's imagination one is almost moved to pronounce them. This causes grave torment to one striving to grow in nearness to God. Just think what the apostle Peter went through when he betrayed Christ, his best friend, and you may grasp at least in part how formidable an enemy the spirit of blasphemy is.

Scrupulosity

There is one more "loathsome spirit" St. John has to identify at the onset of the spiritual night. In Isaiah 19:14 it is called *spiritus vertiginis*. St. John translates this as an ominous darkness sent to people progressing on the way to union that can be their downfall if they are not aware of its insidious power. For this is the bad spirit that not only darkens the senses but also fills one's heart and mind with "a thousand scruples and perplexities" (DN I:14 [3]).

Just as a person burdened with an obsessive-compulsive personality disorder often knows no inner peace, so one may be attacked and agitated incessantly by this false spirit. It catches one in a mesh of intricate arguments about sin and salvation that demand more attention than God. When one argument is seemingly brought to closure, another begins. It is impossible to be content with anything. Any counsel, any idea, is subjected to a thousand tests. No judgment stands for long. Some objection to it arises that must be dealt with immediately. The powers of reason supersede the simplicity of faith. When this happens it is nothing short of horrible. St. John calls such scrupulosity one of the most burdensome effects of the spiritual night. It takes an incredibly skilled master to help a person over this hurdle.

Signals Announcing the Spiritual Night

Having identified some common roadblocks on the journey, St. John explains that generally God will send these stormy trials and temptations in the sensory night to signal us that we may be called to enter this other night. Again he emphasizes that not all people are led by God to the unitive way. One who has passed through such purifying fires and been reformed may be among those God chooses to lead on. The outer senses and the inner faculties must be properly exercised, prepared, and inured for the battles yet to be fought and won by grace.

It would be as unwise to send an amateur into a professional boxing ring as it would be to expect one to step unexperienced into the night of the spirit. The union with divine wisdom that will be granted has to be received by a worthy vessel. The person not tempted, tried, and proven through the trials of the sensory night is at a distinct disadvantage. One's senses are not purified and elevated enough, one's inner life not honed sufficiently in humility, to receive the wisdom of secret contemplation God wants to offer.

Two scripture passages point to this truth, both of which St. John cites. In Sirach 34:9-10 and following, it is said of persons who are not "put to the proof," what do they know? Only one who has experience can speak sensibly. The prophet Jeremiah gives further testimony to the truth that the chastisements of the Lord are not arbitrarily sent to punish us but purposefully allowed to instruct us and to arouse us to repentance (cf. Jer 31:18-19).

When people share their story, it is common to hear them say that without this or that difficult period or failed relationship or financial hardship they would never be where they are today. Who of us would have the courage to face a crisis of major proportions had we the choice to resist it? Yet who of us has not learned something of lasting value from being led by the Mystery to a place we would not have chosen to go?

Faith as Strengthened Through Interior Trials

St. John's own story, especially his horrifying experience of being imprisoned by his own brothers in Toledo (1577-1578), offers vivid testimony to his conviction that such occasions for reformation are small prices to pay for becoming wise through suffering.[1] Faith tells us that God allows us to experience these interior trials for a reason. When we are at our most ineffective, humanly speaking, grace works efficaciously to lead us to a previously unknown level of spiritual maturity.

Once our sensate life is conditioned to forego the link between felt satisfaction and progress on the way of union, we are free to go where God leads us. Our natural weakness causes us to be overly attached to consolations as sure signs of advancement. Now, by means of these many trials, we relinquish the reins of control and place ourselves humbly in the hands of God. Such humility is the best preparation for what the saint calls our "coming exaltation" (DN I:14 [4]).

St. John must continue telling us about these two nights, for he feels as if God has commissioned him to do so. Still he hesitates before taking the next step. He makes clear that no one can say with certainty how long the Mystery intends to keep one in this arena of reformation. It is a state of fasting and penance insofar as the senses are concerned.

The night in question is also as varied as the unique souls who enter it. Not everyone undergoes purgation in the same way or according to the same timetable. Neither are the trials and temptations people experience amenable to set patterns.

God treats each person differently in accordance with the pace of grace in his or her life. All we can say for certain is that whatever form the purgation takes it proceeds in accordance with the ultimately benevolent reforming and transforming will of God.

The imperfections or deformations that must be submitted to divine resculpting may be greater or lesser depending on the life call of the person in question. That is why a spiritual director must treat each one who comes for counsel with respect and discretion. There is only one rule of thumb that a guide can assume: "In the measure of the degree of love to which God wishes to raise a soul, he humbles it with greater or less intensity, or for a longer or shorter period of time" (DN I:15 [5]).

It follows that if a person has a considerable capacity and strength for suffering, as did, for example, Thérèse of Lisieux, then it is likely that God will purge or reform her more intensely and quickly. St. Thérèse's prayer of abandonment, her oblation to merciful love, is an act of pure faith. It is a classical example of what it means to say, "Thy will be done." Its final lines read:

> In order to live in one single act of perfect Love, I OFFER MYSELF AS A VICTIM OF HOLOCAUST TO YOUR MERCIFUL LOVE, asking You to consume me incessantly, allowing the waves of *infinite tenderness* shut up within You to overflow into my soul, and that thus I may become a *martyr* of Your Love, O my God!
>
> May this martyrdom, after having prepared me to appear before You, finally cause me to die and may my soul take its flight without any delay into the eternal embrace of *Your Merciful Love.*
>
> I want, O my *Beloved*, at each beat of my heart to renew this offering to You an infinite number of times, until the shadows having disappeared I may

be able to tell You of my *Love* in an *Eternal Face to Face!*[2]

Those whose faith is not as strong as this may be kept by God in the night for a long time. Augustine of Hippo tells in his *Confessions* how long it took him to reform, and Teresa of Avila describes in her autobiography years of living in spiritual dryness. A contemporary who also struggled to maintain fidelity to his call during a long dark night was Father Walter Ciszek, S.J. This saintly man writes in his own story of a soul, *He Leadeth Me*:

> For my part, I was brought to make this perfect act of faith, this act of complete self-abandonment to his will, of total trust in his love and concern for me and his desire to sustain and protect me, by the experience of a complete despair of my own powers and abilities that had preceded it. I knew I could no longer trust myself, and it seemed only sensible then to trust totally in God. It was the grace God had been offering me all my life, but which I had never really had the courage to accept in full. I had talked of finding and doing his will, but never in the sense of totally giving up my own will. I had talked of trusting him, indeed I truly had trusted him, but never in the sense of abandoning all other sources of support and relying on his grace alone. I could never find it in me, before, to give up self completely. There were always boundaries beyond which I would not go, little hedges marking out what I knew in the depths of my being was a point of no return. God in his providence had been constant in his grace, always providing opportunities for this act of perfect faith and trust in him, always urging me to let go the reins and trust in him alone. I had trusted him, I had co-operated with his grace—but only up to a point. Only when I had

reached a point of total bankruptcy of my own powers had I at last surrendered.[3]

Heeding the Call to Enter the Night If It Comes

While the duration of these nights may extend over a considerable period of time, the experience of people like St. Augustine, St. Teresa, St. Thérèse, and Father Ciszek confirms St. John's insight that God adapts the pace of grace to our capacity to receive it. The purgation one undergoes is less intense over the long haul. Here and there one's temptations abate. God refreshes the senses to prevent one from backsliding. Just when the hot sun seems relentless, a refreshing rain cools the ground. So it is in our relationship to God. It is never too late to mature in Christ. Some arrive at this turn of the road when they are past mid-life. Others never seem to reach the heights to which they may be called in their lifetime. They are neither wholly in the night nor wholly out of it.

Perhaps you and I are among those loved deeply by God but not called to advance beyond what St. Thérèse called the little way of spiritual childhood or what Brother Lawrence of the Resurrection designated the sacrament of the present moment.[4] While advancement to the top of Mount Carmel may not happen in our span of life, St. John assures us that God will still give us a taste of transcendence. For short periods of time and on certain days, these spiritual experiences may make a tremendous difference in our lives. None of us can be the same when we are touched, even briefly, by the finger of God. By enabling us to cope with mild or great temptations, by allowing us to endure the aridity of desert spaces once in a while, God preserves us in humility and self-knowledge.

Our Divine Master knows what we need. When we least expect it, at a time and in a season when we may feel especially lost and alone, a knock comes on our door. The Spirit comes to our aid. Christ consoles us and encourages us not to abandon the quest. We are more likely to give up the futile search for worldly consolations when we taste heavenly food. Such nourishment is enough to prevent us from losing courage. The wonder is that God adapts to our pace of progress, however slow and plodding it may seem.

Where weaker souls are concerned, God acts like a lover, at times drawing near to us in intimacy, at other times seeming to withdraw from us. This game of divine hide and seek arouses our interest. It is a game God plays to exercise us in the meaning of love. As St. John says, "without these withdrawals [we] would not learn to reach [God]" (DN I:14 [5]).

The psalms often address this movement from the presence to the apparent absence of God. For example, the psalmist asks, "Why, O Lord, do you stand aloof? Why hide in times of distress?" (Ps 10:1). God cannot help but hear this desperate plea: "Hide not your face from me" (Ps 27:9) and "Show me the way in which I should walk, for to you I lift up my soul" (Ps 143:8).

In the light of these experiences, we can conclude that nothing God does is done in vain. The road to union is not smoothly paved. It is the road of realism. This experience, like any event that is worthwhile, reminds us that there is no gain without some pain. We cannot hope to follow Christ unless we are willing to take up our cross. If the goal we seek is as consonant and lofty as the union of love, then we must be willing to follow the lead of grace. Usually this means remaining in the sensory night, enduring spiritual aridity and many temptations for a long time. No matter how quickly God leads us on, any time spent outside of the fullness of love feels inexorably long. In this regard, the opening verse of St. John's poem *The Spiritual Canticle* ought to be etched into our Christian consciousness:

> Where have you hidden,
> Beloved, and left me moaning?
> You fled like the stag
> after wounding me;
> I went out calling you, but you
> were gone.[5]

Having explained the obstacles to and conditions for transformation in the sensory night, St. John says at the end of Chapter 14 that it is time to begin his treatise on the dark night of the spirit. Without further delay, let us turn with him as our guide to its commencement.

10

Entering the Spiritual Night

(*The Dark Night*, Book Two, Chapters 1,2, 3)

Only on rare occasions does the journey to union with the Divine resemble a ride on a speeding train. Normally it is a slow process. One does not proceed immediately from the night of sense with its purgative trials and sustained periods of aridity to the night of spirit. Many years may pass in the exercise of what St. John calls the "state of proficients" (DN II:1 [1]). In it, by means of self-renunciation, one departs from the cramped cell of self-centeredness to inhale the refreshing air of freedom in Christ.

To follow God's will, to do one's daily task, however small, in a spirit of cocreation with the Creator, brings with it not only a sense of functional satisfaction but also a taste of transcendent joy. Feelings of freedom, sudden upsurges of interior delight, a foretaste of future graces—these are a few of the gifts given to proficients more frequently than before they entered and passed through the night of the senses. What does this transition time look like from inside the experience? Let me try to summarize in a few points what St. John sees:

1. Neither our imagination nor the inner faculties of memory and anticipation related to it are bound to the practice of strict discursive meditation.

2. Spiritual solicitude or vigilance of the heart happen more spontaneously. This custom begins to become second nature. It requires little, if any, concerted effort.

3. Notwithstanding the importance of meditative techniques, one becomes, even without them, the

beneficiary of good results, the most noticeable of which are "serene, loving contemplation and spiritual delight" (DN II:1 [1]).

4. Commingled with these benefits, like smudges on a smooth pane of glass, are flare-ups of aridity, shadows of pending darkness, rumbles of conflict as ominous as storm clouds on the horizon. When such purgative experiences pass through and over one's spirit, they are more sharp and intense than before because, as St. John suggests, they are "like omens or messengers of the coming night of the spirit" (DN II:1 [1]).

Twilight of the Spiritual Night

At a time when one may feel as if the eye of the storm has passed, as if the time of purgation is at an end, the mystery of transforming love sends messengers to announce that more reformation is in store. The principal part of the process, the night of the spirit, cannot be bypassed, however intense the night of sensory purgation might have been. An alignment has to happen between these two parts of the night so that in the end they will form one *unit* oriented toward *unity* with God and highlight the intrinsic unity of the whole person. For now, the omens of the coming night come and go. Only in the spiritual night itself will they seem excruciatingly prolonged. For now the messages of the night are like the reminders we receive in the mail of a pending event. We read them with interest, taking into account what we are being asked to do. Then we return to our customary routines. The night, like a tempest, blasts its fury for a while then blows out to sea. All is once more serene.

It appears as if God purges some people in this way, by short intervals, because they are called to reach a less lofty degree of love than others. One enters the night of contemplation on fire with the kind of love that burns away lesser attachments and makes one realize that he or she will never be the same. As swiftly as the night descends, so the dawn bathes the sky with soft new light. As the psalmist David affirms, Yahweh sends hail (crystals), or symbols of contemplation, like crumbs (morsels) (cf. Ps 147:17).

It goes without saying that these tastes of dark contemplation can never be as deeply flavored and intensely transforming as what St. John calls "that frightful night of contemplation [he is] about to describe, in which God places the soul purposely in order to bring it to divine union" (DN II:1 [1]). As far as he can tell, God chooses, as it were, from the beginning to place some people in this state and to bring them by way of the cross to the crux of union.

Self-Communications of the Divine to Proficients

Grace seems copious at this point. Persons who are proficient in their walk with the Lord enjoy abundant inflows of inspiration, unmistakable delights in the presence, for example, of the blessed sacrament, and a host of interior gratifications. It is as if God is loving them into a new way of being and living. They receive manifold communications of his presence in their everyday world, many more than they had previously known.

As a result, the life of the spirit overflows into the life of the senses like a bubbling stream surging toward a dry river bed. One receives these signs of God's outpouring love as if through a pure and clear channel. How could one's experience be otherwise? The cleaner the windows of our senses are, the easier the light of the spirit can enter and illumine our whole house.

Despite the cumulative benefits of sensory purgation, it is not enough to ready proficients for the rigor and vigor of God's more refined self-communications. When these are experienced in the sensitive part of one's body, he or she may actually feel sick, suffer a variety of vital symptoms, complain of this or that infirmity, like a weak stomach, and find themselves on the borderline of spiritual fatigue. Quoting the book of Wisdom serves as a reminder to St. John that indeed the mortal body can be a load upon the soul (cf. Wis 9:15):

> Consequently, the communications imparted to proficients cannot be very strong or very intense or very spiritual, as is required for divine union, because of the weakness and corruption of the senses that have their share in them (DN II:1 [2]).

Because communications from God are not able to be received in a purely spiritual way, that is, by the spirit alone, people not yet purified by the night of the spirit may have to cope with such extraordinary phenomena as raptures and transports that rattle one's bones! To all such signs and symptoms of immature faith, St. John offers, already in the *Ascent*, his singular critique: *Nada.*[1]

For those on the way to a more pure and mature faith, such signs are rare. In the perfect they cease altogether. Then the strife is over, the battle has been won; then Christ, the victor, completes what he has begun. One attains freedom of spirit without doing damage to one's senses by means of immoderate asceticism or dependence on felt flights of ecstasy.

To grasp just why proficients must enter the night of the spirit, to understand anew why St. John's teaching on renunciation unlocks the door of liberation, we must assess with his guidance the imperfections and dangers proficients will still encounter.

Detrimental Habits Die Hard

We all have bad habits we find difficult to overcome. Some, like smoking, are addictive. Others, like irritability, are more amenable to reformation. Those hindrances or imperfections that block progress for proficients are dubbed both habitual and actual by St. John. The former have a clinging quality like moss on a stone or dullness on the surface of a crystal chandelier. Imperfect affections—likings for things more than longings for God—remain in the root system of our not yet fully purified spirit. So hidden are they, so subtle and rationalized away, that the night of sensory purgation is not enough to dislodge them. Another night, that of the spirit, has to happen if these alien dispositions are to be redirected.

The first purgation succeeded in pruning the tree of life. The second goes to the ground of the problem that retards its growth. The first purgation removes obvious surface stains; the second deep cleans embedded ones. What has already occurred due to the grace of the night of the senses is to accommodate them to the ways of the spirit. This transformation prepares us for union with God, but it is not enough. Old habits die hard. Stains linger like spots of ink on a white blouse. Even when we wash them well, they can still be seen by a perceptive person.

The stains of the "man of flesh" similarly linger in the spirit. At times they are apparent, as when, for example, one indulges in lustful fantasy or envious comparison. At other times they are almost imperceptible, so unobvious as to be dismissed as unimportant. This would be a mistake. If such deformed dispositions are not reformed by what St. John calls "the soap and strong lye of this purgative night" (DN II:2 [1]), the road to union with God may be severely blocked. For, as the beatitude puts it, only the clean of heart can see God (cf. Mt 5:8).

Beginners as well as proficients have to deal with habits of mind that dull us to the detrimental effects of sin that distract us from God's call, and that make us inattentive to the invitations and challenges of grace. Because in God's eyes we are worth the effort, we may be asked to endure the hardships and conflicts of the night. Odd as this may seem to human reason, the night is a time of concealed illumination, clarification, and recollection for the spirit.

St. John contends that anyone who has not passed beyond the state of proficients still possesses habitual imperfections. These cannot coexist in a perfect state of union with the God of love. We may have trouble with them as long as we live, but we must at least try to overcome them in a spirit of repentance. We can be consoled by the thought that our loving Master always intends to give us the graces we need to start again.

Spiritual Apprehensions as Deceptive

There is yet another stumbling block proficients have to expect. Some will encounter dangers and challenges that arise directly from the spiritual realm insofar as these enter the spirit through the senses. Proficients in the life of prayer are the recipients of many spiritual communications. Apprehensions of the holy are not strange to them. These occur in both the sensory and spiritual dimensions of their being.

For instance, a person on the way to union may see certain signs and wonders, visions that are both imaginative, like the look of Jesus, and spiritual, like white light. The "visions" may be accompanied by warm and wonderful feelings, including a sudden flood of tears. Such gifts are always perceived as undeserved, but they are subject to exaggeration by one's own powers of phantasy. One has to leave room for the fact that they may also be due to demonic seduction. In fact, the devil likes to suggest to proficients that they are special. In this way, the demonic seducer tries to play on their pride and to impress upon them even more exotic, charming, and beguiling flights into near ecstasy.

One has to put these events and feelings into perspective, and, all in all, to renounce them outright. Otherwise they will become impediments to union. The only legitimate point of access to oneness with God is faith, not feelings. Faith is the best defense we can muster to ward off demonic manipulation.

The closer one comes to liberation in God through love, the more one has to guard against the temptation to be the object of other people's attention. The easiest route the devil can use to puff us up is pride. We can be duped into believing, for example, that we are channels for special visions or that we have attained the vain status of being named a seer or prophet. The focus of our attention can be deflected by the demonic from humble submission to God to haughty declarations of divine revelations given to us alone. We presume that the Holy Spirit has chosen to speak to us as if we had been raised providentially to the status of spokesperson of the Most High!

False prophets roam the world in an age like our own, fascinated as it is by the spectacular. Enter the evil one, the prince of deceivers, to puff them up with pride and presumption. St. John's description of this downward spin into deception ought to be memorized by every spiritual director:

> Drawn by vanity and arrogance, they allow themselves to be seen in exterior acts of apparent holiness, such as raptures and other exhibitions. They become audacious with God and lose holy fear, which is the key to and guardian of all the virtues. Illusions and deceptions so multiply in some, and they become so inveterate in them, that it is very doubtful whether they will return to the pure road of virtue and authentic spirituality (DN II:2 [3]).

It is tragic to witness one who is so close to the light and yet so far away. The "holy fear" or awe St. John upholds as the key to spiritual maturity erodes whenever one becomes too sure that he or she has made it. Then it is easy to mistake presumptuous illusion for true openness to the Mystery. One uses the barometer of spiritual apprehensions or affective feelings to determine or foretell one's rate of progress on the road to union. Just when a person is beginning to make some real progress, he or she allows the demonic to interfere with the grace of enlightened humility. The way of the Lord is clear, yet one prefers to follow a disastrous detour.

Steps to Advancement

St. John admits that the imperfections of proficients are so common in this regard and in some cases so resistant to the remedy of the dark night of the spirit that he has to decide either to expound on them for several more pages or to pass over this matter as lightly as he has. He chooses to do the latter because his real purpose is not to repeat the teaching he has presented in *The Ascent* but to establish the absolute necessity of this deeper purgation if one is to advance.

Spiritual blessings, genuine consolations, and self-communications of the Divine ought to evoke our gratitude and rekindle the disposition of awe without themselves becoming the object of our desire. Neither ought we to dwell on them inordinately. As the saint warns, no matter how sincere and strenuous the efforts of proficients may be to deflect attention from themselves to God, they are only human. It is difficult even for them not to make these natural affections and imperfect habits more important than they are.

To ready one for the grace of divine union, to assure that awe erases every trace of arrogance, that humility halts the upsurge of vanity, one has to proceed under the lead of grace into the dark night of spiritual purgation. What St. John calls the lower part of the soul, the region of pretranscendent vital and functional strivings, has to be purified and elevated to the transcendent level of gentle openness to Spirit-inspired aspirations and inspirations. Our lower "I," in the words of Adrian van Kaam, must be accommodated to our higher "I."[2] Only then can we worthily receive these special graces without reducing them to our narrow ranges of understanding or to some closed system of interpretation.

To reach the union God intends, we must let God be God. We have to allow grace to lead us sensually and spiritually into the night of the spirit. St. John articulates precisely why this next step is necessary:

> In this night both the sensory and spiritual parts are despoiled of all these apprehensions and delights, and the soul is made to walk in dark and pure faith, which is the proper and adequate means to divine union, as God says through Hosea: *I will espouse you* (unite you) *to me through faith* [Hos 2:20] (DN II:2 [5]).

Signs of Proficiency

Having expressed the need for this night, the master gives us an overview of what will follow in Book Two. He assumes that he is addressing people who have glimpsed the promised land of spiritual maturity. They are not yet "perfect," but they are certainly "proficient" in the ways of God with us. What are the signs of this "proficiency"?

1. One has already undergone a lower level alteration and is on the way to a higher level transformation. This means that the love of God has allured the senses in such a way that one can no longer be content with the goods of creation. One yearns to know more intimately the Creator.

2. One's senses have been nourished by glimpses and touches of divine goodness. One comprehends that these flow from a transcendent source. They are not of mere human origin. Such communications arise from our human spirit as illumined by the Holy Spirit. They are infused, not acquired by means of any effort or merit on our part.

3. One feels ready to accommodate one's senses (the lower regions of pretranscendence) to the spirit (the higher dimensions of transcendence). One stands in the posture not of master but of servant.

4. Rather than living in piecemeal fashion, it is now the case that each part of the human life form (our capacity to see, hear, touch, smell, and taste) now receives in a new and delightful way nourishment from the Holy Spirit. The self is no longer divided; it is united in at least a minimal way on the level of the transcendent.

5. Whereas before one felt at times a disconnection (as when a lamp plug separates from the electrical outlet) between sense and spirit, one now experiences a flow, a conformity, between these two parts of our being. We, as a whole, socially, vitally, functionally, and transcen-

dently, are ready to proceed along the way of purgation in obedience to God's call. We know not in full what awaits us, but we stand at the cliff's edge of divinely inspired spiritual maturity, ready to take the next step into the abyss of pure faith.

Results of Purgation

St. John further points out some of what he believes may happen during this purgation. Experience tells him that at least the following changes will occur:

1. Our senses and our spirit—the social, vital, functional, and transcendent dimensions of our human life form—will go through a complete process of purification. This occurs whether we expect it or not because one part of the whole cannot be made ready for union with God without every part being affected in a like manner.

2. This purgative reordering of life happens, as it were, from the top down rather than from the bottom up. It begins at the level of the transcendent and touches everything in its wake as a cascading waterfall affects the flow of the river at its base.

3. The night of the senses resulted in a certain reformation, but this was not enough. It reined in and reordered to a degree our inordinate appetites, thus effecting a genuine purgation. Now the remaining imperfections and disorders lodged in the sensory dimensions of the self must be further conformed to the spirit in which they are ultimately rooted. The spirit and its freedom, not the senses and their instincts, are the ultimate signs of distinctive humanness.

During this period of deeper purgation, it is as if the two main parts of our human life form—our senses and our spirit, all that is pretranscendent and all that is always transcending—become one. Purification means in effect reunification. One part of our being cannot be so affected by grace without the other part following suit. In fact, St. John says, "The real purgation of the senses begins with the spirit" (DN II:3 [1]). This is not to say that the night of the senses was without effect. Nothing could be farther from the truth.

It was a necessary beginning, but its completion can only occur in the night of the spirit. The first-level reformation is described by St. John as, in the end, more a "bridling of the appetite" than a lasting purgation.

> The reason is that all the imperfections and disorders of the sensory part are rooted in the spirit and from it receive their strength. All good and evil habits reside in the spirit and until these habits are purged the senses cannot be completely purified of their rebellions and vices (DN II:3 [1]).

St. John insists that the result of the spiritual night is a remarkable integration between the higher and lower levels of the self. Their purification leads to lasting unification. The first night was preparatory. What happened there readies the senses for this final stage of transformation. What was deformed and alienated from God has been reformed by grace. What was disruptive and chaotic is now calm. The sensory or pretranscendent part of our being was in a certain way drawn into the transcendence dynamic, but imperfectly. The senses were made ready to endure whatever purgation or suffering God might ask of one by means of the virtue of fortitude. Prudence, justice, fortitude, and temperance, the cardinal virtues, are necessary to maintain a Christ-centered, gospel-directed life, but of all these gifts the one most needed in the night of the senses is fortitude.

The purgation one has to go through to reform the lower "I" can be long and arduous. One needs to be as fortified for this journey as a mountain climber facing his or her Everest. The climb makes one feel weak at first, but soon the effects of training and practice are rewarded and initial weakness begins to be reformed. One may even discover hitherto unknown pockets of strength.

Accommodating the Senses to the Spirit

In the spiritual realm something similar happens. First the senses undergo reformation. Weakness gives way to determination. Worry exits as trust enters. Security blankets are put in storage as one is willing to take higher and longer leaps of faith. Then, when the sojourner needs it most, God sends him or her the experience of sweet consolation, delightful communion. Were the senses not at all accommodated to the spirit, these onslaughts of love would not reverberate in the deepest recesses of one's heart. Neither would a person have the fortitude or the readiness to endure the new demands of grace.

Even at the stage of proficiency, when one is beginning to enjoy the fruits of transcendent living, the way of communion with God is still, in St. John's words, lowly and natural. He says that the "gold" of our spirit has not yet been sufficiently purified to reflect and radiate the epiphanic presence of the Most High. One is near the crest of the mountain, but one has not yet crossed over to the other side.

Our relationship to God is still inclined to be childish, that is to say, slightly demanding, petulantly expectant that God's way ought to conform to our level of comprehension. Another level of perfection awaits us, for, as the apostle Paul explains:

> When I was a child, I used to talk as a child, think as a child, reason as a child; when I became a man, I put aside childish things. At present we see indistinctly, as in a mirror, but then face to face. At present I know partially; then I shall know fully, as I am fully known (1 Cor 13:11-12).

This seeing face to face, this knowing fully, is what happens when one is wholly united with God, when one reaches the way of perfection. St. John says that such women and men "do mighty works in their spirit." He adds: "... their faculties and works are more divine than human" (DN II:3 [3]). They have been stripped, in the words of Paul, of the "old man," of the "man of flesh," and they have become clothed with the new. They are indeed a "new creation" made in the form and likeness of their Creator (cf. Col 3:9-10). They have put off their "old self," full of deceitful desires, and have adopted a new attitude of mind, becoming more and more like God in righteousness and holiness of truth (cf. Eph 4:22-24). No longer are they conformed to the worldly patterns of the world. With minds and hearts renewed, they are transformed. Their will is to obey God's will for them, for this is good and pleasing and perfect (cf. Rom 12:2).

Forecast of the Night of the Spirit

Forecasting what has to happen for this depth of transformation to occur, St. John lays out, as does an architect the blueprints for a building, what one can expect in the spiritual night:

1. *Divestment.* God will, so to speak, strip one's inner faculties (intellect, memory, and will), one's affections, and one's senses of all counterfeit remnants of willfulness and pride. This will happen simultaneously in the sensory and the spiritual realms. It will affect one both interiorly and exteriorly.

2. *Apparent Abandonment.* It will feel at times as if one has been abandoned by God. This is so because the intellect, once full of answers, is now left in darkness, confused and unsure of the next step. The will, once eager to give all to God, once rewarded by warm, confirming consolations, now languishes in aridity. The memory, once full of sweet residues of encounter with God, once able to recall occasions of nearness to the Divine and the certitude of God's presence, now feels utterly empty. On the affective level, it seems as if all is lost. Affliction replaces affection received and given by God. Bitterness seems to cancel the beauty of a sought after and received touch of love. Anguish seems to deprive one in a cruel way of the warmth and satisfac-

tion once obtained from a seemingly endless storehouse of spiritual blessings.

3. *Privation.* This felt experience of being deprived of knowledge, good memories, and warm feelings is a condition for the possibility of one's receiving a new, spiritual form of life. It readies one to accommodate this new creation. The union of love, the spirit-to-Spirit relationship that alone can satisfy the heart's longing, begins paradoxically at the point when one feels most dislocated from the Divine.

4. *Dark Contemplation.* This remarkable transformation, this shift from one inadequate form of life to another level of distinctive humanness, is not something we can do. It is a gift granted to us by God by means of "a pure and dark contemplation." It is an opening to God that transcends the initiatory night of the senses and leads one to the proficient and potentially perfect night of the spirit. This night, says St. John, "is the principal purification of the soul" (DN II:3 [3]). Now he can explain again and in full the meaning of his opening stanza:

One dark night,
fired with love's urgent longings
—ah, the sheer grace!—
I went out unseen,
my house being now all stilled.

11

Crosses to Bear as Night Descends

(*The Dark Night*, Book Two, Chapters 4 and 5)

As a conductor elicits the recurrent motif in a great symphony, so St. John repeats the opening stanza of a poem etched on his heart by the Divine Engraver. Words once on his lips and always in his mind now beat to the rhythm of every breath.

"One dark night" does not describe a local habitation but a state of being.

"Fired with love's urgent longings" is not a description of passing emotions. It is the lasting disposition of a person for whom life's only meaning has become oneness with the Divine.

"Ah, the sheer grace!" is not an informational theological theme demanding a lengthy treatise. It is a deep sigh welling up from one who has no one and nothing to depend on but God.

"I went out unseen" is not the report of an impartial observer. It is the jubilant proclamation of one who has escaped the wiles of demonic seduction, the press and pull of untamed appetites, the traps of power and possession, the tight knots of self-centered consolations, and a thousand other threads and chains that prevent the solitary bird from soaring free.

"My house being now all stilled" is not the cozy picture of a domicile after dark in which the inhabitants, having taken their Sominex, are soundly asleep! Rather the turmoil we all experience when pretranscendent strivings get the best of us stops, if only for a moment, and we know something of the peace and joy meant for us when Christ becomes our all in all.

Having interpreted this stanza as revelatory of the preceding nights of sense and spirit, St. John now sees it as shedding light on the midnight facet of spiritual or contemplative self-emptying. This is the poverty of spirit to which we must be led if, as the beatitude suggests, the reign of God is to be ours (cf. Mt 5:3).

Initial Effects of Progress

From the perspective of the disciple longing for union with the Trinity, one feels as poor as a church mouse, as abandoned as an orphan, as unsupported as a homeless beggar. This part of one's pilgrimage is painful. The passive night of the spirit leaves intellect, memory, and will in darkness. Imagine the excruciating humiliation of Jesus' bloody walk to Calvary. Could intellect grasp this scandalous act of saving love? Imagine the Lord trying to remember the good times of his youth under the weight of the cross, the laughs exchanged, the tears shed with friends around the fire, the bittersweet taste of salty fish and honey-crusted bread. Could memory offset such affliction and anguish? Imagine the agony the Lord underwent in those final moments before his death, the pain searing through every fiber of his tortured body. Could his willingness to obey the Father restore the sensation of security? When all one sees is darkness, all one can do is to cling pure faith.

One's natural faculties are in a lights out situation, as entombed as prisoners in a maximum security camp. Only in one's heart of hearts does a light burn, a light no prying eyes can detect, no scourgings or thorny crownings can destroy. It is the white light of appreciative abandonment to the Mystery. It is the freely willed offering—accompanied at times by unspeakable suffering—to continue loving God in fidelity to one's call no matter what this commitment demands.

Thus it is that one attains in the most unlikely of circumstances a kind of ecstasy. One goes out of oneself. The lower "self" is at last put in its proper place. It is insufficient to contain what "selfless love" is about to reveal.

To proceed to this milestone on the journey, one has to depart from a "low manner of understanding," from a "feeble way of loving," from a "poor and limited method of finding satisfaction in God" (DN II:4 [1]). Thanks to grace, the two major obstacles that stood in the way—the flesh and the devil—no longer have the power to prevent one's progress. St. John is so happy about this turn of events that he has to burst into song. Only poetry can contain the joy he feels as the recipient of such profound graces.

It takes no less than an experience of "nakedness and poverty of spirit" to still the swirling sea of one's all too brilliant mind games, entrancing passions, headstrong appetites, and controlling affections. What one assumed the real thing to be—*this* is what it means to experience God, *that* really gives me a lot of satisfaction—is now seen as nothing. At the point where human effort ends, divine energy begins to flow more freely. Three signs are indicative of this transformation:

1. *One's ability to think and reason rises to a higher plane of faith.*

Intellectual and intuitive powers, once confined to resolving problems, now behold the far horizon faith alone can disclose. One believes in order to understand, moving, as the saint says, from what is merely human and natural to what is divine.

Purgation fosters transformation. Whereas one used to comprehend life's meaning by virtue of, let us say, a logical proposition or an informational theological assumption, correct but only able to carry one so far, one now understands the journey to eternal life in the light of the formative and sacred wisdom God alone can reveal.

2. *Whereas prior to this transformation one's will was united to God in a rather superficial or lukewarm manner—in a way likely to deflate like a pricked balloon when things did not go according to self-controlled timetables—one now experiences a peculiar strength.*

Neither consolation nor desolation change one's decision to make God the center. Merely human powers of willing, liable to wither in the face of pain, are made strong in the darkness of faith. One really believes in the ultimate benevolence of the divine forming, reforming, and transforming mystery.

No longer does one love in a here-today-gone-tomorrow style. One's love is steady. One's faith cannot be shaken loose from its divine foundation. Such strength is not natural but supernatural. It is a gift of God. It is not ours to command, only ours to obey. It comes to us from the coffers of fortitude, from the prisms of purity, that reside in the Holy Spirit, our comforter and guide.

Thus, in relation to God, our heart moves more in response to divine than human directives. We are less acquisitive and more acquiescent, less pushy and more patient, less controlling and more compassionate.

3. *Memory, once so cluttered with rote responses, ancient wounds, empty images, exhausting expectations, failed illusions, pathetic presumptions, resentful regrets, vapid apologies, sorry trysts, and endless distractions, comes at last to rest.*

No longer bound tooth and nail to the past, our memory becomes a space in which grace can release "presentiments of eternal glory." As St. John concludes: "... all the strength and affections of the soul, by means of this night and purgation of the old man, are renewed with divine qualities and delights" (DN II:4 [2]).

Meaning of the Dark Night of Spirit

Lest we jump too soon toward the distant star of divine union, St. John reminds us that the journey begins with three stark words: "One dark night ... ." And lest we imagine that we can skip this stage by merely repeating the verse, he now spends several chapters explaining that dark contemplation, though ultimately granting light to the soul, does so only by way of the night. Afflictions may in the end advance our flight, but that does not make it less agonizing.

We have to understand what the dark night of the spirit really means. Preparatory longings prompt us to turn outward toward God as a lover cranes her neck to catch sight of the beloved. The pain of longing reaches new proportions when God, like the beloved, returns one's glance. The flow of the encounter reverses. Love no longer goes out from one; it flows overwhelmingly into one.

One feels so small, so unworthy, of this grace. Shame, evocative of repentance and the desire for lasting purgation, clashes with elation and the newly felt awareness that one's old ways are gone with the wind. One cannot turn backwards, though this turn toward the unknown evokes, at least initially, the fear and trembling of which every pilgrim tells.

The inflow of grace, like the inrush of waters in an already flooded stream, washes away with a speed and a fury hitherto unknown, seemingly invincible bad habits and a host of natural and spiritual imperfections.

What is received is infused contemplation, synonymous for St. John with mystical theology. Modes of mastery melt. The Mystery finds new access routes to the inner chambers of one's heart. Through this infusion of grace, God teaches one in secret. The instruction given is as wordless and yet as revealing as that which transpires between friends who really love one another.

The evangelist John knew Jesus and Jesus knew John. John may not have been able to explain in so many words what happened to him at the foot of the cross, but he knew he would never be the same. He received in a glance, as it were, a lifetime's worth of formative wisdom.

This infusion, says St. John, produces two main effects in the soul: The first is preparatory or purgative, the second is reformative or illuminative. Infused contemplation, in other words, readies a person for the unitive way and the love this presupposes by simultaneously completing its purgation and assuring its illumination, that is to say, its radiation already on earth of the lights to come from on high.

Deeper Understanding of This Metaphor

The question one is bound to ask is anticipated by the master: If such contemplation illumines the way to God, if it cleanses channels of faith once clogged by the sludge of formation ignorance, then why does one choose as the only appropriate metaphor to describe what happens the "dark night"?

The reasons St. John gives are as follows:

1. Divine wisdom, infused and transformative, is to the pilgrim-soul night and darkness because its height exceeds or transcends any capacity of our pretranscendent "I" to understand or receive it. This wisdom is and remains infinitely beyond our finite minds. Hence it must be acknowledged by us as pure gift.

2. In the light of God's saving power, we behold without any benefit of defensive cover-ups how base, lowly, and unworthy we are of so gracious a gift. Our love appears puny and impure compared to the divine love we are being shown. Thus the purity of God's self-gift to us, of the Father's having so loved the world that he sent his only begotten Son to redeem us, is so awesome that it becomes afflictive, so bright a light that it becomes dark, so precious that it becomes painful. With the psalmist one asks: Who am I that my Lord should be mindful of me? (cf. Ps 8:5).

Secret Contemplation: Beyond Our Grasp

To validate the first reason, St. John quotes the philosopher Aristotle, the mystical theologian Pseudo-Dionysius, and the psalms of David (cf. DN II:5 [3]).

In his *Metaphysics*, Aristotle suggests that "the clearer and more obvious divine things are in themselves, the darker and more hidden they are to the soul naturally" (DN II:5 [3]). Examples come to St. John's mind that validate this principle. The bright light of the sun blinds the night owl. When we turn our eyes toward sharp sunlight, we soon see only a dark spot.

Our sense of sight can paradoxically benefit from only so much light. It then has to succumb to temporary blindness. When the divine light of contemplation or infused wisdom strikes a not yet illumined interiority, it casts upon one the dense shadow of spiritual darkness. What is happening to one surpasses any category of easy comprehension. Natural understanding has no neat cabinets in which to file supernatural graces, and so the intellect is darkened along with the memory and the will.

Pseudo-Dionysius, in the *Mystical Theology*, and other mystics, like the anonymous author of *The Cloud of Unknowing*, rightly term infused contemplation a "ray of darkness," especially when they try to describe this experience in relation to a soul not yet sufficiently purged and illumined by grace.[1]

In a sense, "ah!" is the only appropriate response because such a supernatural light cannot but overwhelm the intellect. An astronomer who detects the faint glow of a new star in a dark expanse of sky could not be more bewildered. For a moment one feels drained by the wonder of it, depleted of his or her natural vigor, in a state, so to say, of suspended animation, waiting for the process of one's emotions and thoughts to resume.

As for the Psalmist David, the imagery is the same. Clouds, shadows, obscurity—all veil the Godhead; not because the holy of holies is distant from us, but because human intelligence is too weak to grasp the fullness of divinity. Confronted by so bright a light, our eyes—usually so sharp— simply cannot see. Hence we read in Psalm 18:12 that clouds obscure the splendor of God's presence. The result is this paradox: "... when God communicates this bright ray of his secret wisdom to the soul not yet transformed, he causes thick darkness in its intellect" (DN II:5 [3]).

Secret Contemplation: Causes Great Affliction

If in these early stages of the unitive way, divine wisdom darkens human reason, it also evokes the painful truth—so humbling to our pride—that we are neither ready to receive nor worthy of experiencing touches that transcend our grasp. At least at the start of this advanced stage, one senses a stark contrast between the pure gift of divinely infused contemplation and the impure vessel poised to receive it.

One's misery is dubbed "extreme" by St. John because, as his philosophical background confirms, two opposites like light and no light cannot coexist at one and the same time in the same person. Under the siege of such a paradox, one necessarily suffers. One's interiority becomes no less than a "battlefield."

On the one hand, as yet unpurged imperfections vie for attention; on the other hand, the flow of grace leading one closer than ever to perfect love increases in intensity, at times overwhelmingly so. All this requires the kind of careful explanation the master now provides by describing the two chief afflictions one can expect to have to endure:

1. *Sheer Wretchedness.* The light of contemplation, the wisdom it imparts, is by all accounts both bright and pure. Yet the persons toward whom the Holy Spirit bends a wing are inwardly aware that they possess neither of these qualities. Thus one suffers the affliction of feeling utterly disabled and unworthy. How can eyes so weak not suffer pain when they have to behold the relentless brightness of the Beloved?

To suffer because of who one is can be much worse than
the irritation one occasionally feels because of what one does
or does not do. This is the pain of being caught between
contraries: the first infusions of divine contemplation clash
with the remnants of that in us which must still undergo
purgation. The battle that goes on inside of us can be devastating.

One suffers immensely due to the contrast between the
pure light of God's love and the unclean window into which
it so brightly shines. Never have we felt so out of sorts, so
unworthy, wretched, and scarred by sin. For example: Even
though everything in me longs to be with God, it feels as if
God and I are set against one another, as if the one I must love
has turned against me. I grieve as would a widow for her lost
spouse.

St. John suggests that we try to imagine how terrible Job
felt when God tried his faith in this way. We read in Job 7:20
the shock this good man feels when it seems as if God and
he are at opposite ends of the Grand Canyon. Job becomes a
burden unto himself. He cannot stand himself nor can he
stand before God without feeling miserable.

Nothing could be more noticeable than beholding in
God's pure light how smudged with self-centeredness one's
soul still is. It does not take a lecture to convince us how
unworthy we are of meeting God or any other creature made
by God. The deepest source of our grief emerges from the
thought that we may never be able or worthy to come into
the presence of the Most High.

The dark night of the spirit at this point in our journey
plunges us into a vortex of depreciative thoughts, miserable
feelings, and evil temptations from which we think we shall
never escape. While such wretched waves of unworthiness
and incapacity may have been repressed in the past, they
now cannot be denied. The dark night brings them into relief
as would a close-up photograph.

There is no denying the misery we feel. It is as if this sorry
state will somehow last forever, as if our only friend is

darkness, our only possession pain.[2] The psalmist David addresses his own and our plight as follows: "Take away your scourge from me; at the blow of your hand I wasted away" (Ps 39:11).

2. *Sheer Weakness.* We are, after all, only human. It ought to come as no surprise that the natural melts like wax before the supernatural; that our moral character reveals cracks in its veneer when it is confronted by the shining armor protecting the deepest recesses of God's word. The spiritual part of our being, however much it aspires to oneness with God, fails to match by even one fraction the love God has already given to us.

According to St. John, divine contemplation has a kind of force about it that almost blows us away. It subdues us only to strengthen us. What occurs is utterly paradoxical. Confronted by the light of love, it feels as if we may remain forever in the dark. It is as if darkness is the proper place to be, as if restless waiting is the same as being at rest.

As St. John says, "Both the sense and the spirit, as though under an immense and dark load, undergo such agony and pain that the soul would consider death a relief" (DN II:5 [6]). Quoting the prophet Job helps him to put a bit of flesh on the bare bones of this awesome and afflictive confrontation with the Mystery:

> Indeed God has made my courage fail;
> the Almighty has put me in dismay.
> Yes, would that I had vanished in darkness,
> and that thick gloom were before me to
> conceal me (Jb 23:16-17).

Plunged Into the Pain of Loneliness

As if the afflictions of wretchedness and weakness, of oppression and weight, were not enough to endure, one feels utterly alone, cast out of the shelter of God's favor like an unwanted stranger. All of the old props that enabled us to hold our chin up high crumble like matchsticks. The old line of defenses, the usual litany of rationalizations, are like some bad joke, only the laugh is on us. Who will uphold us now?

The night of the spirit is like a room full of mirrors in which we cannot bear to see ourselves as we really are. It is hell when no one takes pity on us, when, as Job so painfully experienced, our friends fail to shade us from the desert sun that sears our inmost spirit like raw meat over a white hot fire. Thus Job alone, covered with sores, not comforted in the least by the well-meaning explanations others offered to excuse his plight, can only cry out the louder: "Pity me, pity me ... for the hand of God has struck me!" (Jb 19:21).

The touch of the Lord is in truth as tender and gentle as the brush of a feather or as cool as fresh water on a fevered brow, but at this moment in the journey to spiritual maturity it feels heavy and hot. The vessel into which sheer grace is being poured is itself in the process of transformation.

Knowing this, God who is all-merciful does not press down on us too forcefully. His touch is ultimately light and invitational, enough to reform us without discouraging us from moving on. Such is the depth of divine compassion: Its wound is gentle, its cautery sweet, for the aim of this purgative contemplation is to grant us the highest of favors, not to chastise us but to divinize us.

12

Other Afflictions of the Night

(*The Dark Night,* Book Two, Chapters 6, 7, 8)

Imagine what chemical and mechanical forces would be required were we asked to change water to wine or apple juice to oil. Transforming such unlikely ingredients is comparable to taking the two extremes (human and divine) and fusing them together in the forge of spiritual transformation. Little wonder one suffers so much. The purgative component of this contemplation comes from the hand of God. The human component—we its receivers—have to be made ready by the Almighty for this transformative process. Old habits and attachments have to be stripped away like layers of paint on an antique chair. Whatever covers the wood has to be removed so that the original lovely surface can be revealed.

On the spiritual level, this depth of conformity to Christ requires that we allow grace to disentangle from our spiritual core the cobwebs of leftover attachments and to dissolve remaining imperfections. This process occurs deep within us in profound darkness. Any time we catch sight of the misery in which we almost chose to live, it feels as if everything about us has to melt away or be done in by the Divine. How else can we become one with Christ?

Feeling Undone

The best scriptural comparison St. John can find is that of Jonah being swallowed by the whale, assimilated like a weak fish in its dark belly (cf. Jon 2:1-2). The outcome of this horrendous event foretells the story of our redemption.

Christ died and was entombed in a burial cave that we might
live. There is no other way for us to attain spiritual rebirth
than to be willing, with Jesus, to enter the sepulcher of death
and await resurrection. To describe the ultimately indescribable depth of this affliction, St. John quotes another
psalm of David:

> The breakers of death surged round about me,
>   the destroying floods overwhelmed me;
> The cords of the nether world enmeshed me,
>   the snares of death overtook me (Ps 18:5-6).

Feeling Rejection

To the sorrowing soul walking through this valley of
darkness it feels as if one has been abandoned by the Mystery.
It is as if a beloved parent throws a child once safe and secure
at home into the darkness of the street at night and slams the
door. The desperation one feels defies expression. Who
would not pity such an outcast?

In this seemingly lifeless hour, the psalms of lamentation
become one's only spiritual food (cf. Ps 88:4-7). So oppressive
is purgative contemplation that one is within inches of feeling utterly lost, without support, and under the shadow of
death, of enduring a kind of living hell, of sensing God's
absence more than his presence.

It takes a supreme effort of the will to continue to abandon oneself to God in faith, hope, and love when the only
responses one appears to receive are chastisement, rejection,
and apparent anger. Though we may feel, as did John the
Baptist, unworthy to untie the Lord's sandal strap (cf. Jn
1:27), does it mean that this affliction will last forever?

Feeling Forsaken

As if misery and rejection were not enough, one has to
bear the added weight of frightening loneliness. It is as if one
has become a lost soul, enveloped in an abyss, forsaken by
God and despised by other people, even one's friends. There
seems to be no relief in sight.

One is like a pilgrim who knows the shrine is within her sight, yet she cannot for the life of her see it. One is like a prisoner who can almost touch the keys to his chains, yet an opening too small for his hand to fit through keeps him from freedom. So the "locks" of our imperfections hinder us from feasting at the sweet table of secret contemplation.

Feeling Utterly Dependent on God

Devastating as it is, "dark contemplation" is an unforgettably formative experience. It enables us to overcome any illusion of independence from God. Compared to the majesty and grandeur of the Most High, we have no choice but to accept once and for all our nothingness. How extremely poor we are! How dependent on God for everything!

This awareness is in itself afflictive. We now know for sure that no temporal good, however small or spectacular, can fulfill us. This lie loses its hold. Neither can mental acumen nor fine health be expected to last forever. Life is limited. Its limits have to catch up with us at some time.

No consolations, not even the highest forms of ecstasy, can satisfy our spiritual longing nor deceive us into believing that anything or anyone less than God can be our all in all. Such pleasures, powers, and possessions are now put in their proper, pretranscendent place.

More vivid than any of these goods is the conflicting evidence of our imperfections, the inner emptiness that haunts us, the spiritual dryness that causes us to feel overcome. Our powers of apprehension, our intellects, memories, and wills, lack animation and ambition. Everything is an effort. What is most focal to us is what we would most like to forget: the terrible possibility that, despite his promise to be always with those he loves, perhaps God has abandoned us after all.

St. John offers a sober summary of the afflictions so far described, ones he himself certainly had to endure:

> Since God here purges both the sensory and spiritual substance of the soul, and its interior and

exterior faculties, it is appropriately brought into
emptiness, poverty, and abandonment in these
parts, and left in dryness and darkness. For the
sensory part is purified by aridity, the faculties by
the void of their apprehensions, and the spirit by
thick darkness (DN II:6 [4]).

Dark Contemplation Purges Our Affections

It would be impossible for a person to enter this tunnel
without losing hope that there is an exit were it not for the
fact that what is happening is, to use St. John's word, "fitting." "It has to be this way" is not a defeatist statement, an
exercise in passive acceptance, or a lazy resistance to the
challenge contemplation offers us for growth. While one's
suffering is as anguishing as that of a person hanging in
midair, gasping for breath, one cannot doubt that God allows
the void and the suffering to happen for good reason.

Neither physical supports nor prior functional ambitions, neither spiritual apprehensions nor rational expectations, can contain the fire of contemplation that is out of our
control. The consuming fire that can remove rust from metal
or clear a corn field in a flash has no difficulty dealing with
the inordinate affections or habitual imperfections we may
have contracted over a lifetime. These pockets of pride have
lodged themselves in hidden corners of our soul, so much so
that we may not even know anymore that they are there—but
God does.

Purification means that we have to make ready the inner
room in which our Divine Guest wants to reside. This space
will have an "occupied" sign on it unless we empty it of
ultimately unimportant items like the control buttons to
which we cling. Handing these over to God can be reason
enough for torment, but the freedom we shall eventually feel
makes this suffering immaterial.

The prophet Ezekiel accepts that flesh and bone, the
sensory and the spiritual parts of our soul, have to be burnt
in the fire, consumed and destroyed, if the transcendent is to

be revealed (cf. Ez 24:10-11). This fire afflicts us sorely because it annihilates the last remnants of the passions and imperfections that block our union with God and prevent us from receiving the legacy of loving and liberated surrender we are meant to enjoy. There is no better or faster way to walk to freedom than to allow God to unfasten the knapsack of passions and imperfections that weigh us down.

What keeps a miner sifting though buckets of silt is the promise of gold. The Lord sees that promise in us, and so does St. John. Both believe that if we enter the forge of purgation we will be transformed from dross into pure gold. This method of annihilation only destroys what is superfluous anyway. Thus no matter how terrible it feels, we can see what is happening to us as a formation opportunity.[1]

The Mystery challenges us to seek what is appreciable in this process by first trusting that suffering has a meaning, even though we may feel as weary as David did (cf. Ps 69:1-4). Then we can wait and see what God has in store for one who does not give up hope.

In due course, the gospel promise reveals itself to us as both trustworthy and true. God humbles us, to be sure, but only so that he can exalt us (cf. Mt 23:12). We may have to be led as far as the jaws of death to find the meaning of mature faith, but these will not clamp down until our hour has come.

The spiritual death we have to undergo is the entrance to new life. The intensity of the darkness that has to engulf us in order to free us waxes and wanes. We can be sure in the process that God will never test us beyond our capacity to endure. Though St. John says that we may be led at times to the brink of the "nether world" (cf. Ps 55:16), we shall be saved by the benevolent love that gives us a second chance. That is why the purgation offered to us in the dark night is comparable to purgatory itself.

St. John goes so far as to suggest that one may undergo during this relatively brief span of time what would require many more purgations in the life to come. In the same breath, he affirms that we ought not to be afraid of the dark night. It comes to us as God's gift to save us from worse troubles. All we can do is trust, as times passes, that the suffering we must undergo is a blessing, that every affliction serves in the long run to advance our ascent to God.

The Nights Test Our Faith

The struggle to remain faithful under the duress of darkness stretches our will to the breaking point. Mary did not understand the message of the angel, but she willed without hesitation to let be what was happening to her (cf. Lk 1:38). In the Garden of Gethsemane, Jesus asked that the cup of suffering pass him by, adding immediately that not his will but the Father's be done (cf. Mt 26:39). We are free to resist these divine invitations, to refuse these challenges, or to say *yes* to God in self-giving surrender. Our will is the bridge and the barrier over which mature faith must pass.

Adding to the struggle involved is the power of memory to recall what is weakest in us. Doubts plague us, too. Are we or are we not strong enough to remain faithful during this affliction? Not only do we have flashbacks of the bad things we have done, we also find ourselves fantasizing about how good life used to be, how we once seemed to find favor with God. What did we do to deserve such a fate? Instead of self-surrender, which strengthens our will, we risk self-pity, which weakens us all the more.

If we are not careful, we may start to wish for signs and wonders, subtle or dramatic consolations, proofs from God that our suffering is acceptable. Thus, to quote the title of one of Sören Kierkegaard's edifying discourses, instead of practicing the "purity of heart that wills one thing," we become doubleminded.[2] It is no use trying to comprehend this apparent loss of divine favor. We have to accept our sorry state and make the best of it, lamenting our pain, as Job did (cf. Jb 16:12-17), yet trusting the gain God will help us to derive from it.

Holy scripture cites passage after passage from the psalms, the prophets, the parables of Jesus, the perils of Paul, passages too numerous for St. John to mention, to narrate the stresses and strains of the night. Yet, as he insists, none of these descriptions can capture the essence of the dark night experience.

A text that comes close to doing so—one cited line by line by him—is from Lamentations 3:1-20. In its verses one finds verbalized such experiences as having one's bones broken, being sent among the dead, bound with heavy ropes, preyed upon by bears and lions. Jeremiah laments feeling desolate, stung with arrows, scorned by the people. His teeth are knocked out. His only food is ashes. He can no longer remember what the good life was like. His longing for God seems frustrated at every turn, finished. He is one lump of affliction.

In this long passage St. John seems to find the best description of what he himself felt like when he was a prisoner in his own community. Anyone who has gone through the night of faith knows of what he speaks. How, then, ought we to treat ourselves and others in this midnight hour?

Suffering With Compassion

While in due course we may understand why God has led us into this night of nights, what precedes the shift from darkness to light is a suffering so intense that one's heart would have to be as brittle as flint not to feel compassion. The burden will become a blessing; God will bring "the gloom forth to the light," as Job discovered (cf. Jb 12:22); the darkness will give way to the dawn; the night will shine as the day, as David confirmed (cf. Ps 139:12), but these reliefs recede into the background. Focal in one's experience are excessive doubts and unspeakable tribulations with no end in sight (cf. Lam 3:18).

It is as if one has been flung into a cell in solitary confinement with the key cast into the sea. The psalmist, too, describes this state as one of despair, anguish, and heartbreak (cf. Ps 143:3-4). Such suffering, whatever else it may signify, is surely a transforming event.

Seeking Direction

Where can one find a learned, wise, and experienced spiritual guide like St. John? Astute analysis of the dark night is not the usual topic of Sunday preaching. Spiritual directors of such high caliber are a scarce commodity. Experts can predict with a certain statistical objectivity that things will take a turn for the better, but it is hard for one to believe this is true without sound doctrine and practical counsel to support such claims. When one is in a desert dying of thirst, a thimbleful of water offers no relief.

Similarly, words of consolation fall flat. Future promises sound like polite bromides because unprepared directors really do not understand the extent of one's misery. Happy forecasts, meant to alleviate present pains, evoke only greater misery. They offer no relief from the hellish, hapless predicament of spiritual purgation.

St. John admits that there is no remedy for this sickness. It is over when the Lord says it is over, and not before. Other than patient endurance and deep prayerfulness, there is nothing one can do or say that brings any real respite. St. John, who knew firsthand of what he was speaking, says people in this state:

> ... resemble one who is imprisoned in a dark dungeon, bound hands and feet, and able neither to move nor see nor feel any favor from heaven or earth. They remain in this condition until their spirit is humbled, softened, and purified, until it becomes so delicate, simple, and refined that it can be one with the Spirit of God, according to the degree of union of love that God, in his mercy, desires to grant (DN II:7 [3]).

The initiative for this action rests with God alone. The degree of suffering depends on the degree of union to which God wants to lead one. Accordingly, one has to endure more or less aggravation, a shorter or longer duration of purgation.

If we consider the life of Teresa of Avila, it ought to come as no surprise to hear St. John say that to be truly efficacious, purgative contemplation or the passive night of the spirit may last for some years. The saint tells us in her autobiography what it was like to live in the darkness of faith and not despair. At intervals decreed by grace, the intense pace of purgation may go into low gear and give way to smoother rhythms of illumination with perhaps a few waves of union. For a brief but blessed time, one may feel the shackles dropping, the prison doors being flung open to let in light.

A sense of sweet peace passes over one like a cool minted drink on a hot, humid day. The felt depths of friendship with the Divine return. The Alone communicates with the alone, as if there had been no break. It is right and proper that one accept these illuminative, lights on experiences, as signs of the spiritual wholeness purgation intends to produce[3] This is good food for the journey. It validates Christ's promise to give us life, and life abundantly (cf. Jn 10:10). It is worth waiting and hoping for such peace and joy.

St. John confesses that at times these foretastes of heaven on earth are so intense that one begins to believe the worst is behind him or her. When graces come in the form of trials, it is as if one will never be freed from their weight nor be able to accept them fully as blessings. When graces come in the form of spiritual goods, one is inclined to believe that the night has ended and that with the coming of the dawn every kind of blessing on earth and in heaven will be bestowed. How great it would be to build a tent on this holy ground and stay there forever (cf. Ps 61:5 and Mt 17:4).

Making Honest Appraisals in the Midnight Hour

Honest appraisals of our life at this time help to ready us for the midnight hour God allows to occur for reasons St. John will now explain. What happens at this point in the process is complex.

On the one hand, the experience of renewed friendship with God is so powerful that it wipes out the former feelings of loss and abandonment. It is the same with physical pain. A mother agonizes as she gives birth, but the joy of her newborn's first cry quickly replaces the suffering she had to endure. She still feels weak, her body has to recover, but her spirit rejoices.

Though the journey to God has received new impetus, our inmost spirit has not yet been thoroughly cleansed of needs and desires associated with mere sensate satisfactions. Received consolations are beautiful, but we can rely too much on their bounty. We are not as yet sufficiently detached. We can still be swayed by spiritual delights and the residues of satisfaction they leave in our senses.

Though in truth we have changed, though we are not nearly as weak as we were prior to the reception of purgative contemplation, though we may think we have attained new heights of union along with an abundance of spiritual goods, we had better be on guard. God knows that we are still not capable of seeing the tentacles of imperfection, the root systems of impurity, and the ulterior motives buried deep in our hearts. We are inclined to think that our trials have ended, but many more are in store.

Trials Greater Than the First

On some level we know that the desert has not yet been crossed, though we succeed for a while in keeping this intuition under wraps. When we honestly appraise what we are feeling, we may be able to admit that the purity of heart for which we have prayed is not yet ours. No matter how tranquil we may feel following some communication from on high, we sense that it cannot forever conceal the fact that we still know that something is lacking. The roots of self-centeredness run deeper than we would like to believe.

The awareness that something else remains to be done keeps us from enjoying to the full the abundance of grace we have already received. It feels as if an enemy within, though pacified for a time, is soon to awake from its slumber and cause us a lot of trouble.

And this is true, for when a person feels safest and least expects it, the purgation returns to engulf the soul in another degree more severe, dark, and piteous than the former and which lasts for another period of time, perhaps longer than the first (DN II:7 [6]).

Now almost nothing can dissuade us from believing that our blessings have disappeared like raindrops in the ocean. The first trial was terrible. Then for a while it ended, and we felt elated, nearly convinced that we had nothing left to be purged so thoroughly—and now this! How could one not conclude, as this second degree of anguish descends, that the window of opportunity has slammed shut forever? Good-bye former blessings! Now the spirit flatly dismisses any thought contrary to this conviction. Cut loose are the last remnants of attachments to anything that stands in the way of God's holy will.

St. John compares this posture of humble submission to what it must feel like to the souls in purgatory who doubt they will ever be freed from their afflictions and lifted to heaven. They, like we, possess faith, hope, and love but because they feel deprived of God's presence, these virtues bring them no comfort. They, like we, love God but this fact bestows no felt blessing because they think God does not love them. They, like we, are only sure that they are unworthy of being loved by God. Seeing themselves as people thus deprived of divine care, feeling misery to be their only bed, they can see no reason not to be rejected and found abject in God's eyes.

Truly one must pity those who suffer this purgation. They know they love God. Ask, and they would die a thousand deaths for his sake. Yet they see no relief in sight. The more they love God, the worse they feel. This is their paradoxical reality: Their love for God is so great that they have no other concern, yet they are unable to feel that God loves them. This is a terrible state. It pulverizes what may once have been a strong self-image. One feels despite all the books one may read or the sermons one may hear that there is nothing in him or her deserving of the love of God.

So bad is this state that one lives in the conviction that there is every reason for God to abhor him or her and the same goes for other creatures. Written in capital letters are all the reasons one should be scorned by the same God for whom one desperately longs and toward whom one only wishes to turn with love.

Afflictions of the Darkest Hour

What if all one wanted to do was to pray to God and to profess pure love and fidelity and what if one were prevented from doing so because the same dark night which evoked these needs impeded their expression? Such is the cloud under which one must now live, a cloud so thick that seemingly not even one ray of sunshine can pass through it (cf. Lam 3:44). This suffering knows no bounds. It is as if the words with which we want to beseech God get stuck in our throats. Even when a small squeak surfaces, we are convinced God neither hears nor pays attention to it (cf. Lam 3:8).

The problem may be that we are trying too hard to make contact with the Holy on a wavelength that sufficed before but fails now. The best we might do is to be still. St. John says "... this is not the time to speak with God, but the time to put one's mouth in the dust ..." (DN II:8 [1]).

Such silence may release hope, provided we are willing to suffer through purgation with patience. We need to ease up a bit, for now it is God's turn to work in us, to take all the initiative. We can do nothing for the moment. We can neither pray vocally, nor pay attention to spiritual matters, nor do much but function minimally to sustain our temporal needs and everyday duties.

Whereas we used to feel rather in control of our lives and works, we now find ourselves so absorbed in the current bereavements that we forget what time of day it is. Long periods pass without our knowing what we did or what we were thinking about. We try to concentrate on a task, we do our best, but we have trouble deciding when to do something or how to do it.

What does this switch from doing to being, from controlling everything to finding ourselves in the experience of nothingness do to us? At least four points of formative transition have to be taken into account according to St. John:

Incipient Transformation

The night of the spirit enables *three* necessary deprivations to occur so that *three* necessary transformations may happen in due course:

The *intellect* "does not know" as it formerly did; the light of "knowing" gives way to the transcendent wonder of "not knowing," which results in a new, never before experienced, higher form of wisdom, the secrets of which are yet to be explored.

The *will* "does not love" as it used to because its affections are being detached in darkness from all inordinate attachments. The result will be a purer, more inclusive, Christ-like manner of loving rooted in a remarkable bond of union with God.

The *memory* "does not remember" as it did previously by virtue of a series of discursive facts that led to knowledge about God. One now anticipates more of what God has in store for those transformed by grace. All one really wants or cares to remember is God, who was, is, and always will be. Nothing else is of ultimate concern because everything is being annihilated by the night (cf. Ps 73:14).

The result of this "unknowing" is a kind of forgetfulness in the memory. Dark contemplation, like a "black hole" in the heavens, so absorbs one's attention and affection that one's powers of recollection fall into a state of abstraction or oblivion. There are several reasons why this happens:

First of all, to receive the union of love that is divine, the human vessel must be made ready. Our inner powers have to be reshaped by the light of contemplation, which paradoxically shines the brightest in the dark.

Secondly, to prepare the proper room for our Divine Guest, we have to withdraw temporarily from the affections we feel for other creatures and from our limited apprehensions of them. God wants to teach us a new way of seeing and loving, one that is transcendent instead of merely pretranscendent or purely functional.

How long this absorption lasts is dependent on the intensity of the contemplation God wishes to grant one. The time this transformation takes is wholly God's to determine. For St. John the "more or less" depends on this:

> The more simply and purely the divine light strikes the soul, the more it darkens and empties and annihilates it in its particular apprehensions and affections concerning both earthly and heavenly things; and, also, the less simply and purely it shines, the less it deprives and darkens the soul (DN II:8 [2]).

The brighter and more purely God's light shines within one's interiority, the darker this light is. By the same token, when the light is less bright, there is less darkness in one's perception of it. This paradox repeats an ancient principle cited by the saint and integral to the apophatic way, namely, the more evident the transcendent is in itself, the less understandable it is to our functional or inferior intellect (cf. DN II:8 [2]).

To illustrate this truth St. John uses a familiar example: that of sunlight beaming through a pane of glass. The more free it is of particles of dust, the harder it is to see. The ray is detectable to the degree that the air is full of dusty things. This is so because light waves as such are invisible to the naked eye. We see light, says St. John, because it strikes or reflects this or that object. Without such contact we could see neither the light nor the thing in its path.

In short, the less dust there is in a room, the harder it is to see the power of the light. When there are no objects to refract a ray of sunlight, it remains invisible to us.

Apophatic Contemplation

So it is when the divine ray of contemplation strikes our human nature: It surpasses all we know. We are deprived of our typical ways of affective attachment and apprehension. Natural lights do not reflect what is supernatural. Thus are intellect, memory, and will uplifted to the "More Than" without our understanding how this happens. We are left in darkness. There is a void within us, even though something awesome is occurring. We are being purged and illumined on the highest level, yet we think that all is in darkness. The light of grace radiates through open windows into the room we have readied for God, yet because there is nothing left in us from which it can refract, it appears as if the darkness is too profound to penetrate. This is not the whole story by any means.

Knowing by Faith, Not by Sight

When and if the divine light that shines in the dark finds some object on which to focus its beam, say some truth or some falsehood, no matter how subtle, one understands it more clearly than one did before one was in this darkness. The darkness of faith enables us to see with a clarity previously unknown. We recognize our imperfections more quickly the more conscious we are of God's perfect "dark light." It is invisible to lower reason and focal consciousness; it is able to penetrate our higher reason and trans-focal consciousness to such a degree that we see ourselves and God in a new way. We begin to understand why the darkness is not a problem to be overcome by seeking, for example, felt consolations, but a great gift to be cherished.

This paradoxical light that shines best in the midnight hour is so simple and pure, so general and unaffected by any degree of human cleverness, that it has to be of God. No particular object, however intelligible to us on a natural or supernatural plane, can restrict its intensity. Especially when one's sensate and spiritual powers of apprehension have been purged by the "happy" afflictions of the dark night, we reach a new level of awareness, a more refined way of reasoning.

Simply said, "The soul with universality and great facility perceives and penetrates *anything earthly or heavenly that is presented to it*" (DN II:8 [5], Italics mine). In terms of spiritual direction, this gift would be referred to as the ability to read the heart. In terms of preaching, it would be the capacity to direct hearts through hearing. Other gifts (healing, prophecy, teaching) are marks of this graced transformation.

According to the apostle Paul, such a person can penetrate "even the depths of God" (1 Cor 2:10). The book of Wisdom assures us that this way of "seeing into" is so general, pure, and simple that it can grasp and touch the whole (cf. Wis 7:22-25). One does not deflect the light by trying to focus it only on this or that thing or affection.

Richly Blessed Poverty

All of the above characteristics can be subsumed under the canopy of poverty of spirit. Having been purged of every form of self-deception, having had annihilated by the dark night all proud pockets of particular knowledge, possessive affections, pleasures, and powers, one knows from long, often excruciating experience that nothing but God can satisfy our heart. This was the conclusion reached by Teresa of Avila in her oft-quoted prayer:

> Let nothing disturb you
> Nothing affright you
> All things pass:
> God never changes.
> Patience obtains everything.
> One who has God
> lacks nothing
> God alone suffices.[4]

Not to understand anything in particular is for the time being not a source of sadness, since it seems as if one knows in general what really matters. It is not a hardship to remain in this cloud of unknowing nor does it make any sense to shun or fear the darkness. All one has to do is to maintain vigilance of heart, wait upon the Mystery with equanimity, and trust in the divine plan for one's life.

In this posture of humility, says St. John, one resonates with the words of Paul, who said he had nothing yet possessed all things (cf. 2 Cor 6:10). In the same vein, St. John's eloquent though excruciating description of the dark night experience ends with these few tranquil, convincing, and consoling words: "Such poverty of spirit deserves this blessedness" (DN II:8 [5]).

13

Paradoxical Reality: The Darkness That Is the Light

(*The Dark Night*, Book Two, Chapters 9 and 10)

Joy in suffering, hope in despair, life in death—such paradoxes make perfect sense to one whose faith has been tried by fire. Having described the dreadful afflictions of the dark night, St. John now erases them like chalk dust on slate by explaining their deeper meaning. Without faith what he knows to be true experientially might appear ridiculous. With faith it makes perfect sense to say that this night, where so much has happened to make one sad, will end up making one feel glad. This happy night darkens intellect, memory, and will on one level—that of the functional with its routine facts, defenses, and wish fulfillments—only to impart light to the spirit on another level: that of the transcendent.

Powerlessness Becomes Powerful Through Grace

Persons educated by the darkness to depend wholly on God acknowledge being powerless but see a higher purpose in this lack of control. They are now light enough to be lifted up by God. Shattered expectations may leave us feeling miserable, but this lowliness allows God to draw us to higher planes pride can never attain.

By mere human standards, these stark reminders of our finitude make us feel minuscule as church mice. At times our minds are as empty of thoughts as rivulets reduced to clay by a relentless sun. Our possessions fail to comfort us. To own something seems as irrelevant as to own nothing. Our natural affections for all things great and small do not disappear but neither do they satisfy a deeper yearning.

God allows these restless desires to remain unsatisfied so that we will wait in readiness to receive the touch of grace that alone enables us to enjoy everything under the heavens and on the earth as a gift. Because nothing we have or know has the power to encapsulate us, we are free to treasure everything. All becomes praiseworthy and precious to an appreciative eye. Loosened from the depleting demands of self-centeredness by the power of transforming grace, we can treat ourselves and others with patience and compassion. Such freedom of spirit ignites the power in us to praise God always—for to God alone belongs the glory (cf. Rom 11:36).[1]

Helpful Comparison

In trying to describe how open we must be to receive grace, St. John compares the process to a natural compound like water. It is made up of hydrogen and oxygen, yet when these elements are commingled in the water we drink, we cannot as a rule distinguish this or that color or odor or taste. Separate elements have become one. In the same way, all the natural acts, habits, and affections we have acquired over a lifetime must be so purified that our human spirit can freely and fully be in touch with the Holy Spirit.

Wisdom divine must have found a home in our hearts if we can taste its delights to such an eminent degree. Much in us that resisted Christ's call—pride, prejudice, pettiness, deprecation—must have undergone purgation, for without it we would never be able to experience such an abundance of peace and joy.

Experience has taught us that whether our attachment to any object as ultimate is the size of a thin thread or a triple-linked chain the result is the same: no freedom of spirit, no possibility of receiving the intimacy of divine union, no uplift of our poor spirit by the power of perfect love that contains in itself every delight we humans could desire.

To underline this truth, St. John reminds us that because they could not shake themselves loose from the scraps of food they found in Egypt, the children of Israel almost missed tasting the manna in the desert God sent to satisfy their hunger (cf. Ex 16:3-4 and Wis 16:20-21). Our own pitiful pouncing on this or that impermanent taste or partial truth seems to suggest that after all there is perhaps nothing new under the sun! It is hard to believe that we still settle for less (this attachment, that bit of knowledge or praise, such and such a fleeting apprehension) when we are called to enjoy so much more. Why do we persist in being deceived by distractions when God lays before us a banquet of spiritual delights?

We may still fail to see that these higher, transcendent affections, these spirit-filled sentiments, apprehensions, aspirations, and inspirations, are of another order of reality. Entrance to this kind of freedom and likeness to God requires that we sever certain ties to the pretranscendent that we may have absolutized. The harm inordinate attachments cause is due to the fact, as St. John frequently says, that "two contraries" cannot exist in one and the same person. For example, we cannot simultaneously invest all our energy in functional outcomes and expect to have any stamina left to pursue transcendent meanings. Transformation has to bring us to a new point of convergence where the ambitions of the "managing me" become the servants of my aspirations to be a disciple of Christ and to do whatever he asks on a day-to-day basis.[2]

To pass on to this plane of integration and the appreciative dispositions it grants, we have to allow the dark nights to annihilate and undo the lowly ways of pretranscendent responses to life's meaning. Painful as it may be, these old traits have to be put into storage once and for all. We have to welcome being led by contemplation into a cave where for a while it is dark and lonely. Our throats, symbolizing the vital dimension, are dry. Our wants and needs, sentinels of the functional, are in conflict. Our spirits—forecasters of transcendent freedom—feel empty. Yet through all this agony there is a voice in us that will not stop singing.

Paradoxically, the light that flashed on in the midst of this darkness is so lofty, bright, and bold that the radiant beams of the stronger floodlights pale in comparison. Compared to the divine light of faith, hope, and love in which we are destined by the Divine to live, all the natural lights disclosed by our human intellects seem as dull as bare low-watt bulbs in a windowless banquet hall.

Process of Profound Reformation

Let us examine with St. John's help this movement from darkness to light. The goal to which we are being drawn by grace is as multifaceted as a diamond. It is first of all the divine intent that our higher reason reach union with the light by which the pure of heart see God. To enable the attainment of this state of perfection is the work "dark contemplation" has to accomplish by shutting off, so to speak, some natural light switches and reducing to obscurity our self-inflated answers to every question, thus opening our minds to the Mystery.

Such a process of reformation follows no set schedule. According to St. John, the darkness lasts as long as it takes to expel and erase the usual way in which we understand things with the help of lower reason. Modes of logical mastery are habit-forming because they also feed into our pride and its "I-can-do-it" mentality. For as long as we persist in the mindset of a manager rather than deferring to what is "More Than," we can expect the purgation to last. In God's time we may see that all that we know is what we do not know.[3]

This paradoxical illumination does not weaken our ability to think; it actually gives us fresh insights and inner strength. We understand without understanding, as if we stood under the sun benefiting from its brightness without getting burnt. What harms us is not the light that comes from God, but the darkness through which we must pass. That can be as frightening as it is painful. At this level of reformation, the darkness is not superficial and passing but substantial and profound. As St. John says, "… it is felt in the deep substance of the spirit" (DN II:9 [3]).

Refinements of the Will
Enabling Us to Mirror the Mystery

The affections of the will, our longings and loves, must undergo similar refinements if we are to mirror the mystery of oneness with Christ. The gross must become subtle, the rough delicate, the exterior interior. Every affection and feeling, every desire, whether secret or spoken, has to pass through the refining fires of the dark night. There, in accordance with the divine plan to release us from bare affections and to teach us the way of true love, we shall have to endure purgation in order to enjoy illumination and union.

Who would trade passing, fickle feelings for lasting and sublime affections and delights? These do not belong to our fallen nature—they are gifts that signify the depth of Christ's redeeming love. There is no way for us to experience such love unless, like Christ, we are left in the dryness and distress the Lord had to endure.

In times of trial and deprivation our ability to love God with natural waves of affection is stretched to the limit. It takes nothing short of supernatural acts of the will to say *yes* to God amidst an inconsistency as shocking as the suffering of the innocent. Such consent is essential if the demon of depreciation is to desiccate like snakeskin on a desert road.

Contemplation of the divine is comparable at this stage of transformation to fire. It burns but does not destroy as when Tobias put the fish heart in the flames (cf. Tb 6:17). It is as if we are given the chance to start our life anew. Purgation renders the complex simple, the impure pure. It cleanses our palate of base tastes so we can experience the sweet delights of divine love. It redirects our attachments so that we can touch the hand of God from whence all good gifts pour forth.

When the dark night pushes away obstacles like a snowplow clearing a rough country road, it is easy to see why the soul beholds itself transformed by touches that can be nothing less than divine. The promise of what awaits us following the passage through and beyond the darkness is remarkable. The dark night, to be perfectly clear, is a preparation for—not the conclusion of—union with God. To be worthy of crossing the threshold to such communion, one has to be in a properly disposed state, otherwise the splendor and delight God wants to bestow on us would be too overwhelming to endure, let alone to enjoy. It would be like throwing "pearls before swine" (Mt 7:6).

The simple truth is that "These delights surpass all the abundance the soul can possess naturally ..." (DN II:9 [4]). Both the prophet Isaiah (64:3) and the apostle Paul (1 Cor 2:9) knew that our eyes could not see, nor could our ears hear, nor could it enter into our hearts what God has prepared for those who love him.

We approach at this point the core of the paradoxical reality out of which this entire text emerges. The person so led by grace must be made empty to be full; poor to be rich; purged of every customary support and consolation to be empowered by divine energy; lacking self-sustaining apprehensions to attend to earthly and heavenly revelations from on high.

> Thus empty [one] is truly poor in spirit and stripped of the old self, and thereby able to live that new and blessed life which is the state of union with God, attained by means of this night (DN II:9 [4]).

What does this new person look like? Who are we and who have we become when God is our all in all?

Preliminary Signs of Transformation

1. *Radiation of Christ.* Over and above our everyday experiences and natural knowledge ("Here is the journal I keep on spiritual reading; this is the way I like to clean my house; here's how I prefer to chair a meeting ..."), we draw water from another well. It is as if we are in tune with the

music of the spheres. We overflow with sentiments and expressions that seem to arise from a divine source. We seem more able to radiate Christ to others even when we are doing, as they do, the most ordinary things.

2. *Divine Refinement.* This "sixth sense" or epiphanic sensitivity continues to refine all of our common and natural experiences. We see the same things everyone does, but with a difference. We are aware of their divine source. We hear the same tunes but march to a different drummer, one more divine than merely human.

3. *Certitude of Presence.* Though we have been placed in terrible distress by the tremors of the night, we have grown inexplicably sure of God's presence with and within us.

Refinements of the Memory
Resulting From Initial Transformation

In the light of these changes, we can assess more realistically what happens to the spiritual faculty of memory. We seem more prone to put aside or relegate to the background facts and happenings that used to be perfectly agreeable and peace-giving in order to process what has caused us to feel alienated from other people and things. We feel different from them. We see events in a new light. It is as if we are at once at home and in a foreign land. The night has withdrawn us from our usual way of working and praying. We experience human events, as does everyone else, but we interpret them from a divine perspective. That is what makes us different. Affliction catapults us out of commonality.

There is something fascinating in this power of faithful endurance. Are we being condemned by the Divine or charmed? Are we imagining this paradox of good news in the face of sadness and suffering, or is what we see and hear of God a proper source of wonder?

To enter this land of likeness can be unnerving. The familiar is both customary and strange. We are at home yet lost in a new territory that has been here all along without our recognizing it. Our usual way of knowing and experiencing things is on hold. We are both formed and informed by insights that seem more appropriate to the next world than to this one.

In a word, we can say that to suffer such afflictive purgations in the memory is to be spiritually reborn (cf. Jn 3:3-7). As our old selfish self flows out, our new divinely attuned self flows in. Through suffering we see. We receive the grace of salvation in the throes of purgation. We know, as did the prophet Isaiah, that the pains of labor have brought forth new life and release from sin (cf. Is 26:17-19).

Refinements of the Intellect
Resulting From Initial Transformation

Nothing we have known heretofore can compare to the new plateau of peace granted by the contemplative night. It is as if the practice sessions are over and we are now ready to accept the invitation to play with the symphony. The quality of our peace is so sublime and transcendent that it "surpasses all understanding" (Phil 4:7). What we formerly called wholeness or oneness or peace was as shot full of imperfections as a hunting target.

This seeming peace, though sensory and spiritual, had to be purged, disturbed, and taken away so that the Divine could demonstrate through the distress of the night another paradox: When we seem to have "forgotten what happiness is" (Lam 3:17), when we feel as far removed from rest as a glacier from the equator, it is then that we may receive God's own peace, a gift the world can neither understand nor give.

The way to this place of peaceful presence is along the route of painful disturbance. We cannot see the dawn of a new day in the Lord unless we pass through a night when we must cope with our fears of darkness, our evil imaginings of pending doom, the inner tugs of war between that of us willing to take any risk to meet God and that of us wanting only a safe haven.

So overwhelming is our apprehension, so miserable do we feel at this midnight hour, that we almost accept as an

irreversible truth that we are lost. The litany of our lamentations is long and far from ludicrous:

1. My cup of blessings is empty now and forever.

2. My spirit moans as a wailing widow with deep
sorrow.

3. The clamor and roar of my distress rivals Niagara
Falls at flood time.

4. I sometimes have no choice but to wail aloud.

5. I cannot stop the flow of my tears, even if I had the
strength to do so.

6. Moments of relief are few and far between. I know
what the psalmist David must have felt when he spoke
of being afflicted and humbled, when he roared with the
anguish of his heart (Ps 38:9).

All of these moans and groans, these fears and feelings
of distrust, signify profound, soul-wrenching suffering comparable to the wail of an animal whose foot is caught in a trap.
The pain can be sudden and piercing. The cry of the heart in
its groaning (cf. Jb 3:24) can arouse enough pity to fill an
empty reservoir to overflowing. In St. John's words:

> As the waters sometimes overflow in such a way
> that they inundate everything, this roaring and
> feeling so increases that in seeping through and
> flooding everything, they fill all one's deep affec-
> tions and energies with indescribable spiritual an-
> guish and suffering (DN II:9 [7]).

Called to Faith Amidst the Afflictions
of the Dark Night

Anyone who has felt this way knows that hope for a new
day grows more dim with each passing moment. The
prophet Job offers a prime example of one pierced to the
quick by seemingly useless suffering, so intense that he
cannot sleep (cf. Jb 30:17). Doubts and fears tear his will to
shreds. He cannot rest no matter how much he wants to, for

the war within continues to rage. His whole being is like a combat zone.

Can we trust the truth of the paradoxical reality now proposed by the master? Do we believe that the suffering we must undergo is proportionate to the peace that awaits us? Do we accept with a disposition of appreciative abandonment to the Mystery that this pain penetrates our soul like rain on parched land because the love we shall possess through grace will be as pure and refined as the labor that produced it? No marble stone ever became a graceful work of art without intense chiseling by a master craftsman like Michelangelo. For "commensurate with the solidity of the edifice is the energy involved in the work" (DN II:9 [9]).

Faith alone can convince us that on this withering vine reside grapes that will ripen and produce fine wine. Only trust in a greater good can sustain us when, like Job (30:16, 27) our inmost parts are so afflicted that we almost give up hope. St. John reiterates his point as firmly as a woodcarver chips away at a log in which he sees the shape of a wondrous statue.

To journey as high on the mountain as we are able to the state of perfection, we have to plunge into a valley as deep as the night of purgative affliction. To reach the possession and enjoyment of everything, we have to walk the way of dispossession and energy-depleting deprivation. To bless God as the source of all our gifts and virtues, we have to overcome every trace of reliance on our own power. Thus the paradoxes that promote pure faith cannot be avoided: God's seeming absence is a sign of divine nearness; emptiness is a pointer to fullness; poverty of spirit is the opening to a wealth of wisdom.

Perhaps it is safe to say that paradox is God's idea of play. It is like a game of hide and seek. Just when we think all good has been removed from reach, we are ready to receive the grace of a fresh start. Just when we are convinced that our life is nearly over—and no preaching or teaching can convince us otherwise—we catch the first glimpse of a turn-around occurring. Just when calculative reason and clear logic make us conclude that for whatever reason there are no more blessings in store for us (cf. Lam 3:18), an abundant avalanche of goodness reduces us to wonder.

Pushing the Limits of Paradox

Because paradox intrigues a mind as astute as St. John's, he feels obliged to probe its mystery somewhat further. He himself ponders why something as pleasant and positive as the light of contemplation, why something that unites us with the Beloved and gives us every blessing, has to produce such painful and negative effects, at least in these initial stages. What is happening here?

The saint begins to respond to this question by telling us again what is *not* going on. Contemplation or the divine inflow cannot of itself produce pain; it is the essence of sweetness, the bestower of delight. The reason why we experience such distasteful effects is not the fault of contemplation, but of the weak vessel into which its holy waters have to be poured. The well is so deep, the water in it so pure, that it cannot be drawn up in a cracked cup. We are as a rule inadequately prepared for the event of taking a drink that intends to transform us. In us exist elements contrary to the process of our being illumined by divine grace. For these reasons it ought to come as no surprise that for a while it feels as if our only friend is darkness.

To further delineate the mysterious link between love, purgation, and the secret knowledge that is contemplation, St. John turns again to the device of comparison. He says that the divine light for which contemplatives can find no words, can be described as having the same effect on a soul as fire would have on a log of wood. If the wood is wet it will smolder; if it is too dry it will crumble into dust. The wood has to be properly treated for it to burn well and produce heat. So, too, our inner room has to be placed by grace in a state of readiness to receive the gift of union with God.

Provided the wood is of high quality to begin with, the match, once struck, bursts into flame and the fire, once applied to the logs, first dehumidifies them, then dispels the last traces of moisture, and then sends up as smoke any remaining water. As the heat intensifies, the wood begins to turn black, dark, gnarled, and ugly. It may even smell odd, but by drying the wood in this manner, the fire enables it to burn brightly and to expel elements that evaporate rather than emit heat. In due course, by this process of enkindling and heating from without, the fire and the wood, as it were, become one.

The fire with all its warmth and beauty transforms once cold, damp wood into itself. Thus changed, the wood becomes neither active nor passive. It transcends these either-or categories. Though still quantifiable as wood due to its density, the log possesses the quality and gives off heat with as much intensity as does the fire. Dry itself, it dries what is hung before it. Hot itself, it radiates through and warms a whole room. Brilliant itself, it illumines the darkness. Light itself, it produces light in its surroundings. Remember, however, it is not the wood as such which produces these benefits: it is the fire.

By analogy, St. John sees in his meditation on the log and the flame a direct parallel to what happens in us thanks to the divine and loving fire of contemplation. Before this grace can transform us, it has to purge us of bad habits and sins that block its flow. In the process it brings to the fore for purification that which, from the viewpoint of goodness, truth, and beauty, is wicked, deceptive, and ugly. To see oneself in this state is to know how terrible sin can be. No words can capture its unsightliness.

This burning has a double effect: It brings to focal awareness deformed dispositions that have created a network of self-centered defenses and rationalizations that delay humble attunement to God; and it gives us a glimpse into how tenacious the hold of sin is in our lives and how long a time of reformation we may need to uproot it. To both expel

and annihilate these causes of chronic, often unack-
nowledged unhappiness, a special illumination is needed.

The dark night of divine contemplation, like a field set
afire to make it more fertile, has to provide light so that we
can see the avenue to our liberation. While to the untrained
eye, one may look the same, and no worse for the process, to
the person involved, there is no doubt that he or she is
abhorrent to God, deserving of chastisement, and unworthy
of such a relationship. At this stage of the purification
process, the burnt log is so ugly it is difficult to believe in the
pending glory of its flaming beauty.

Summary of the Purgative Process

Not wanting to slide over the value of this analogy, St.
John offers seven paradoxical points of comparison as a
conclusion to his analysis of the first verse of the first stanza
of his poem, the words of which ought by now to be imprinted on our hearts: "One dark night."

1. *Preparation for Transformation*. Hard as it is to believe,
one and the same light purges and transforms. In the beginning stages of spiritual deepening, the Mystery, like fire, has
to prepare us, as it does the wood, to be radically altered.
Without this pain there can be no progress.

2. *Exterior Purification*. The source of our suffering is not
the Mystery, who is wholly benevolent, but our own weakness and imperfection. Wisdom reminds us that all things
work together for the good for those who love God (cf. Wis
7:11). Just as the log of wood cannot give off heat until it is
transformed, so we cannot expect to receive the light and
delight of contemplative union unless purgation precedes
transformation. We suffer intensely because we are destined
to be united with the highest expression of love and wisdom
the human mind, heart, and spirit can attain. The good we
are destined to possess requires that our journey to it be every
bit as disturbing as it will be transforming.

3. *Termination of Suffering*. Consider the doctrine of purgatory as a continuation of the reformation begun on earth.[4]

As long as one has deformations and imperfections to overcome, one will have to suffer the application of refining fire (cf. Mal 3:2). St. John compares deformations to the fuel that catches flame. Once it disappears there is nothing left to burn. We may experience the same effect. Once the deformed dispositions and bad habits that drew us into the dark night have by God's grace been transformed, the suffering associated with this purification will terminate.

4. *Enkindling With Love.* The love that purifies is the same love that enkindles more and more warmth. In the same way, the wood becomes hotter as the fire prepares it for burning. Unlike inert matter that cannot reflect on what is happening to it, we might on occasion catch sight of the method to this apparent divine madness.

When the light of contemplation shines momentarily less intensely, we can peek over the edge of the horizon and glimpse what is really being achieved by this work. These pause-and-assess moments are comparable, the saint says, to what happens when an ironworker stops, takes the metal out of the forge, and examines how much work he has done and what there is left to achieve. So too, one is able, if not in the midst of the purification process, then during such assessments, to see the good that God has wrought. "So too, when the flame stops acting upon the wood, there is a chance to see how much the wood has been enkindled by it" (DN II:10 [6]).

5. *Interior Purgation.* Times of respite must not be mistaken for the permanent release enjoyed in the state of union. After such alleviation of exterior purgation there comes a new onslaught of intense purification. Now is the time when the fire of love returns to consume what must be purified from within if one is to become transparent with love's true light. One's suffering at this time becomes intimate (only God can know this about me); subtle (I cannot hide this side of my stubborn resistance any longer); and spiritual (I am being led to a place I did not want to go).

Since inward burning is proportionate in its intensity to the inwardness, subtlety, and deep-rootedness of the spiritual imperfections divine transforming love intends to reform, there is a link between such interior purgation and the action of fire upon wood. As St. John understands it, the more the fire penetrates into the wood, the more intense and vehement it has to be. It takes as much effort to prepare the innermost part of a log for burning as it does for God to welcome once and for all a wayward son or daughter.

6. *Consciousness of Nothingness*. At this level of refinement, it seems as if all one is conscious of is one's own nothingness. The time of blessed splendor is past. So sensitive is one's formative conscience that every slip seems to be a pointer to just how full of evil one still is. This is a bitter pill to swallow, but it does cure one of any leftover, self-centered illusions.

The wood is now so like the consuming fire that its own identity seems as fragile as air. For all this loss and lamentation, one will soon discover that the more intimate the purification, the more intense will be one's pleasure in God alone. Joy beyond all telling awaits one for whom, to again cite St. Teresa's prayer: "God alone suffices." The journey to this high place requires nothing less than a lifetime of experience.

7. *Recurrence and Return*. Though one knows ample joy during intervals in the purification process—a joy so profound it seems as if the bitter aloes of the dark night are gone forever—one suspects that some sinful roots in need of recurrent reformation remain. One adverts here and there, especially under pressure, to some old patterns. Hence one's joy cannot be complete—neither here and now nor by life's earthly end. New dark nights await in the wings to assail one when further purification is necessary.

Usually one's intuition of the return of the night can be trusted. St. John does not believe that those inner rivers of the soul that have been cleansed of deformed dispositions can successfully cover up portions yet to be reformed. He calls to mind the vast difference between the inmost part of the wood, still to be enflamed and illumined as compared to the parts of the log already burnt away. The fire still has work to do. We are sinners in need of redemption until our dying day.

Faith and the Fire of Love

With each interior purging the process repeats itself. One thinks all its good has come crashing to a halt. One assumes that the blessings promised by the Mystery have been fulfilled long ago and that there is nothing beyond the present cross to anticipate.

It takes profound faith to proclaim the good news of yet another Easter morn when all one sees are Gethsemane and Golgotha. At the foot of the cross, overcome by inner pain, feeling abandoned by the Mystery, one is momentarily blinded to the good. Pure faith is the only way to behold, amidst such functional blindness, the bigger picture.

From the start, St. John has insisted that faith is the only proximate means to union with God. Once again he soberly proves his point. What he teaches us goes far beyond the naive conclusions of "New Age spirituality"[5] and its blithe counsel to pursue one's bliss through various projects of self-salvation.[6]

Having sounded this sober warning, St. John is now ready to move to the second verse of his poem. He has described to the best of his ability the mysterious forming, reforming, and transforming properties of the dark night. It is time to leave these experiences behind and to initiate a lighter discussion of "the fruit of the soul's tears and the happy traits about which it begins to sing in [this] second verse: 'fired with love's urgent longings'" (DN II:10 [10]).

14

The Passion of Divine Love: Tracing the Transformative Effects of Contemplative Purgation

(*The Dark Night*, Book Two, Chapters 11, 12, 13)

The bonds of love between a seeker of God and the God by whom one is sought are impossible to break. In Francis Thompson's poem, "The Hound of Heaven," strong feet follow after the one who flees and hides his face "with unhurrying chase, and unperturbed pace … ."[1]

Divine love continues to spark the embers of urgent longing that have led us thus far on the journey begun "one dark night." Like fire enkindling twigs set for burning, so love penetrates to our bones and marrow, to the core of our being, under the steady outpouring of grace released by God in the contemplative night.

The fire of love is at once painful and purifying. It affects the sensory as well as the spiritual parts of our human life form, though in a different degree, gradually accommodating all that is pretranscendent to the transcendent.[2]

Purification of such an intense kind occurs in our inmost spirit. This cleansing redirects our transcendence dynamic, freeing it from all encapsulating, lesser satisfactions and pointing it toward the lasting fulfillment awaiting us when we love God with our whole being and our neighbors as ourselves.

What St. John wants us to understand at this juncture of the journey is that however confused and conflicted we may feel because of the darkness, we are coming closer to the light of union with God. Though love wounds us purgatively, it does so only to propel us passionately toward the transcendent. If someone were to ask us what is happening to us now, our answer might be, "Nothing, yet everything."

Characteristics of Consuming Love

The love with which we love God and God loves us is so passionate and intense that mystics like St. John compare it to the experience of humanly falling in love. Similarly, our emotions run the gamut from inflamed hearts to flustered minds.

This love is received, as it were, passively while generating strong passions. One can do nothing to stir up such deep affection; it comes to one like flint sparking fire. Characteristic of this union is one's capacity to mirror the Mystery. Such love is not a product of our own making; it is a reflection of God's action in us.

Previously our longing for God was a source of suffering; now it evokes awe-filled delight. God infuses the warmth we feel within as well as the newfound strength, equanimity, and energy that ready us to witness to the gospel in the world. The Lord finds in us a worthy and welcome dwelling place. The dark night enables us to feel its flames without being consumed. The cross becomes the sign of our communion with Christ. The night tames our inordinate attachments and teaches us the meaning of transforming love.

Now no temporal substitute for the transcendent attracts us as ultimate. Love has made it impossible for us to be fooled. Some may think of us as incapacitated, but we have never felt freer or more capable of completing any task God sets before us.

The fact that we are unable to be content with any person, event, or thing separated from God makes us more appreciative of life and world as filled with divine gifts and blessings.

Having been reduced to the "least of these" by the dark night, we are better able to empathize with our own and others' vulnerability (cf. Mt 25:40). Still the easy road no longer attracts us. We would rather enter God's house through the narrow door (cf. Lk 13:24).

Purgation as a Key to Liberation

Purgation, like the weaning of a child or the pruning of a vine, has to happen at the right time and be wrought by a delicate yet decisive hand. God's "technique" seems to demand profound detachment learnt from the repeated experience of our having to leave everything behind for the sake of finding it again, albeit in an entirely new way, as hidden in the mystery of God's eternal, providential care. Such detachment is never depreciative. By withdrawing our desires from lesser goods, we come to appreciate the higher good toward which they are pointing.

Purgation as liberating enables us to see things not as possessions but as pointers to their unpossessed Source by whose power all that is comes to be. We would neither seek union with God nor persevere in faith through pain and suffering were it not for the fact that God has loved us first (cf. 1 Jn 4:7-12) and freed us by means of purgation from the sticky web of illusory desires.

The union with God to which we are being led by grace cannot be blown away like the scattered leaves of fickle satisfactions, here today and gone tomorrow. Purgation strengthens us, as it did the psalmist David, to focus solely on serving God (cf. Ps 59:10). Nothing can be withheld—no ability, no desire, no gift of intellect, no memory, and no affection of the will. We know from experience that any satisfaction to be found outside of God has a life as limited as a dying battery. In due time it will simply run out of energy.

Living the Great Commandment

In attempting to describe how remarkable and strong this flame of love in the spirit can be, St. John writes his own version of the first commandment (cf. Dt 6:5), making sure to add that such inclusive love neither disdains anything human nor excludes anyone from its circle of fire. To the contrary, the master says that:

> God gathers together all the strength, faculties, and appetites of the soul, spiritual and sensory alike, that the energy and power of this whole har-monious composite may be employed in this love (DN II:11 [4]).

It is hard to imagine how all the movements of the spirit and all the impulses of our appetitive nature come together in this expression of fervent love, but they do. Paradoxically the wound of love makes one well. The touch that reduces our pride to dust draws us to lucid transcendence. All of our passions are aroused by and directed toward union with the Divine, but at the beginning, burning replaces bliss. We are more aware of the fire than of the force of love behind it.

At times we find ourselves surrounded again by dark-ness and plagued by doubt. We know that God will never withdraw his love from us, but because we feel so few consolations it seems as if we shall never cross over to the promised land or enjoy its milk and honey.

St. John, using an image from Psalm 59:15-17, compares our hunger for God to the sighs and howls of starving dogs wandering through a city. The more the fiery winds and flames of love dry up our spirit, the greater our need for Christ Jesus to come and give us a drink. There are no words to express what it feels like when one's whole being becomes one long howl for the Holy. St. John's own version of Psalm 63:2 phrases how much he pines for God, saying, *"My soul thirsts for you; in how many ways does my flesh long for you"* (DN II:11 [5]).

Love's Urgent Longings

All of this leads to the fact that one's deepest self is "fired" as iron in a forge "with love's urgent longings." St. John makes a point of saying that this kind of passion affects one much more profoundly than merely "an urgent longing of love" (DN II:11 [6]).

The difference to which he points would be the same as that between romantically flirting and falling in love so deeply that one is willing to make a lifelong commitment. The love one feels for God shuns casual complacency. It is at once unspeakably satisfying and a source of suffering. The wound that stings is also consoling because it comes from the Beloved.

The man Job voices this give-and-take of love when he describes endless nights of waiting in sorrow commingled with anticipation (cf. Jb 6:2-9). It is as if one is in a small, walled room that grows more narrow day by day, not unlike St. John's own prison cell. He must have known through experience what the book of Job reveals. At the epicenter of this event of seeming abandonment by God, one's affliction appears almost fatal. One's suffering seems unaccompanied by comfort. As darkness descends anew, hope almost fades that some good may manifest itself.

Comparison With Purgatory

St. John compares the contemplative night to the doctrine of purgatory in which he deeply believes. This burning of love increases one's anxiety and affliction for two reasons:

> 1. Especially in this day and age, when we stroll at night along a strange, dark road, we feel apprehensive. We fear shadowed places in a park. We can taste our fear when a twig snaps behind us. Multiply such human fears a hundredfold and you may sense the doubts one feels of ever being rescued from the pit of spiritual darkness.

> 2. At the same time, one is aware that the wondrous stirring that wounds the senses and spirit also enflames them with love.

Describing these two ways of suffering, the prophet Isaiah tells how he at one and the same time desired God in the night and felt miserable, how he watched for God's appearance at the crack of dawn while feeling stretched to the limit by anticipatory desire (cf. Is 26:9). For this reason St. John says of this purgative experience that:

> ... in the midst of these dark and loving afflictions, the soul feels a certain companionship and an interior strength; these so fortify and accompany it that when this weight of anxious darkness passes, the soul often feels alone, empty, and weak. The reason is that since the strength and efficacy of the dark fire of love that assails it is communicated and impressed on it passively, the darkness, strength, and warmth of love cease when the assault terminates (DN II:11 [7]).

How could anyone endure such a draining, life-changing, lonely experience were it not for the felt presence of an all-embracing love and the promise that this passive purgation will end with the gift of new life?

The analogy with purgatory further helps St. John to capture this time of transition between passion and promise. He says that the dark material fire that purges souls in the life to come to ready them for heaven's light is comparable to the dark spiritual fire he has been describing as at once loving and wounding. Whereas the cleansing in the hereafter is seen by him more in terms of a conflagration, that which occurs in this life is seen as an initially painful illumination of love.

The psalmist David asked God, therefore, to create in him a clean heart (cf. Ps 51:12), a heart on fire with the love of God and as receptive to grace as a shiny, clear window is to the rays of the sun. In his Sermon on the Mount, Jesus, too, blesses the clean of heart and promises that they will see God (cf. Mt 5:8). The prophet Jeremiah seems to see the same connection between the purgative way and the infused graces by which God bestows mystical wisdom. In Lamentations 1:13, he names the fire sent into his bones as an emissary of divine instruction. Similarly, the psalmist David links trial by fire and the bestowal of loving wisdom, saying that though God rains a "burning blast" of brimstone on the wicked, "the upright shall see his face" (Ps 11: 6-7).

Glad Side of This Sad Night

The night of contemplation cannot be ultimately anything but a night of consolation if it means that God infuses love and wisdom in persons according to their capacity and need. As the fire of love purges us of every trace of formation ignorance, of every refusal or forgetfulness of our true transcendent nature, it illumines us at the same time with love and the light of mystical knowledge.

The best and only cure for our blindness is an encounter with the wisdom of the living God. It descends like light waves in the heavens to us on earth. St. John accepts as a doctrine of faith that messengers (angels) of God impart inspirations as wondrous as rays of sunshine passing through many windows at once. Naturally the intensity of the communication depends on how close or how far a window is from the sun and on the density and quality of the glass through which it shines.

It follows, therefore, that the closer a spirit is to God, the more transparent it becomes to his overall communication of love. The lower we are in this hierarchy of spirits, the fainter will be the illumination we reflect and the more difficult it becomes to receive and give witness to the fullness of God's love.

Angels as pure spirits receive this inflow with little anguish, but this is not the case with us. Our nature, since the fall, is impure, fallible, and weak. The communications of God impact upon most of us as does sun upon a person sick and bleary-eyed. We wince and blink but our pain, as St. John explains, has a purpose.

The same fire of love that enamors and afflicts us refines our receptivity. If grace allows, we may become almost as open as angels are to its gracious inflow. This happy state is for the time being only a promise. At this stage loving knowledge, the gift of contemplation, can only be received by us in a less delightful state of spiritual distress, hunger, and thirst for God.

Process of Passing Through the Purgative Night

What happens prior to the point when these urgent longings are stilled?

1. Early in the purgative process, as we have seen, the fire has to dry out and prepare the wood for the application of the flame to enkindle it.

2. As time passes, one grows more enamored of God. The fire begins to radiate warmth, which is a sign of deepening love and intimacy with God.

3. As darkness overtakes the intellect and faith alone carries one forward, the mystical knowledge of love being infused by the Divine does two things: It enflames the will with affective longing, and it wounds our lower powers of reason by illuminating the intellect with a knowledge and light beyond its ability to grasp. The will in turn is re-enkindled with fervor.

4. Throughout this time of transformation, the will remains passive or receptive. It is like a living flame of love, afire with the transcendent knowledge granted undeservedly to it, yet incapable as yet of articulation. The words of the psalmist David capture something of what happens to intellect and will at this time:

I kept dumb and silent;
I refrained from rash speech.
    But my grief was stirred up;
hot grew my heart within me;
in my thoughts, a fire blazed forth (Ps 39:3-4).

At the end of this explanation, St. John describes the turning point from distress to delight. As love enkindles and ignites mind and heart, reason and affection, intellect and will, something wonderful happens. We experience, in the words of the saint, "a certain touch of the divinity." One stands on the threshold of "the perfection of the union of love for which the soul hopes (DN II:12 [6]).

Beyond Trials to the Divine

According to St. John, one cannot experience the union of love until one has passed through the trials of purgation and tasted the delights of illumination. Consider true friendship in this context. It remains a fair-weather affair unless two people are willing to put it to the test of time and the trial of trust. The relationship has to grow beyond the stage of feeling good to gain in maturity. Over the course of the years, the level of intimacy, care, and concern enjoyed by the friends has to reach such a refined state that one is willing to lay down one's life for the other, as Jesus did (cf. Jn 15:13).

Extensive trials thus prepare one for the infused touches of God. These life-transforming pointers to the "More Than" defy explanation, yet they give to one who has suffered with and for Christ every reason to rejoice. The will now loves without the intellect comprehending how, as once the intellect had willed to remain faithful without feeling anything but aridity.

These experiences and others like them occur in the night of contemplative purgation. When divine light acts upon the intellect or higher reason, it leaves lower reason groping in the dark for an explanation. Only higher reason receives the gift of faith-inspired wisdom. St. John concludes:

> All of this is similar to feeling the warmth of fire without seeing its light or seeing the light without feeling the fire's heat. The Lord works in this way because he infuses contemplation as he wills (DN II:12 [7]).

Delightful Effects of the Dark Night

While keeping in mind the afflictions of the night, St. John seems eager to assure us of its delightful effects. What wondrous gifts has God prepared for those who walk in the footsteps of the Lord?

1. *Serenity.* Mystical knowledge, while not initially dispelling aridity, does not leave the intellect or the will in distress. In fact the opposite occurs. Even without feeling the actual union of love, one rests in the serene assurance that God is near. The serenity of soul granted to one whose faith has been formed, reformed, and transformed by fire is ineffable but absolutely foolproof. The felt experience of encounter with the living God happens when and as God determines. It leaves a residue of peace and equanimity that proportionately increases one's capacity for tolerating restlessness and aridity.

2. *Simultaneity.* Contemplation affects at one and the same time the intellect and the will. It forges a strong faith while enkindling a tender love. To the degree that both faculties are purged, the resulting union will be more perfect.

At the start of this transformation process, designated by St. John as "purgative contemplation," the will burns with longing, before the higher intellect, inspired by faith, comprehends what is occurring. Though both faculties are being simultaneously purged, there is a distinction. Because our will is free, we can conceivably resist or refuse this invitation of grace. It appeals to us both passively and passionately, but we are not forced to listen. The method the Spirit seems to prefer is more indirect than direct, more subtle than overt.

God enkindles the flame of love in the substance of our soul. This draws us toward the Beloved almost irresistibly. At times, seemingly against our will, we begin to fall in love with the God who wounds and woos at the same time, in whose presence we feel both afflicted and affectionate. That is why St. John refers to this enkindling as a "passion of love" rather than as "a free act of the will" (DN II:13 [3]).

One is captivated by God as young lovers are by one another. One would not trade all the freedom in the world for being thus bound. Like a bird in flight, one is carried high into the clouds by the force of this passion, buoyed up on thermal currents by the impetus of true love. The need to understand fades into the background. One's sole concern becomes the fulfillment of one's desire for God. Free exercise of one's will appears important only if it satisfies the passion of love.

The intellect takes this experience in without seeking to comprehend it. Who can explain why anyone falls in love? The passion is primary, its consequences are secondary, its effects are delightful.

3. *Suffering*. True love, as everyone would agree, is unthinkable without some kind of suffering, even when the fire of love is purely spiritual. This is not to say that the senses are oblivious to such passion. To the contrary, everything that affects our spirit affects our senses and vice versa. The difference is that this desire for union with the Divine evokes a suffering far greater than anything experienced in the night of the senses.

One knows in the depth of one's being that not to find God in this way is to forfeit everything that makes life worth living. Thus the soul's greatest suffering, its trial of trials, is to imagine that one has lost God or been abandoned by the Mystery.

4. *Boldness*. It takes boldness not to feel bitter about why God would hide himself when we are seeking him with all our heart. It takes perseverance to get past the temptation to think that God is angry at us or indifferent to our suffering. It takes courage to make yet another act of appreciative abandonment to the Mystery. Thus inebriated by love and the desire for deeper oneness with God, one forgets oneself and proceeds into the night without undue concern for one's well-being.

5. *Inebriation*. This effect is illustrated for St. John by the story of Mary Magdalene. Her love for Jesus was stronger

than the pull of her past, promiscuous life. She did not care what either prominent people or peasants thought of her. All she knew was that she had to bathe the feet of Jesus, the teacher, whom she loved with all her heart. Her inebriation enabled her to reach him. The wound of love drew her toward his healing touch without delay (cf. Lk 7:37-38).

After the crucifixion and burial of Jesus, nothing could stop her from going to the tomb to anoint his body—neither the stone sealing it nor the soldiers guarding it. Thus at daybreak it was she whom Christ chose over all others to announce the resurrection (cf. Mt 28:1-10; Mk 16:1-8; Jn 20:11-18). She was not even embarrassed to ask the gardener if people had stolen the body. She had to know where he was (cf. Jn 20:15). For her no question or concern was foolish if it brought her closer to his side.

Love thus inebriated has these traits: It is strong and vehement. Nothing seems impossible to it. It assumes that everyone feels the same way. It has no room for lukewarmness. When in the Songs of Songs the bride searches for her Beloved, she assumes that everyone she questions feels the same intensity of desire (cf. Sg 3:3; 5:8). So, too, does Mary's love for the Lord manifest this ardent quality. Nothing could keep her from being with Jesus. She had to know where he was so she could seek him without delay.

The spiritually maturing person, who is advancing on the way, feels like this:

> The wounded soul rises up at night, in this purgative darkness according to the affections of the will; as the lioness or she-bear that goes in search of her cubs when they are taken away and cannot be found [2 Sm 17:8; Hos 13:8], it anxiously and forcibly goes out in search of its God (DN II:13 [8]).

6. *Impatience.* One sees here a commingling of passivity (being captivated by God) and activity (going in search of God). While one feels more the absence than the presence of God, one has no inclination to run away from the chase.

When a person in imminent danger of perishing knows help is within reach, he or she cries out impatiently to whomever can hear.

This experience of impatient love is another delightful effect of the night. One tells God in no uncertain terms that it is impossible to fight the good fight, to keep the faith, to run the race to the finish (cf. 2 Tm 4:7), without some sign of his love. Like Rachel weeping for her children (cf. Jer 31:15), so the impatient lover ceaselessly reminds God of her need.

7. *Conjunction.* Despite the fact that we feel miserable and undeserving of God's grace, surrounded by darkness, and in need of ongoing purgation, we have no doubt that our destiny is to be joined to God. The force driving us to love this boldly, this impatiently, will not subside in intensity until we are united with and assimilated to the object of our desire: union with God, who is love (cf. 1 Jn 4:8).

Until such conjunction is attained, our hunger and thirst for holiness will not be assuaged. This desire enflames our heart with new daring. It does not matter if our intellect remains in unknowing or if our will has to endure the pain of feeling unworthy. Union with the light, oneness with the God of love, are the only goals worth pursuing despite the trials we have to pass through to reach them.

Dispelling Deceptions

When divine light strikes the soul and throws it paradoxically into deeper darkness, it is because something in us is not yet ready for transcendent transformation.

At first we can see only what is closest to us—not the mercy of God but our own misery. In due course our eyes will stay riveted on the light and its holy source, but for now we have to wait until the Mystery draws our hidden sins out of the shadows of self-deception into the transforming circle of light.

It is an act of God's mercy to enable this self-insight to lead us to repentance and conversion. With the dispelling of these blind spots, deceptions, and imperfections, we can enjoy the delightful effects of this happy night of contemplation as God intends. Its manifold blessings and benefits begin to appear as morning-glories at the crack of dawn. According to St. John,

> ... God grants the soul a favor by cleansing and curing it. He cleanses it with a strong lye and a bitter purge in its sensory and spiritual parts of all imperfect affections and habits relative to temporal, natural, sensory, and spiritual things. He does this by darkening the interior faculties and emptying them of all these objects, and by restraining and drying up the sensory and spiritual affections, and by weakening and refining the natural forces of the soul with respect to these things (DN II:13 [11]).

It would be impossible to accomplish this liberation on the basis of our own lights. This is a work of sheer grace: to help us to die to all that is not God so that we may live with all in God.

Becoming a New Creation

Once we have shed our old skin, God can clothe us anew (cf. Eph 4:24), restore our youthful enthusiasm, and make us fly like an eagle (cf. Ps 103:5). The reformation God set out to accomplish is complete when:

> 1. Our human intellect is so illumined by a supernatural light that it can reason, act, and decide only by virtue of its oneness with God.

> 2. Our will is so informed by the love of God, so united with the will of God, that it loves no longer in a merely human way but in a way that is divine. This conversion of heart so affects our memory, our affections, and our desires that these inner channels now operate in accordance with the will of God. We begin to approximate on earth the union of mind and will that characterizes the saints in heaven.

Thus does God make of us a new creation (cf. Eph 4:24). Now that Christ has become our light and our salvation, we are able to do the Father's will in this world. Now that the house of our senses is as still as a mountain lake on a windless day, we are ready to follow our Beloved with the carefreeness characteristic of the children of God. So let us depart in secret, unseen by the prying eyes of our lower desires.

15

Stillness and Security Only Divine Darkness Can Dispense

(*The Dark Night*, Book Two, Chapters 14, 15, 16)

Is there a bridge between the gift of sheer grace and the conditions that make its reception more certain? For St. John this bridge is stillness. It may mean for a while having to endure suffering without complaint, trusting that out of it will come something creative. At least it means that we cease trying to master the Mystery and wait upon its leading of us. An escape from the house of lower level living has to occur if we are to cross over to the high places of contemplative union with God. As our senses go to sleep, as our reason, memory, and will fall silent in awesome wonder, we are made ready by grace to depart for the land of likeness to God.

One Must Travel in the Dark

To move lightly and with the least hindrance, we have to leave the land of unlikeness when it is dark. Such a departure is easy at night because everyone in the house is off guard and asleep. It was on a night like this that the saint really did escape from his prison cell in the Carmelite monastery of Toledo to the convent of the sisters of the Teresian reform, who gave him safe haven.[1] In this experience of St. John we find a metaphor fitting for the inner journey we are called to make to God. How does this heroic release come to pass? Let me convey the answer in the form of a story.

* * *

Once upon a time a brave and beautiful princess was cast into prison by her jealous sisters. They accused her of treason because she had attracted the attention of a rival of her father, the prince of a neighboring kingdom with whom she hoped to achieve an alliance for the good of all the people. What really aroused the ire of her sisters was that she had found favor with the humble and handsome prince, who already spoke of her as his "beloved."

In her heart the princess knew she would someday be his bride. This desire grew stronger with each passing hour she spent in the dark dungeon where no visitors came, not even her father the king.

Recalling her prince, he who would end her pain, the princess planned to escape. Nothing could keep her from being reunited with her lover. He waited for her outside the prison walls. He was alone, in solitude, and she wanted nothing more than to be in his presence. So strong was her determination, so intense was her desire, that she knew she had to leave not only the dungeon but also the security of her childhood home.

One dark night, aided by a kind jailer and guided by a mysterious light, she slipped out of the cell, tiptoed through the castle where everyone seemed to have fallen asleep, and fled into the freedom of the night, even as dawn edged over the horizon.

Suffering had released her from inner bondage to selfish passions and foolish plans. Her lower needs had undergone a transformation during days and nights of deprivation in the dungeon. These worldly concerns had filled her inner life like an overcrowded room, but that was behind her now. During the lonely hours of having to face herself before God, she came to see that what mattered were not passing pleasures, powers, or possessions but only her love for him, the one she knew so well. Now that she was free, no member of her household could hinder her pursuit or block her departure. She had been released by love.

* * *

The moral of the story is that we all have to seek release from whomever or whatever hinders us from making the journey to God. Is it the world in which we live? Is it the human condition? Is it envy or greed, gluttony or lust in their overt and subtle forms? What most often hampers us comes from within. Our own household—peopled as it is by security needs, fears, excessive attachments, controlling thoughts, and idle dreams—is our worst enemy (cf. Mt 10:36). This truth is not hidden from St. John:

> The operations and movements of these members had to be put to sleep in order not to keep the soul from receiving the supernatural goods of the union of love of God, for this union cannot be wrought while they are awake and active (DN II:14 [1]).

God Alone Can Effect the Work of Transformation

Despite the fallenness of the human condition and our penchant to resist the promptings of grace, God calls us to the perfection of love. All natural talents, excellent as they may be, cannot effect in any way the supernatural goods and graces offered to us by the generosity of God.

As the principal agent of our heart's transformation, only God can infuse the graces necessary for contemplative union. Lest we interfere with these divine operations, his way is now more secret, more silent. All counter moves on our part to control the uncontrollable prove to be futile. This miracle of transformation, if it occurs at all, is the Lord's doing.

We learn in the darkness of the night that our human gifts, sensual and spiritual, must pass through the way of purgation to be worthy of receiving this divine infusion. For our part it is necessary to remain in a posture of humility and openness to any stirring of grace. Above all, we have to temper our urge to interfere with what God is doing for us, and not indulge in lower level inclinations or self-saving attempts to push against the pace of grace.[2] Let's return now to our story.

* * *

As the princess stepped across the castle moat at dawn to reach the waiting arms of her lover, she realized that what brought her to this place of liberation was not her own effort but God's grace. Who else could have lulled to sleep the members of her inner and outer household?

To enable this happy departure to occur, it was necessary for God to reform her hitherto recalcitrant passions, wrongly placed affections, and self-absorbed desires to be the focus of everyone's attention.

She now had to admit that she wanted to do the good deed, not merely for her father, but to gain the court's praise. Reconciliation between rivals is a worthy goal, but it must occur in accordance with God's timetable, not her own.

The princess' first obligation was to pursue spiritual union. She had to allow divine grace to reform her disjointed sensory and spiritual parts and to transform her heart.

This restoration was not for public consumption. It happened in the darkness of the night without her being seen by anyone. Something in the princess must have been put to sleep or mortified so that the best in her could come to fruition.

No one or no thing in the lower tier of her senses could now impede her departure for the land of freedom that awaited her coming.

* * *

This release from the limits of sense-bound perception is a grace only one who has savored it can fully appreciate. A person once addicted to drugs or alcohol might sense the elation St. John feels. Such a recovering person knows how wretched it is to worship only at the altar of an empty promise of satisfaction, to be the slave of a substance.

St. John speaks of such suffering in terms of his having been subject to the tugs and twitches of his lower appetites, to his pretranscendent impulses, compulsions, and ambitions. Anyone who has had this experience will understand why the freedom of the life of the spirit is so important and why it bestows gifts and goods that last a lifetime.

Splendid Results of Reformation

Passage through this "horrendous night" makes one feel in retrospect like singing or telling in poetry why what happened was a great grace and how it has become life-transforming.

There is a happy ending to this story, one with a twist worthy of the best fairy tale.

One would think that a person heading into the darkness runs the risk of never finding her way through it, of being lost forever. The tension builds because the heroine of the tale has to endure many torments. The night has its share of horrific sensations. The heroine has to push past spasms of doubt inwardly. Fear mounts outwardly. The tension rises to such a feverish pitch that escape seems a hopeless dream.

Then the unthinkable occurs. Rather than being undone by the dark night, it becomes the instrument of one's redemption. Through suffering one grows wise. In groping for the light, one sees the tunnel's end. At the time and place the Mystery has prepared, one stumbles upon a well-trod bridge to freedom. Out of chaos comes creativity, out of death, new life.

Symbols of the Night
of Renunciation/Liberation

Several things happen to our heroine. St. John depicts her plight in symbolic terms that he will carefully analyze:

1. *Clothing.* While journeying though the night, the color of one's clothing (that is to say, one's apparent identity) is radically changed, to the point where one's true self shines forth.

2. *Ladder.* The way one departs from the prison of mere pretranscendent dispositions and actions is by means of a secret ladder, the location of which no one in the house of the senses knows. This ladder is a symbol for the living faith that gives one the courage to depart in concealment in the first place.

Without faith our princess would never have been able to execute her escape plan successfully. Without hope she would not have felt a strange security, a reason-defying certitude, that all would be well. Without love her limiting desires, old wants, and exhausting passions would not have gone to sleep.

Had she remained on edge, in need of controlling the departure or its outcome, the members of her household would have been shaken awake and she would never have been allowed nor enabled to depart.

It is marvelous to know that though one walks in darkness one still feels secure. Normally this is not true. Try turning off all the lights at night and finding the bathroom without tripping. We feel anything but secure, but such is not the case at this stage of St. John's description of the soul's journey to God.

The Night as God's Emissary of Transformation

It has already been established that one's escape from pretranscendent living is possible only because the night—as God's emissary of transformation—darkens the natural light of our sensory (exterior) and spiritual (interior) formation powers so that, through purgation, these same assets can be illumined by the transcendent supernaturally.

Once lower level appetites are put to sleep, deadened, and deprived of their ability to find ultimate satisfaction in anything less than God, real growth in spiritual maturity can begin to take place.

The night limits the image-making meanderings of our discursive and fantastic minds. It subdues the binding efforts of the memory to imprison us in the past. It lifts our once proud intellect into the humbling mist of the "I-don't-know-what/which is so gladly found."[3] It causes our will, once stuck in the mire of willfulness or in the loose muck of will-lessness, to feel the hot air of aridity that makes us painfully aware of how empty and out of control we really are.[4]

It is as if a dense fog hangs over our bodies, minds, and hearts. Our spirit is sorely afflicted. We worry because God seems to be withdrawing from us when we most need him to be near us. And yet, as St. John's verse asserts, in this darkness one walks with an air of calm and quiet security. How is such poise possible under the circumstances? What is its source?

Why There Is Security in the Night

Say you are hiking over rough terrain when all of a sudden you lose your footing, slide down a steep embankment, and plunge into a deep hole that proves to be the entrance to a hidden cave. Recovering from your fall and in despair of being rescued, you realize that you will have to rely on God's help and your own ingenuity, fired by the desire to escape this trap and survive.

Night descends. You are in total darkness. The light on which your senses, especially sight depends, disappears. You grope to find a resting place. You huddle in a small crevice of rock that holds your body's heat and wait for the dawn. You feel so vulnerable, lost, and alone that tears run down your dirty cheeks.

Cancelled is every project you felt was important. Gone from memory, intellect, and will are the intense desires that drove you to satisfy your basic needs, organize your business affairs, and control your destiny to a high degree. Your heart aches for the presence of any human being—friend or foe.

Food and drink, now rationed to a minimum, are no longer taken for granted. Every detail of your life demands attention, and the night offers a seemingly endless space for self-reflection.

Time slows to a snail's pace. As midnight nears, you feel your inmost self almost departing from your senses and your spirit. It is as if you are being drawn to a higher plane of reason and faith. Though you have nothing and feel as if you are nothing, you sense a strange kind of liberation. It is as if your night vision clicks into gear and you can see with inner eyes.

Each breath becomes a prayer. The light is dim yet its power to illumine you inwardly is as bright as a beacon. Part of you (your senses and your spiritual faculties) is for all intents and purposes asleep, and yet you (the higher you often imprisoned by lower desires) are awake.

You could not feel more deadened and deprived of comfort than you are now. It is impossible to find pleasure in anything. The wall of rock against which you lean is cold and damp. You cannot see your hand in front of your face. The silence is so thick you could cut it with a knife. Your mouth feels as dry as sawdust.

Inwardly your thoughts race from one topic to the next. You are distracted by one fantasy or one flash of memory after another. You are unable to think in a discursive, carefully reasoned fashion, yet you feel certain that things will get better, though how, you do not know.

As the darkness intensifies and your discomfort becomes nearly unbearable, it feels as if you are going literally out of your mind. The truckload of memories to which you could cling comes to a halt. The channels of reason that helped you to plan your escape clog up. Your mind goes blank. What is happening to you is impossible to understand. It seems ludicrous to calculate how far you have to climb at the midpoint of this night you now believe will never end.

Your will to live does not weaken, but your capacity to be in charge feels constrained. Though the illusion of independence explodes in a thousand fragments, one more cracked and arid than the next, your awareness of being dependent on God soars to dazzling heights.

There is that part of you that is as empty as a broken bottle and as useless as an old shoe, but there is also more happening to you now than you can imagine.

It is as if a dense, heavy cloud invades the already darkened cave to attack the last remnant of your human efforts to free yourself. This obscuring of all that used to give you comfort threatens to draw you away from God, but this threat never materializes because, much to your amazement, there comes over you a feeling of security.

In the gloom of the cave you sense a friendly presence. Is it God? Is it God's messenger, the guardian angel to whom you prayed as a child? Who knows? All you can say is that there is no place to go but toward its light.

Outside the cave your appetites led you every which way. All you wanted to do was to gratify them as quickly as time and money would allow. Your calculating mind raced from point to point, intent on fulfilling every whim and ambition. You relied on your affections or your imagination, on your mental acumen, on your indomitable will to get you where you had to go.

Now there is nothing to befriend but darkness, and this strange, loving presence. Your life used to be torn between excess (too much) and defect (not enough). You would change your course or sing another tune, depending on which way your wants would lead you. You were the captive of inordinate inclinations and, until now, you did not know it.

In the cave all such operations and movements are impeded. Here it is impossible to make such foolish mistakes. It is high time to be freed from the false promises of your pretranscendent existence. You no longer want your captors (the world, the flesh, the devil) to keep you locked in prison. The Mystery is beckoning you beyond your old worldly ways and me-centered wishes. The devil is losing the ground he gained when your soul was at war with itself, overrun by the fierce fight between this or that affection or desire.

Since these are now dying, the devil departs, and again that wave of inner peace, not of your making, soothes your fears and makes you content to wait upon the Lord. You doze off to sleep just as the sun starts to rise.

The Night Protects Us From Evil

This rendition of St. John's text is a way of explaining his conviction that "In the measure that the soul walks in darkness and emptiness in its natural operations, it walks securely" (DN II:16 [3]).

For St. John the prophet Hosea (13:9) seems to suggest in so many words that we are our own worst enemies. Trying to satisfy rapacious senses and inordinate appetites leads only to entrapment in mere pretranscendent living. The distance between us and the land of transcendent freedom widens. Inhibiting our way is any form of resistance to God's saving grace. Propelling us forward is the dark night that prevents evil from getting the best of us. It enables the graces of union with God to pierce through the seemingly impenetrable barriers raised between us and the Divine due to self-centered preoccupation.

Thanks to the dark night, appetites that once dominated our desires and actions are tamed to such a degree that they become appreciative receptors of divine epiphanies. Once blind, we now see. Faculties that used to puff us up with pride and willful modes of control are made so humble in the night that they can be called "heavenly" by St. John.

We remember God's goodness instead of being distracted by a thousand ultimately unimportant things. We observe a change in ourselves that could come only from the grace we are given to lift high the cross of Christ. The best part of us feels secure because we no longer rely on possessions or pride, personal power or presumption to make us happy. True joy replaces empty, passing gratifications of this or that deceptive desire.

It is as if a powerful force is protecting us from many other evils. Like creatures whose vision is better at night than during the day, we no longer mind walking in darkness. It helps us not to go astray or to betray the call God issues to us.

Led by grace, we reach a point of no return, spiritually speaking. What used to be a solid pavement becomes a motorized walkway. We begin to advance rapidly and to live virtuously.

Darkness Draws Us Into a Process of Divinization

Obviously the dark night is God's way of offering us all that is good and profitable for our salvation. God assures us at every turn that we do not need to be afraid of the dark because we are walking the road to spiritual maturity with Christ as our companion. Notwithstanding these wonderful benefits of the night, St. John asks the very questions that may have plagued our minds:

Why does God need to draw over us this veil of not knowing, of not seeing, of not understanding? Why must he dampen our desires by virtue of so much disappointment and suffering, humanly speaking? Do we have to be covered with a veritable blanket of sorrow? Is it only through adversity that we humans can see the stars? Why must it be that we derive no satisfaction even from good gifts, and that we find any effort to stay attentive to the promise of release so exhausting? Why, when we ought to know better, are we still tempted to focus on other less important things, or to feel the push and pull of untamed desires?

The answers the saint gives to such oft-voiced questions are at once simple and complex. To expect that a lot of excitation will accompany the outpouring of spiritual graces is naive. We want clashing drums and cymbals, but the Lord chooses to come to one who is worthy with a "tiny whispering sound" (1 Kgs 19:12).

Because our pretranscendent human ways of sensing and understanding are both limited and tarnished by sin, we cannot take in the full transcendent excellence of divine self-communications. What is received by us can only be received in accordance with our natural gifts and limits. That is to say, even if God were to lavish us with supernatural delights, we would be unable—except under the most exceptional circumstances—to receive them in other than a base and somewhat self-centered way.

God cannot accommodate to our human minds the sublime mystery he is, but he can offer us another gift—a purer way of loving—through the purgation and illumination that happens in the dark night. At the high point of this transformation process, the beatitude, "Blessed are the clean of heart, for they will see God" (Mt 5:8), takes on a new significance. Our human life form, weakened and wasted by bad choices and actions counter to God's intent, undergoes a profound transformation. We are able to receive supernatural touches and tastes of the transcendent that mystics like Symeon the New Theologian identify as the grace of divinization.[5]

This mysterious process, of which God is the principal agent, purposefully darkens our usual ways of perception and action. It weans us away from narcissistic desires and enables us to grow beyond the babyhood of the spiritual life. This process purges lowly modes of comprehension bound to pretranscendent pleasures and powers so that we can behold the "More Than." It annihilates the last remnants of lower level living so that the divine seeds planted in our hearts since baptism may come to full bloom.

The process of divinization releases us from the hold of counterfeit forms of life and enables us to radiate the bright light of the Christ-form. St. John concludes:

> Thus all these faculties and appetites of the soul are tempered and prepared for the sublime reception, experience, and savor of the divine and supernatural, which cannot be received until the old self dies (DN II:16 [4]).

Indescribable Benefits of Divine Communications

One can almost hear St. John breathing a sigh of relief as he shifts from the chore of analyzing the devastation of the dark night to the delight of acknowledging its indescribable benefits.

He finds in the letter of James (1:17) confirmation of his conviction that the source of every transforming encounter we shall ever experience is the "Father of lights." Neither our human yearnings nor our free choices can account for the depth and origin of the divine communications that make our spiritual life a reservoir of peace and joy, prompting us to share with others something of the goods we have received from God.

Humanly speaking, you could be the brightest person on earth, engage in esoteric theological debate, or be the recipient of a thousand spiritual delights and still not bring about in any way this communication. On this high plane the goods derived from the darkness do not proceed from us to God; they come from God to us.

By focusing attention on our Divine Source, St. John keeps us humble. He wants us to see that just because we might feel inclined to turn toward God or to use our minds to think about him, with all the satisfaction derived from so doing, it does not mean that our desires or actions are, of necessity, supernatural. To the contrary, what we deem "spiritual" may be all too human.

While we have a natural capacity to direct our attention, appetites, and thoughts toward any object, including something like a spiritual communication, it does not mean that God is the source of our satisfaction. As a person once told me, "I knew a spiritual director who could speak as enthusiastically about bananas as he could about Meister Eckhart's doctrine of the birth of the Word in the soul."[6]

Communications from on high do not originate in any natural inclination of ours but in God alone. This helps us to understand why such encounters are often life-transforming. For proof we need only recall Moses' encounter with Yahweh before the burning bush (Ex 3:2-3) or Mary's annunciation experience (Lk 1:26-38).

Signs of Being in Communion With the Mystery

Are there some signs by which we can recognize the difference between movements and inner stirrings that are merely natural and those which evidence that one is truly in communion with the Mystery who is almighty God?

St. John suggests by way of reply that we can be reasonably sure that the interior aspirations and inspirations now moving us are from God if our soul is (1) *obscured* (the dark night of the senses); (2) *put to sleep* (the dark night of the spirit); (3) *pacified* as to its natural ability; and (4) *weakened* in all its operations. Only then can we safely presuppose that the strength and courage we receive are from the Mystery and not a product of our own making. At such times the dynamics of self-actualization grind to a halt while the dynamics of spiritual ascendancy are placed in high gear by a hand mightier than ours will ever be.

Let's look at some of the signs of dark contemplation in more detail:

1. *God Guides Us When We Can No Longer See.* God wants to show us that affliction is not a closed door. Neither is it an occasion for masochism or errant asceticism. Rather the Mystery wants us to see that when our desires are scattered like thistles in the wind, when our inclinations to move in one or the other direction run into roadblocks, when our minds and memories, our musts and shoulds, feel as incapacitated as rusty machines incapable of any productivity, that is no reason to feel afflicted! Rather we should think of these breakdowns as breakthroughs. These times of grinding to a halt humanly offer us great graces spiritually.[7]

God sees what we only now begin to comprehend. This is his way of freeing us from ourselves and our proclivity to act as if we, by ourselves alone, had to do everything. The "I-can-do-it-alone mentality," however well it may have succeeded in the past, never really gave us complete and perfect security. Our plans were always in some measure pushy and self-centered. Our attempts to take charge were at best awkward.

What a delight it now is to let God take us by the hand and guide us through the darkness! What a relief that we do not have to do so on our own power! We are happy to be led, as if we were blind, along a way and to a place we know not. Never could we have hoped to be in this land of likeness to the Divine had we relied on reaching it by ourselves. Had we eyes like eagles or feet like gazelles, it would have made no difference. God had to take the lead.

2. *God Encourages Us to Befriend the Unknown.* By now it should be clear that the persons to whom St. John refers walk as securely in darkness as in the light of day. There is another asset to this experience as well. Every time one receives some new grace or pursues the right path, it turns out to be the way one least understands. "I" would never have chosen this path to transformation. Surely "I" would have been lost, but God's leading was right from the start.

The experience of absolute certitude, grounded in pure faith and trust in God, is so new that one would never have chosen to pursue it. Yet it is this unknown passage that has drawn one, albeit blindly, across the desert to the promised land of freedom.

By getting lost one was found. This happens because to reach such unknown territory, to travel unmapped roads, it is impossible to be guided by a know-how one does not have.

Once when I was driving in a foreign country whose road signs I could not even read, I doubted every turn. Whenever I could, I sought the guidance of others. To reach my destination—a small retreat house near Kyoto, Japan—I had to talk myself into not turning around. This meant that I had to take the risk of driving on unexplored roads. I could not understand unfamiliar markings. I had to seek help and finally to follow a stranger who seemed to know where I wanted to go.

St. John uses the example of an apprentice learning a new art or trade. He has to struggle from the start. He has to plunge into the pain of making many mistakes rather than relying on what he had mastered previously. If budding artists or laborers balk at bracketing their former proficiency, they cannot expect to make progress.

It is almost a truism to say that for one to advance in holiness one has to walk in darkness. Since God is the master and guide on this journey, we have great cause to rejoice. Is it not a wonder that comprehension comes in obscurity and certitude in confusion?

3. *God Turns the Obstacle of Suffering Into a Formation Opportunity.* Whereas one used to assume that suffering cancels the feeling of security, one now knows from experience that scars do turn into stars if our faith stays firm. Only one who has been at the foot of the cross would have the courage to say that "Suffering is a surer and even more advantageous road than that of joy and action" (DN II:16 [9]).

This is so for two reasons: When we suffer, we turn to God to give us strength whereas when we are in charge we rely too much on our own always imperfect decisions and deeds. When we suffer, we usually practice such virtues as prudence and fortitude and in the process acquire many others. Suffering purifies our selfishness if we imitate the Lord. It makes us wiser and more cautious. No real maturity is possible without taking advantage of this formation opportunity.

4. *God Both Protects Us and Frees Us From Being Duped by False Promises.* The seasoned traveler who has been to the desert and survived its extremes of hot and cold walks across this desolate terrain with a security no casual tourist can muster. It is as if one is so absorbed by the light within and the wisdom it evokes that one forgets the desolation incurred in the crossing. Every step brings one closer to one's destination.

Similarly, the night of contemplation brings us so near to God that we feel protected and freed from all that is not God. It is as if we have to undergo the pain of an illness to appreciate what it means to be healthy. God in his wisdom puts us on a strict diet. It requires abstinence and may even make us lose our appetite for a while. During this training period, readying us for the most intense duration of our desert walk, we have to be treated with a tender yet tough hand.

What happens is not unlike the care of a sick person whom all members of the household esteem. For her own good, they keep her indoors, knowing that a chill would only make things worse. They try not to disturb her rest nor to distract her with needless worry or suspicious whisperings. They give her small portions of prescribed food—substantial, if not tasty—trusting that in due course a spiritual healing will happen, perhaps complemented by a physical cure. One's dearest companion is, of course, the Lord.

5. *God Woos Our Hearts in Hiddenness.* Anyone who has to endure profound suffering and sorrow knows that it can harden our hearts. As far as St. John is concerned, this is neither the only nor the correct response. The special gift of "dark contemplation" convinces us as no other experience can how near to us God is, how he safeguards us like a mother does her child, how much care we receive from Christ whether we are conscious of it or not.

In our fallible, fallen condition, it may seem as if the darkness that surrounds us is as thick as an impenetrable cloud that obscures everything from sight. Yet it is in this very cloud that we come to know God more than we know ourselves. Just as our human eyes are too weak to stare into the sun without seeing a blind spot, so the closer we come to God the more dazzled we are by the radiance of love's pure light. The more we approach it, the more hidden it is.

The psalmist David declares, therefore, that God makes darkness his hiding place. In Psalm 18:12, St. John finds ample evidence from holy scripture that "The dark water in the clouds of the air signifies dark contemplation and divine wisdom ..." (DN II:16 [11]). For St. John these metaphors signify the paradox that divine wisdom (light) radiates through the gift of Christ-centered contemplation (dark). The more direct and undeniable God's self-communication is, the less able we are to plumb its depths.

The Light of lights bestows upon us a clarity of purpose, a pristine truth, beyond what any reasoning process can reach. It is conveyed in what the Bible depicts as "foolishness" from the human perspective (cf. 1 Cor 2:14). What happens is that our pretranscendent intellect reaches its limit when God sets before our inner eye transcendent knowledge. This moves us to new clarifying heights of faith, even as our human understanding remains shrouded in misty lowlands.

That we could be so miserable and yet so caught up in the Mystery, so in danger of losing our direction and yet so led into the light of truth, is a wonder to St. John:

> The clearest and truest things are the darkest and most dubious to us, and consequently we flee from what most suits us. We embrace what fills our eyes with the most light and satisfaction and run after what is the very worst thing for us, and we fall at every step (DN II:16 [12]).

It is humbling to hear words such as these from a master who identifies with our human condition. How often we think we have found something or someone who offers us a ticket to happiness, only to learn that we have boarded the wrong train. We are in danger of never arriving at our destination. Fear is overcome if we live by faith.

We have to shut our eyes, trust God as one would a perfect guide, and believe—though we are in a dark tunnel—that there is light on the other side. We plunge into the darkness, convinced that we are lost, only to find the way that will lead us to where God wants us to go.

It is as if the dark "night" becomes a shining "knight" who safeguards our passage by warding off our old enemies—the world, the flesh, and the devil. The darkness also saves us from being victimized by the counterfeit pride-form that would separate us from God.[8]

Darkness serves as the divine dwelling place. It safeguards us. It offsets our understandable insecurity. It shields us from harming ourselves and keeps us from being harmed by others (cf. Ps 31:20-21).

When people's words and deeds distract our attentiveness to God, we can hide from them behind the fortification offered by the contemplative night. Its shielding, protective power prevents us from evoking the rancor of lying tongues or fueling their fires by our defensiveness.

Absorbed in God's love, we have neither time for nor any interest in idle gossip. The dark waters that conceal yet reveal the divine presence are more fascinating to us than the news reports that rivet people's attention. Distractions do not divide the heart of one whose appetites and affections have been weaned from baby food and tasted grown-up fare.

As the beneficiaries of darkness, our faculties are freed from any and all imperfections that are contrary to spiritual maturity, whether these are self-originating or have other causes as their source. Is it any wonder that such a person can say without a shadow of a doubt that the journey on which he or she has embarked in darkness results in one's feeling perfectly secure?

6. *God Gives Us the Gift of True Determination.* It is one thing to start out on a long trip, another to complete it. Yet, if St. John is any example, we can believe that almost from the beginning of this obscure, painful, and dark pursuit God graces us with a special gift: that of fortitude.

There are many points at which we could throw in the towel and end the trip. It is dark but the Lord seems to know exactly when we need a drink or a period of rest to refresh and fortify us for the remainder of the journey. Whatever else happens to us, of this we are sure: Somewhere near the start of this transforming experience we are conscious of receiving the gift of true grit or, as Teresa of Avila would say, of "determined determination."[9] Of this gift St. John writes:

> From the outset individuals are conscious of a true determination and power to do nothing they recognize as an offense against God and to omit nothing that seems to be for his service (DN II:16 [14]).

The night enkindles in our hearts marks of character no one can miss. We are as vigilant as air traffic controllers when it comes to caring for and committing ourselves to do what most pleases God. Short of scrupulosity, it is safe to say that the lover will ponder many times over how he or she may have angered or offended the Beloved.

The relationship between the soul and God is tender, courteous, gentle, and solicitous, always placing God first in one's life and offering him homage.

Of no concern to contemplatives are *my* wishes, *my* needs, *my* stamina, *my* mindsets. Such objects of self-centered gratification fall by the wayside, for one is now centered on God from whom all good comes.

7. *God Unites Us to Himself in Love.* The seventh and final benefit of dark contemplation is the best, namely, the pilgrim-soul "goes out from itself and from all created things to the sweet and delightful union with God through love" (DN II:16 [14]). This growth in freedom not only occurs in darkness with the greatest feeling of security; it also happens in secrecy with the help of a "ladder," a key symbol of St. John upon which I shall reflect in the next chapter.

16

The Secret Wisdom of Dark Contemplation

(*The Dark Night*, Book Two, Chapters 17 and 18)

Three images of the night intrigue St. John: Its wisdom can neither be taught nor understood because it is *secret*; its movement toward transcendence is upward as when one climbs a *ladder*; it leaves us as mysteriously as it came, with this difference: We seemingly look like everyone else but in truth we are in *disguise*. The first two images pertain to the dark night of contemplation as it affects us; the third has to do with the way we are to behave when this holy night of reformation and transformation enfolds us. It removes all traces of our old clothing, that is, the way we used to see and hear things, and gives us new garments. These disguise us from our enemies—the world, the flesh, and the devil—so that we can do the work of God.

Dark Contemplation Is Secret

Like two lovers who slip out of their respective dwellings in secret to meet one another, so is this union of love between us and God shrouded in mystery or secrecy. Another name for "dark contemplation" is "mystical theology," understood, though never fully, by the likes of a Thomas Aquinas. It was St. Thomas who said that compared to the gift of divinely infused love his entire *Summa* in the field of informational (systematic, moral, doctrinal) theology was as worthless as straw.[1] This is like saying that the depth of transformation undergone by the soul thanks to this divine communication remains secret to the sharpest intellect. None

of our faculties can grasp it: not the mind with its razor-edged
rationality and its reservoir of words; not the memory with
its wondrous powers of retention of one's own and
humanity's insights and experiences; not the will with its
attractive ways of calling attention to our desires.

This wondrous gift of union is in no manner an acquisition of ours; it is infused by the Holy Spirit in a way that
changes us forever, though we neither know nor grasp how
this happens. However exhaustive an explanation we may
try to devise, the depth of this experience remains a secret,
even to the devil:

> Indeed, not only does the soul fail to understand,
> but no one understands, not even the devil, since
> the Master who teaches the soul dwells within it
> substantially where neither the devil nor the natural
> senses nor the intellect can reach (DN II:17 [2]).

When one has returned by night to the land of likeness
to God lost by sin, it would seem as if he or she could give a
step by step description of the process, but there is only so
much one can say. Human limits keep us at the edge of divine
wisdom and power. Who can penetrate the mind of God or
see God's face and live (cf. Ex 33:20)?

Our ability to understand the deep things of God is
always an inability and, therefore, this contemplation is
called secret. It retains a residue of utter transcendence and
follows what mystical theologians traditionally name the
"apophatic way" or the way of unknowing.[2]

Effects of Secret Contemplation on the Soul

What we can discern are the effects this transformation
produces in the soul. The wisdom and work of love are first
of all purgative. In the dark nights of our life, understood as
genuinely graced events used by the Spirit to free us from the
prison of pride and the illusion of unmitigated control, something happens that is important enough to require a line by
line analysis by St. John.

However, caught as we are in the straits of purgation—a kind of secret cave where God reforms our heart—it is hard to say exactly what is happening. We know only that the end result is a freedom of spirit that makes our suffering a source of sweetness—strange as it may seem.

After a while the time of purgation passes, though there is always more of us to reform. Then there emerges another effect that is like sunrise after a storm: that of illumination.[3] The wonder of God's transforming plan for our life is suddenly clear. Our ears are opened; our eyes can see. Yet even now the self-communication of God remains ineffable.

> Not only does a person feel unwilling to give expression to this wisdom, but one finds no adequate means or similes to signify so sublime an understanding and delicate a spiritual feeling (DN II:17 [3]).

If a poet of St. John's caliber says he cannot convey this experience in the tools of his trade—words—then what of us? If he, a spiritual guide of such excellence, cannot find the proper comparisons to express the profundity of what has transpired, is it any wonder that such wisdom retains its mystery? No matter what we say of it there is an ocean of meaning that remains unexpressed.

Though the words he does write are grounded in firsthand experience, St. John is still hesitant to attempt to tell what this secret knowledge is. Even he can only grasp so much of it. The difficulty has to do, among other things, with the way we receive knowledge. The interior wisdom in question is, in truth, not complex but simple, not gnostic or for a special few, but general and, at least in principle, available to all, not quantifiable and selective but qualitative and spiritual. It enters our minds and hearts through the power of the Holy Spirit; hence it is infused and, therefore, not confined to a sensory genre or image.

It is not possible for our imagination to form an exact picture of this spirit-filled process. It is not as if one can say infused contemplation is, fill in the blank, and then describe it as one would the bejeweled lid of a box and its glittering contents. This sublime wisdom does not enter our interiority through any faculty. It is not possible to name it except by virtue of certain figures of speech. Light is perhaps the most apt metaphor.

The odd thing is that even without these usual routes of reason, the one who receives "secret wisdom" has no doubt that he or she intuits clearly and tastes fully the wondrous sense and sweet delight of this heavenly wisdom. St. John continues to grope for the words he says are not there to depict this sublime occurrence by telling a story. Let me put it in my own words.

The Journey to Union Continues

Once upon a time a pilgrim en route to a sacred shine he had never seen before began to imagine what it might be like. First he pictured it this way, then that. Having never been to a comparable place, he had no likeness with which to compare it. He surmised that all this guesswork would end when he actually arrived.

Suddenly he came to the place of his heart's longing. He prayed in silence and in song. A love the likes of which he had never known stirred within him. The irony was that when people at home asked him to describe where he had been he could not do so. He had no name for it. Every attempt was a new failure. He understood then that what had happened to him was utterly transforming. People could see it in his face. He had experienced something profoundly intense and life-giving, but as much as he tried, he could not describe how this holy place had touched him, though it had made an indelible imprint upon all of his senses. Above all, he could not find any adequate expression for the feeling of love that had entered his heart, pierced him to the quick, and brought tears to his eyes. Such is the problem:

> The language of God has this trait: Since it is very spiritual and intimate to the soul, transcending everything sensory, it immediately silences the en-

tire ability and harmonious composite of the exterior and interior senses (DN II:17 [3]).

Silence is the space of divine, transforming grace. It is the
only adequate framework for ineffability. St. John finds his
own experiences in this regard verified by sacred scripture.

When Yahweh addressed the prophet Jeremiah, he was
stunned speechless and could only utter the sound, "ah!" (cf.
Jer 1:6). When Moses beheld the bush that burned but was
not consumed, speech also failed to come forth. Neither
imaginatively nor through his senses could he render in any
adequate way what exactly occurred during this extraordinary exchange with the Divine (cf. Ex 4:10-13). He knew only
that his life had been irrevocably altered. Any attempt to
communicate directly this infusion of grace, as we read in the
Acts of the Apostles (cf. Acts 7:30-34), would have been to
Moses not even worth considering. Moses' interior imaginative ability might as well have belonged to one of his sheep
when it came to being able to say what he now understood
of God. None of his inner or outer receptors were capable of
receiving this knowledge. It had been infused in him and the
effect was life-changing.

As St. John puts it, "the wisdom of this contemplation is
the language of God" (DN II:7 [4]). It is Pure Spirit speaking
to our human spirit, the Alone with the alone. It makes
perfect sense that anything less than spirit—like the realm of
the senses—cannot perceive and articulate in full the
apophatic depth of what is "More Than" the sum of any
number of any parts.

The wisdom of which St. John speaks is, therefore, a
secret to the senses. Neither tongue nor eye has the know-
how to speak of it or to describe it. Even if one wants to do
so, its essence is beyond words. Even a God-fearing person
of good heart, one who has been led to the place of wisdom
and wants to give a faithful account of it to an experienced
spiritual director, will find himself or herself hard pressed to
describe it. It pains them to even try to speak of their experience since often the gift of contemplation granted to them

is so simple that any word about it would make it overly complex. Their awareness that "It is the Lord" happens so quickly and gently that they are sometimes no more aware of it than one would be of a cool breeze touching one's cheek on a summer's eve.

All our pilgrim might tell, for example, is this: "I can't quite say what happened. I only know that I feel a peace and harmony I hope never ends. I thought I would come home bubbling over with words and all I want is to be quiet. I am aware of God's presence continually. I feel content. I want nothing more. God is enough for me."

Such generalities preserve the ineffability of the experience of infused contemplation. To dissect it would be to despoil it. When and if one receives a lesser kind of divine communication, something as particular as a vision, a locution, or a spiritual feeling, then perhaps more details can be given. This is because our senses participate in some way in this kind of phenomena. Pure contemplation is different. It is and remains an indescribable secret.

Hidden in God

There is another reason to label such infusion "secret." Not only is mystical wisdom a secret unto itself, according to St. John it also has a way of hiding the soul within itself. Besides the effects thus far noted, characteristic of this wisdom is its capacity to engulf "souls in its secret abyss" (DN II:17 [6]).

When Moses came down from Mount Sinai bearing the Ten Commandments, the people were instantly aware that he had been to a place light-years away from the ordinary nuts and bolts of their idolatrous existence. He had been to the mountain and the fact that "the skin of his face had become radiant" (Ex 34:29) proved it.

It was the same when John the Baptist returned like a wild man of God from the desert wilderness and preached to the people to repent and prepare the way of the Lord (cf. Jn 1:23). To be led by God to this place of transforming grace is like being catapulted to a distant uninhabited planet. The plain on which one stands is immense, as vast as a desert with no known boundaries or an ocean with ever receding shores. To be brought here by the Mystery is a favor beyond any earned merit. The more solitary this experience is, the more conscious one is of being dwarfed while savoring its delights.

If only for a brief duration, like the time the disciples saw Jesus transfigured before their eyes (cf. Mt 17:1-8), one feels elevated above all creaturely wants, hidden in the cleft of a rock, held in the palm of God's hand, raised up above every temporal creature on eagle's wings—and, were it one's personal decision to make—never wanting to build one's tent anywhere but on this site. Here we can only assume that St. John is writing about himself:

> Souls are so elevated and exalted by this abyss of wisdom, which leads them into the heart of the science of love, that they realize that all the conditions of creatures in relation to this supreme knowing and divine experience are very base, and they perceive the lowliness, deficiency, and inadequacy of all the terms and words used in this life to deal with divine things (DN II:17 [6]).

In his poetry, the saint also tries to speak of this unspeakable transformation with a poignancy few have ever grasped:

> After I have known it
> love works so in me
> that whether things go well or badly
> love turns them to one sweetness
> transforming the soul in itself.
> And so in its delighting flame
> which I am feeling within me,
> swiftly, with nothing spared,
> *I am wholly being consumed.*[4]

Turning to Tradition to Tell the "Secret"

In this commentary on the dark night, as well as in many of his poems, St. John makes clear how impossible it is even to approximate what took place without the illumination offered by the long tradition of mystical theology. With it comes at least some comprehension however poor, and some experience however mundane, of divine things. No natural means, be they both wise and lofty, can tell of these things as they are in themselves. Masters like Thomas Aquinas and Pseudo-Dionysius confirm that such experiences are always beyond our feeble attempts to describe them. Not even one who has beheld the truth and been transformed by its effects would profess to grasp anything of its essence.

Once again, the saint concludes, this wisdom in its fullness remains always and forevermore a secret. In the deepest sense of this term, it is supernatural. It is the way by which we are guided to the perfection of union with God and to communion with all the saints and every member of the Body of Christ.

We advance toward the Divine, humanly speaking, not by way of what we know but by way of what we do not know and cannot control. We enjoy the grace of this place of perfection, but we are ignorant as to how we got there or why we have been so favored by our Lord. All of our knowing brings us face to face with the unknowable. We may have thought we were on familiar ground while we were in the process of acquiring contemplative dispositions, but now that we have, so to speak, been handed the prize, our sense of awe reaches overwhelming proportions.

The prophet Baruch must have felt this way when he acknowledged that no one can really teach the ways of wisdom or think through her paths (cf. Bar 3:31). So, too, was the psalmist forced to say to Yahweh that his light shines over the entire world, that he blinks, so to say, and the earth shakes under our feet, that neither his way nor his path can be known by any creature in a categorical sense (cf. Ps 77:18-19).

In his meditation on this psalm text, St. John says of secret wisdom:

1. Like the lightning of God that brightens a world dark with sin, so divine contemplation illumines the farthest reaches of our soul and casts out the shadowy hold of *self*-consciousness.

2. This illumination does not happen automatically. It must be preceded by the shaking and trembling of purgation, and it is painful.

3. The way one must follow to go to God does not match the solidity of the earth but the fluidity of the sea. To follow Christ means to step out into both calm and raging waters. It is to walk in footsteps we often do not see except with the eyes of faith.

4. Ultimately the way is beyond human reason. Where God wants to take us is a hidden and a secret place—a space not available for scrutiny by the senses but utterly inviting to the spirit. After all, to walk on water is a miracle our bodily senses cannot comprehend. It requires an act of pure faith (cf. Mt 14:22-31).

5. God leaves his traces in anyone he chooses to bring to himself in this intimate way. Such a one is touched by the finger of God and transformed forever. Walking in the footsteps of Christ is in the end only possible because the Lord leads us and carries us. He makes us, who are small, great with faith. He gives us the gift of union. We are filled with the traces of God, with a wisdom so transcendent, a union of love so transforming that it makes us almost unrecognizable to ourselves.

The figure of Job comes to mind, enabling St. John to underline his conviction that God exalts the humble and perfects in them his wonderful ways (cf. Jb 37:14-16). Those poor in spirit and pure of heart are, in so many words, the keepers of the secret wisdom that is infused contemplation.

Contemplative Love Is a Ladder

Because this wisdom is hidden from human schemes and reasons, it has the character of secrecy surrounding it. A second way to describe it is to use the image of a ladder. This invention is useful for everything from climbing trees to picking ripe fruit to pillaging a fortress full of treasure. For St. John the ladder is an apt symbol for "secret contemplation." Only by means of grace can one ascend to the Transcendent and taste in some measure already here on earth the treasures of heaven. If the union of love is the prize, then one who climbs the ladder to the highest rung will possess it in Christ.[5]

Another text suggests the validity of this image to the master. In Psalm 84:5-8, we are told that the one who receives God's favor has to be ready to make the ascent from this valley of tears to the mount of perfection, climbing up to its summit step by step until the God of gods is beheld on Zion. God is the treasure in the fortress. His name is Holy. To meet him is to know what we must do to live in fidelity to our call to serve the Lord in the ordinary circumstances of lay, religious, and clerical life, as single or married people, as biological or spiritual parents, as young or old, as female or male.

There are many reasons to compare this secret wisdom to a ladder. The first is that we can both ascend and descend on it. The divine communications that infused contemplation implants in our soul extol us in God (ascent) and humiliate us within ourselves (descent). St. John confirms with holy scripture that if a communication is truly from God it will at one and the same time both humble and exalt us.

The paradox of secret wisdom is inescapable. On this road, "to descend is to ascend and to ascend is to descend, since those who humble themselves are exalted and those who exalt themselves are humbled [Lk 14:11]" (DN II:18 [2]). First we have to be humbled by God, descending from pride and pompous presumption through the grace of the dark night; only then can we be raised up (cf. Prv 18:12).

If this is true of the spiritual life, then it holds as well for our daily routine (actions). Life in general suffers many ups and downs. Nipping at the heels of the harvest is the threat of drought. It's as if God gives us periods of relative calm to ready us to endure the conflicts that are to come. Prosperity may be a forewarning that penury waits in the wings. Misery may be in line after abundance. Torment may not be far behind tranquility. After a feast comes famine and vice versa. As St. John soberly announces:

> This is the ordinary procedure in the state of contemplation until one arrives at the quiet state; the soul never remains in one state, but everything is ascent and descent (DN II:18 [3]).

Ups and Downs of the Restless Heart

What is the reason for this unrest? It is at once easy to understand because God is our goal and hard to grasp because of our sinful condition. The union of love, the state of perfection, consists of two components: one is God's perfect love of us; the other is our contempt for self as separated in any way from God. This ambiguity makes no sense unless we adore who God is and accept who we are. Before we can run to the top of the mountain, we have to learn how to walk in the valley of truth.

When we lean on the strong arm of the Lord and let his love lead us home, we feel the exaltation of one who breathes in sweet, bracing mountain air. When we see that we have not walked in this truth but in a lie of our own making, we experience the self-humiliation without which there can be no self-transformation. Only when we have attained with God's grace and our freely given consent the lasting dispositions of a heart perfected in love do the ascent and descent of the ladder come to a halt. There is no more reason to climb up than there is to climb down because by that time we won't have to fret. We will have reached our goal. We will have been united with God for all eternity, for he "is at the end of the ladder and it is in him that the ladder rests" (DN II:18 [4]).

St. John sees this image of a "ladder of contemplation" prefigured in the story of Jacob, who saw such an image in his sleep, a stairway on which the angels of God were ascending and descending in a two-way pattern: from God to us and from us to God (cf. Gn 28:12-13). St. John notes that these events as recorded in scripture happened at night while Jacob was in a deep sleep. The story also tells us that the way we ascend to God is a mystery revealed in dreams but leaving only tell-tale traces in tomes of human knowledge.

What seems the worst thing that can happen to us—a night of disillusion and ego-desperation, an annihilation of expectation, a mortification of desires—becomes the basis of our ascent to freedom. Ordinarily loss is only loss. In this story of spiritual release, it is a gain. We would anticipate that the best spirituality would be about self-actualization, inner consolation, satisfaction, prosperity, success, and other "New Age" slogans. We learn the truth from the classical tradition. Such spiritualized selfism represents not the end of the line but that from which we have to ascend. This means descending into the sobering depths of the dark night where we see ourselves as we are. Only then can we let go of all that we are not and allow grace to release our real identity, the name by which we have been called by God from the beginning.

The Science of Love

St. John does not simply say casually, he "declares" emphatically, that this ladder of secret contemplation has as its "principal property," its chief characteristic, the fact that it points to "a science of love" or "an infused loving knowledge that both illumines and enamors the soul, elevating it step by step unto God, its Creator" (DN II:18 [5]).

In the following chapter, we shall climb these steps with St. John as our guide, noting as he does their signs and effects one after the other, so that a director or a directee can recognize on which of these rungs he or she is at any given time.

This knowledge is invaluable to anyone receiving or practicing the art and discipline of spiritual direction in private or in common.[6]

In this teaching, St. John will follow the classical tradition represented by such masters as Bernard of Clairvaux and Thomas Aquinas, both of whose works he cites.[7] The powers of natural reason and logical analysis are in this case only pretranscendent tools at the disposal of higher reason and faith on the level of the transcendent. That is why, even as he describes these steps, St. John maintains their secrecy. He acknowledges that when all is said and done, the ladder of love retains its apophatic depth and its secrets since God alone holds it, measures it, and weighs it. If by this ladder we climb to heaven, then it is only in heaven that we shall grasp each of its rungs—except the last, since it belongs only to the Godhead to know its sublime reaches.

17

The Mystical Ladder of Love

(*The Dark Night*, Book Two, Chapters 19 and 20)

St. John uses the image of the ladder of love with its ten rungs to show us how a lover of God can reach the full maturity of spiritual intimacy only by ascending from lower to higher levels of faith, hope, and love. One's incentives are confidence, courage, and constancy; one's guide is the Holy Spirit.

Step One: Longing for God

At some point in life, perhaps after we have tasted success, chased a lot of stars, and sought happiness in the wrong places, we may acknowledge the ache we feel deep within for something more. This is the grace of a "transcendence crisis."[1] Nothing satisfies us as we thought it would—not anyone or anything, no matter how great. Why hasn't this relationship been enough to fill my emptiness? What made me think this house or that position could make me perfectly happy?

If we are open to God's call at such "so what?" moments, if we can own our sorrow of soul without feeling too afraid, we may be ready to hoist our two feet onto the first rung of the ladder of love. Why we feel sick at heart is understandable. Nothing, literally no-thing, thus far has given us more than a teasing glimpse of the land of likeness. Lucky for us, we are "sick in an advantageous way" (DN II:19 [1]). We are like the bride in the Song of Songs who was "faint with love" (Sg 5:8) or the Desert Fathers weeping for their sins.[2]

Physically we may feel fine; functionally we know if we pushed ourselves to new limits, we could make it; but spiritually we sense there is something terribly wrong with us. God's love for us is so overwhelming that by contrast our life seems wretchedly superficial, so much so that at times it feels as if we are dead inside. Of what use are our foolish pursuits compared to the heroism of a converted heart?

When we are brought this low by grace, we can be sure that the spirit of love is nearby, waiting in the wings to lift us to the high places of renewed zeal for life and freedom (cf. Jn 11:4). If we but acknowledge our weakness, Christ will be our strength (cf. 2 Cor 12:9-10). God values this sickness more than a thousand days of perfect health. It is a sign that we do not want to succumb to the languor that makes us indifferent to our salvation or the lukewarmness that deadens our will to obey God's call. Such disobedience is the sour fruit of sin. Our stubborn clinging to things that are less than God, as if they were the be all and end all of consonant living, snaps like a dry twig underfoot. We must seek another way.

When languish replaces languor, it is a sure sign that our lives are taking a turn for the best. Now is the time to mount the first rung of the ladder for that for which we languish is God alone. Finite fulfillments are put to rest as we seek the far horizon where the Infinite awaits our coming. The psalmist David gives words to what we feel, for he, too, languishes for release from sin, for forgiveness and redemption (cf. Ps 119:81).

St. John offers us an apt analogy for what occurs at this crisis moment. He sees this sickness as a formation opportunity. Just as sick persons change color and lose their appetite for food, so on this first step of love's ladder our inner life undergoes reformation, that is, our past dispositions "change color" or turn over a new leaf that detaches us from all that would direct us away from God. Thus we lose our appetite for less interesting food.

Continuing the analogy, the saint suggests that one does not become this sick without an accompanying "excess of heat" or a fever. He compares this state of our being overcome by God's grace to a high fever. Only his touch can cool our brow and lead us to this first rung of the ladder. This grace is freely given like bountiful rain (cf. Ps 68:9-10). We can resist it; we can refuse it. Yet nothing is more depressing at this point than the thought of persisting in our old ways.

There is, in fact, every reason to flow with the rain of grace that descends from above. Its coolness will help us to let go of exhausting idols of our own making. The sickness of heart we feel in relation to the things to which we had previously clung is like good medicine. It makes us strong enough to climb the "ladder of contemplation." It is as if we have no choice to do so since we are unable "to find satisfaction, support, consolation, or a resting place in anything" (DN II:19 [1]). Restless in spirit, quickened in heart, we do not walk, we run to catch the first rung and soon climb to the next.

Step Two: Searching for the Beloved Without Ceasing

The lover of God has to leave the relative safety of the first rung and risk to climb higher. There is no guarantee that her search will be rewarded, but there is no turning back. Though at first she may not find him, she has no choice but to persevere. So intense is the passion repentance produces, that she will search unceasingly if that is what God wants (cf. Sg 3:1-2).

The lover leaves no stone unturned. She tracks down every possible trace of her Beloved's presence. She pays no attention to distractions, stopping at nothing until she wins the prize (cf. Ps 105:4). She questions every person who may have seen him, follows any lead that seems promising, and, like a good detective, does not cease her search until the missing person (the Mystery that is Christ) has been found (cf. Sg 3:3-4).

St. John observes that when Mary Magdalene saw that the stone was moved away from the tomb, she did not linger but ran immediately to Peter and John for help to find her Lord (cf. Jn 20:1-2). So solicitous is this second level of looking that every epiphany of the Mystery arouses a more urgent expectation.

> In all [her] thoughts [she] turns immediately to the Beloved; in all converse and business [she] at once speaks about the Beloved; when eating, sleeping, keeping vigil, or doing anything else, [she] centers all [her] care on the Beloved ... (DN II:19 [2]).

Yearning and seeking are life-transforming dispositions. They help us to convalesce from the infirmities of the past and to gain strength for the harder climb that is to come. The ascent continues, but not without the sweat of further purification.

Step Three: Performing Good
Works With Fervor

For the true mystic, contemplation of the Most High does not meet the test of authenticity unless it results in an outflow of charity in good works. Detached from the captivity of counterproductive self-centeredness, one's formation energy can be reattached to other more Christ-like pursuits. These may include, for example, the spiritual and corporal works of mercy, almsgiving, volunteer services, or whatever expression of love makes use of one's gifts and talents for the sake of serving the Lord.

Initially we may be motivated to do work out of fear of displeasing God. Love soon casts out this kind of fear and replaces it with care for others out of love for God. No matter how many works we do in God's name, they always seem small in number and quality compared to what has already been done for us by the Beloved. Many works seem but a few. Years spent in the service of the Most High seem like a day. Failure does not worry persons who work to fulfill the commandments of love God sets before us (cf. Ps 112:1). Humility of this depth overflows our hearts and enhances our generosity.

St. John cites the example of Jacob who served Yahweh for seven years more than the seven he had already served— all because of love and an unbreakable promise to obey God's call (cf. Gn 29:20, 30). If Jacob could do so much with so little certitude of the outcome, why can't we do even a little more?

In the light of God's abundant care, we cannot avoid feeling upset and pained by the paltry offerings we give to God by comparison. Nothing God asks seems too much for one who is in love. So lofty is this encounter between the soul and God that "if it were licit [souls] would destroy themselves a thousand times for God and be greatly consoled" (DN II:19 [3]).

The exaggeration is effective because it drives home St. John's point: Compared to the love with which God loves us, all of our works seem useless. Unless we climb this third rung of the ladder, we can never be certain that the tentacles of pride have been properly clipped. It is good for us to think that we are worse than other Christians and that God deserves much more than we seem ready to give.

What protects us from becoming self-centered is the remembrance that though we may perform many good works, all of them are imperfect and wanting. The results are at times confusing and painful, as if we are spinning our wheels and not accomplishing anything.

In this way all the glory attached to any meritorious act goes to God. We remain lowly and subservient. The result is wonderfully freeing. This step removes us from three of the grossest by-products of pride: prejudice, presumption, and the harsh condemnation of other people. This kind of solicitude prepares us for the next step. It gives us the courage we need to persevere. We must draw upon a divine source of strength to resist the temptation to cease climbing at the first sign of suffering.

Step Four: Pursuing God With
or Without Consolation

A major paradox on this rung of the ladder of love is that one becomes accustomed to suffering for the sake of Christ. This continual self-stripping, contrary to popular opinion is not wearisome. Love, to paraphrase St. Augustine, makes the heaviest burden light, a familiar truth repeated in holy scripture (cf. Sg 8:6) and cited by St. John (cf. DN II:19 [4]). The bride whose heart is imprinted with the seal of the Beloved finds that her love is stronger than death. No work is too much. Her desire to emulate God in all things is as durable as flint.

What amazes St. John about this step is that it fills us with enough formation energy to keep our flesh under the rule of the spirit. It enables us to resist the false promises promulgated by either the world or the devil. We enjoy a kind of holy equanimity, neither seeking consolation nor trying to escape desolation. What is, is. If satisfaction comes in prayer, we receive it with gratitude, as we do the other favors of God, but we neither seek for these nor expect them to be guaranteed. As it is, we hardly know how to thank God for the abundance of graces already given to us, so why would we ask for more?

Our attention shifts from having to receive gifts from God to seeing how receptive we can be to the Divine Giver. We ask: "How can I begin to serve God as he deserves?" We think: "How can I thank God for the love he has shown?" Whatever the cost, on this rung of the ladder we want only to exclaim with a saint like Francis of Assisi, "My Lord and my God! My God and my All!"

Why so many fail to climb this fourth rung is that they still overtly or secretly are in search not of God alone but also of their own gratification. What they desire are the favors and gifts of God, not the God who grants them.

By contrast, those who make the climb want to be pleasing to God, no matter the cost to themselves. Yet, as St. John laments, how many of us are willing to set aside our own interests? Friends of God on this step of love's ladder are relatively few. He explains why:

> What is lacking is not that You, O my God, desire to grant us favors again, but that we do not make use of them for your service alone and thus oblige you to grant them to us continually (DN II:19 [4]).

What makes this degree of love so elevated is that one remains absolutely dependent on God for everything. Love of the Divine has become so genuine, so lacking in selfish motives, that we are willing to follow Christ, no matter the suffering this kind of discipleship may require. What we do we do for his sake, not our own.

As a result, the blessing God bestows on the heart of the suffering servant is ineffable joy. This is conveyed in delightful spiritual encounters that call to mind Mary's visitation to her cousin Elizabeth when the child in her womb leapt for joy (cf. Lk 1:39-45). Christ's love for us is so immense that he cannot stand to see us suffer for long without some response. Recall the way Yahweh eyed with compassion the prophet Jeremiah and remembered him when he felt as if he were perishing in the desert (cf. Jer 15:19-21).

The desert of internal detachment creates space for grace in our lives. We stride across it resolutely because we have a goal to reach. We do not pause in our pursuit of the Beloved nor rest for long in any oasis. So enflamed with love are we on this fourth step that we can imagine going in no other direction than upward to the fifth.

Step Five: Ascending Higher With Incessant Hunger

At this midpoint of the ascent—if such is conceivable—one's desire to be with God in an eternity of delight grows exceedingly more impatient. One is filled with a longing that is almost overwhelming. The desire to see God, to be one with the Mystery, is so ardent that any delay—be it as short as a traffic signal or as long as a terminal illness—is both tiresome and annoying. What keeps the bride going is the belief that she may at any moment find the Beloved. When her desire is frustrated even slightly, she is distraught. Her longing is intense. She feels as faint as the psalmist, who longs to dwell in the house of the Lord (cf. Ps 84:2-4). At this midpoint, one offers God an ultimatum only a saint could utter, for "On this step the lover must either see its love or die" (DN II:19 [5]). Such was the tone used by Rachel when she expressed to Jacob her immense longing for children (cf. Gn 30:1).

The suffering God's holy ones undergo on this step is comparable to the rapacious hunger of unfed dogs circling a city filled with food, only to find all entrances blocked (cf. Ps 59:7). This rung of the ladder is thus named "hunger." The soul in transit to a still higher plane of love and freedom finds that no other food but the sight of God can satisfy it. One has no choice but to proceed to the sixth step.

Step Six: Running Swiftly to God

The pace of the climb now quickens. We no longer have to pull ourselves up to God rung by rung. We are running swiftly. What encourages us to move upward toward the Infinite is the experience of many divine touches.

Like a highly trained athlete who stretches effortlessly toward the finish line, so we run without fainting into the arms of the God who is our hope. Love invigorates us like a high-energy drink revives a runner. It feels as if we are jet-propelled, as if we could take flight without any trouble.

The prophet Isaiah tells us that we shall renew our strength and ascend on eagle's wings; we shall fly and not faint (cf. Is 40:31). The psalmist confirms this imagery by comparing our desire for God to that of a deer racing toward a flowing spring to quench its thirst (cf. Ps 42:2-3).

St. John says the reason for this swiftness is twofold: It is due to a dramatic increase in self-giving or charity and to the fact that our heart is almost completely purified. Unburdened by iniquity, we can run like stallions toward the winner's circle. Our heart beats faster, our pulse races, our lungs expand with air because we are speeding toward our goal—the rung of adherence to the way of God's commands (cf. Ps 119:32). In short order we come to the seventh step.

Step Seven: Moving Upward
With Ardent Boldness

The old adage that familiarity breeds contempt is simply not true on the ladder of love. The closer one comes to the goal of union, the more ardent and bold is one's felt relationship of intimacy with God. No cautionary type of direction can convince one so in love to wait nor can it prove to one that it would be wise to rest a while or retreat. Such advice seems as foolish as trying to convince a bride that she should be ashamed of declaring her love in public.

None of this makes sense to a person whose love has expanded beyond any care for self-preservation or protection. Any risk of going higher is now worth it. All that matters is to try to match God's graces with equally ardent daring. No climb is too difficult, no ladder too high when the goal is pure love. Thus Paul writes in his epistle to the Corinthians that charity knows no bounds: It believes in, hopes for, and endures all things (cf. 1 Cor 13:7).

St. John seems to think that Moses took this seventh step when he begged God to either forgive the Israelites for their iniquity or to strike his name from the book of life (cf. Ex 32:32). That was no small threat! Abraham must have felt something of the same boldness when he bargained with God, like a merchant haggling over the price of wares, to save the city (cf. Gn 18:23-32). Certainly the shepherd-warrior David could not be accused of being shy. He declared quite matter-of-factly that if one takes delight in God, if one makes God one's all in all, one can be absolutely sure that God will grant in one way or another the petitions of our heart (cf. Ps 37:4). Then, too, with the bold confidence only a young lover could muster, the bride asks the Beloved to kiss her with the kiss of his mouth (cf. Sg 1:2).

At this stage of the ascent, St. John offers only one note of caution:

> It is illicit for the soul to become daring on this step if it does not perceive the divine favor of the king's scepter held out toward it [Es 5:2; 8:4], for it might then fall down the steps it has already climbed (DN II:20 [2]).

The blessing and burden of this step entails at one and the same time maintaining holy boldness while conserving our humility. We may feel as relaxed and daring as a trapeze artist twirling under the big top, provided our ardent longing for God matches our trust in his helping hand. If this disposition of appreciative abandonment has captured our heart, we need not doubt it will captivate the heart of the Beloved and lead us to deepest union.

Step Eight: Holding on to the Beloved

When we have sought something or someone for a long time and at last found them, we want to hold on to them for dear life. On this step, love has at last impelled the bride to capture her Beloved. Nothing could make her let go of him save God's own decree. She has found the one for whom she has longed with her whole heart and soul and to him only will she cling.

On this eighth rung, the soul's desire for union is realized to the highest degree possible in this life—if only for short, endurable stretches of time. Touches of intense union are of necessity intermittent. Were they to be prolonged beyond a brief duration, one might no longer be in this life.

Because of the intensity of this encounter and all that it demands by way of ongoing formation, reformation, and transformation, even those who arrive at its height may find they can maintain such an intensity only for a short while. Then they have to turn back, whether they want to or not.

St. John explains the reason for this tension between laying hold of the Beloved and having to let go in this way: "If one were to remain on this step, a certain glory would be possessed in this life; and so the soul rests on it for only short periods of time" (DN II:20 [3]).

Such was the experience of the prophet Daniel. He was a man with desires as great as any lover, but God had to order him to stay on this step and not to go any farther (cf. Dn 10:7-11). That was because the next step can be considered the closest one comes to heaven on earth. It belongs only to those God himself deems among the perfect to reach it.

Step Nine: Burning Gently in God

With our limited human intelligence we wonder: "How can anything burn gently? Isn't fire fierce, searing, appalling, frightening?" To the naked eye there is no doubt that flames destroy all that is in their wake, yet burning with love is re-creative. It wounds tenderly. It is as delightful as the heart-warming ardor of genuine love. Between two old friends, words of affection are no longer confined to the limits of expression. They have returned to the depths of silence where exchanges beyond words signify both union and communion.

So it is when the Holy Spirit perfects the oneness of the soul with God. In holy scripture, notably when we read the account of the first Pentecost (cf. Acts 2:1-13), and in the writings of the spiritual masters (John quotes, for example, St. Gregory), it is said that when the apostles received the Holy Spirit their hearts burned gently within them. They were on fire, but they were not consumed physically. Rather they were empowered by the intensity of love's flame to go forth and tell the world the Good News: Christ has died, Christ is risen, Christ will come again.

Once more the master is at a loss for words to describe the goods and graces enjoyed by souls in this perfect state. Were volumes to be written of this experience, still more volumes would be needed to contain what is left unsaid and so on to infinity. Thus the ninth step marks the crossing of the threshold to the tenth which, quite simply, "is no longer in this life" (DN II:20 [4]).

Step Ten: Seeing God Clearly

The highest rung of the ladder of love represents what happens when our earthly life is assimilated into the life to come and the saved behold in ceaseless splendor the Beatific Vision. Once we reach this blessed sight, we shall possess it completely because our soul will have left our body and been reunited with the God who made us. Such souls, whose hearts are pure, who have been purged through love in the dark nights, are more blessed than they could know. They may bypass purgatory and enter the courts of God singing for joy.

This vision, says St. John, "is the cause of the soul's complete likeness to God" (DN II:20 [5]). One has returned fully to the land of likeness where the clean of heart see God (cf. Mt. 5:8). This wondrous vision is the foundation for the claim made in 1 John 3:2 that we shall be like God.

Likeness does not mean equality, for we are and remain, also in eternity, the children or the "creatures" of God our Creator. It does not mean, to use St. John's phrasing, that we will have the same capacity as God. This is impossible. It means only that in becoming like the one in whose form and image we are made, we shall be wholly divinized "through participation" (DN II:20 [5]).

This, then, is a description and an interpretation of the secret ladder alluded to in St. John's poem. On these higher steps it is really not a secret anymore. The life-changing effects love has wrought reveal more than we thought possible to see on our faith journey.

Picture yourself peeking over the top of the ladder of love and actually beholding the mysteries once veiled from sight. St. John tells us that at this height nothing is kept from us because we are already being assimilated to the delights of the next life. He hears anew the words of the Lord that on that day we will have no more questions to ask (cf. Jn 16:23) because we shall see God face to face.

Until that day, the saint says, it does not matter how high we ascend on the mount of perfection. "Something will still be hidden in proportion to one's lack of total assimilation to the divine essence" (DN II:20 [6]). Given the insights we receive from ascetical-mystical theology, given the experiences associated with love's formative secrets, is it any wonder that "ecstasy" (or the soul's going out of itself and away from all things) happens as an expected result of our ascent to God? This is so because love, like fire, flashes upward "as though longing to be engulfed in its center" (DN II:20 [6]).

18

Souls in Disguise: Escape From Alienation Into the Embrace of Love Divine

(*The Dark Night*, Book Two, Chapters 21 and 22)

Like the author of a mystery novel who poses the one question that exposes the entire plot, so St. John asks of his own poem: Why does the soul say that it departed by the secret ladder "disguised"? Why was this "cover-up" necessary? From whom or what was one trying to escape by donning another garb? Why did the seeker have to hide who he was by appearing in a different guise?

A double intention seems to be at work here. By "dressing" in a certain way one is more likely to attract the attention of the Beloved. The aspiration to gain the favor of God is a good way to offset any form of alienation. Outer wear of this sort shows one's good will. A disguise is also in order to enable one on the way to hide from rivals, enemies, and alienating forces bent on preventing one from fulfilling one's God-given destiny to attain freedom of spirit in all things.

Thus one has no choice, as it were, but to become a "spy for the Eternal," to use Sören Kierkegaard's term.[1] The "spy" chooses symbolic garments that signify for whom one feels undying affection and voluntary allegiance. At the same time a good disguise can provide the best cover under which to outwit one's adversaries, these being, in classical terms, the world, the flesh, and the devil.

On the deepest level, persons pledged to the service of God—women and men who love the Lord and long to win his favor—have to appear in such a way that, in a manner of speaking, their supernatural affections for the Spirit hide every natural flaw. Secure in this disguise, one can better sidestep the pitfalls and obstacles that would block the final stages of the ascent to freedom.

Thus, in respect for the power of the symbol, St. John suggests that the best thing we can do is to clothe ourselves in three protective and primary colors: white for faith, green for hope, and red for charity. These make a fitting tunic to be worn by the "knight" of the night. Such lovely colors catch God's eye favorably and enable us to advance safely. They fortify us against the powers that would deter us from seeing God, since as long as we live we are vulnerable to temptation.

The Whiteness of Faith

The garment closest to one's heart has to be pure white. The color of this inner tunic corresponds to the purity of one's faith. By now our faith ought to be so clear, so confident, so utterly at one with God that we are blind to any alien thought put forth by our doubting intellect or any sinful deed prompted by the devil. Wrapped in the warm white robes of faith, we can withstand the cold ploys of the demonic and absorb as wood does fire the forming energy of the Divine.

Under the guise and guidance of faith, we can no longer ignore the gentle yet firm prodding of our transcendence dynamic. What is merely pretranscendent loses its hold on our heart. Demonic seductions have less and less power over us. Faith, like a good radar system, immediately signals us when something we do or say or leave undone is likely to hinder our union with God.

The efforts of the most formidable enemy, whose lies are legion, are thwarted by faith. St. John calls it the soul's "strong protection" (DN II:21 [4]). He claims that faith guards us more than any other virtue against the wily, alienating tricks of the tempter. Mighty and astute an enemy as is the Prince of Deceit, his evil ways are as putty in the hands of a person who has been led through the night of pure faith to the place of grace where God greets us as friends (cf. Jn 15:14-15).

The apostle Peter, who was not yet robed in pure faith, betrayed Christ not once but three times (cf. Mk 14:66-72). He had to endure the pains of hell during his dark night, but this episode taught him, as no other lesson could, what it means to believe in Jesus Christ. Pure faith safeguarded this repentant fisher of souls from further temptation. He wrote to the early Christians in 1 Peter 5:9 that they too had to resist Satan and remain steadfast in the faith. How badly we need in our time to listen to the same two directives!

Faith, according to St. John, is like a foundation garment. We have to wear it under all of our other clothing. This white garment is a symbol that we have earned the favor of God, that union sought has become union found.

Paul writes in Hebrews 11:6 that it is impossible to please God unless we live by faith. St. John reminds us of the prophecy of Hosea 2:21-22, confirming that if we desire to be espoused to and united with God, we must be interiorly clothed in faith. Thus dressed, it is as impossible for us not to please God as it would be for a knight like Don Quixote not to defend his fair lady, Dulcinea.

By way of review, St. John assures us that no one can leave the realm of superficial living and enter the region of darkness unless he or she is clothed in this white garment from the start. Faith is, after all, the only proximate means to union with God.[2] It draws us to the light that is divine without the glow of intellectual lights flashing on. We believe even though we do not understand.

We walk by faith and not by sight most truly when heaven's doors seem closed to us and God is as hidden as desert blooms in a drought. We are driven forward by this virtue even when we derive no satisfaction from our spiritual reading of the scriptures nor from the writings of acknowledged masters.

Faith is a multifaceted wonder. In enables us to maintain constancy or perseverance in appreciative abandonment to the Mystery in times of suffering. It prevents us from being discouraged in the midst of trials as simple as having our patience stretched to the breaking point by an elderly parent or as profound as the dark night itself. It provides a buffer zone preventing us from failing, as Peter did, to follow Christ in obedient discipleship wherever he leads us.

Our faith has to be tested in the furnace of tribulation. So it was for the first believers, and so it must be for us. When things go our way, free of troubles, faith comes easily. We need to experience what it means to really let God be God when in truth we have nowhere else to turn. Then we know what the psalmist David means when he says that he kept the hard sayings of God solely because he heard with a faithful heart the words commanded by his own lips (cf. Ps 17:4-5).

The Greenness of Hope

Were we dressing for battle, our choice of garb could not be better. Our protective undergarment is the white tunic of faith. Over this we must put on a green coat of mail. This color symbolizes hope. By wearing it we defend ourselves from the world as a place where God is forgotten. We are freed from its power to push us to make mundane, temporal satisfactions ultimate. Dressed in a green garment as fresh as a newly mown meadow, we set our eyes on the horizon of eternity the world cannot grasp. This color gives us the courage we need to pursue our heart's longing and the valor to do so without retreating when the going gets tough.

When a nomad parched and forlorn after a seemingly endless desert crossing spots all at once an oasis greening amidst the sand, when he knows it is not a mirage but a miracle, he feels surging through his veins a burst of energy. He hastens toward this heaven-sent place as full of hope as anyone who has been tested in the desert and lived to tell the tale.

Compared to what awaits us at the heavenly table, the morsels we gather on earth seem worthless, as brown and sunburnt as unwatered prairie grass. Wearing a coat of heaven-sent hope enables us to divest ourselves of the tattered garments of worldly waste, symbols of shattered promises of peace and joy we never attained.

Hope is the virtue that prevents us from setting our hearts on this world as the final aim of living. Knowing how much more awaits us in the life to come, we shed all clothing that would kill or erode this hope. Thus we learn the great lesson of Christian commitment: how to live in this world in service to God while at the same time rising above the things of the world (cf. Jn 15:19). I mean things insofar as they are seen as merely worldly rather than as epiphanic pointers to the Most High. We thus comprehend from experience what it means to care for the persons, situations, and things entrusted to us by God without tarnishing our green veneer of hope for the home he has prepared for us from the beginning.

Because the livery of hope disguises us from the worldliness of the world, we are protected from another formidable adversary on the way to our goal. We wear what St. Paul calls "the helmet that is hope for salvation" (1 Thes 5:8). Hope is like this piece of armor. It protects our head from rolling side to side in the face of an endless array of worldly distractions. By looking straight before us, we are not likely to lose our way. Thus, as St. John concludes:

> Hope has this characteristic: It covers all the senses of a person's head so that they do not become absorbed in any worldly thing, nor is there any way some arrow from the world might wound them (DN II:21 [7]).

With eyes set on heaven's door, we are no longer doomed to a life of gross dissipation. Hope directs our eyes heavenward (cf. Ps 25:15). In hoping for nothing but God, we see everything in God. We beseech the Mystery to bestow mercy on all who place their trust in God. He alone can relieve the misery wrought upon us so often by a God-rejecting versus a God-fearing world (cf. Ps 123:3-4).

Picture what happens when God gazes upon this spritely creature in green. How could he resist, so to speak, giving us all we need to grow in holiness when we place our hope in him?

The bride thus wounds the heart of the Beloved with the depth of her hope. The look in her eye (cf. Sg 4:9) stops him short because he knows from the way she is dressed that she belongs wholly to him. Had the bride chosen another color, the symbolism would not be the same. Green says, in effect, that God is her goal, that without God she is nothing and attains nothing. Only to the degree that our hope is unrelenting can we be confident that our moves in this mundane world will be on target. With grace to guide us we shall be victors, not victims. We shall win the crown God has in store for us.

Had we no hope, the night in its terrors would swallow us whole. We could not resist the lies of the world that would dissuade us from seeking God. When we put on the green livery of hope, our pockets are empty of any other possession; our steps seek no other support than the solid pavement of pure trust.

Paradoxically, we are carefree while still caring. We accept God as our ultimate care-giver. Hence there is no reason not to hope, no matter how many strikes we may seem to have against us. Even when our tongues taste only dust, as did the prophet Jeremiah's (cf. Lam 3:29), we do not hunger or thirst, for we know that in the kingdom of heaven we shall have our fill (cf. Mt 5:6).

The Redness of Charity

Our outfit remains incomplete until we put over our white undergarment and green coat, as the crowning touch of our disguise, the most precious garment of all: the red toga of charity. Not only does this third color enhance the beauty of the other two, it also brings us in a mystical sense into God's private chambers.

Dressed in the livery of love, we enter the "wine cellars of charity" and become properly intoxicated.[3] At this peak of perfection, we are both protected and concealed from another adversary: the "flesh" or that of us which refuses to submit itself to the transforming power of the spirit. The "flesh" would cling instead to a poor substitute: self-love obsessed by everything but God.

Charity saves us from making such a tragic miscalculation. Not only does it correct our course, it also fortifies faith and hope. Clad so elegantly, we now worthily go forth to meet the Beloved. By his glance we know how pleasing we look. The king now comes to us resplendent in the purple robes of royalty (cf. Sg 3:10), readying a seat for us alongside himself.

The red toga also serves to remind us that the journey to God began when our heart was set on fire with love's urgent longings. We grabbed onto the rungs of the secret ladder and would not let go until we reached the top. There the Beloved drew us, his saved people, to perfect union with the Trinity.

All these symbols converge in the night. White, green, and red, standing for faith, hope, and love, are the colors associated with the purification of intellect, memory, and will. Because these virtues serve to snatch us away from all that is less than God, they are destined at the same time to join us to God. How does this happen?

1. *Faith*, as we have seen, shuts off the lights of natural understanding in the intellect and puts us in touch with the Transcendent. It mocks our low-level attempts to master the Mystery and readies us for a higher meeting with divine wisdom.

2. *Hope* is like a magnet attracting the filaments of memory away from all creaturely wants. It empties our minds of past accomplishments and turns our attention toward that which we as yet do not possess (cf. Rom 8:24-25). Hope frees us to remember who we are most deeply and to anticipate where we are going. It thus

prepares our memory for union with the Most High now and in the life to come.

3. The role of *charity* is twofold: It rescues our appetites and affections from lasting encapsulation in whatever is not God; and it centers the full thrust of our love on God in whose light we can appreciate and live the rest of the commandment—to love others as we love ourselves. Thus charity redirects our will to its proper end. It unites us with God and all the people of God through love.

Without wearing the pure white of faith, the bright green of hope, and the deep red of charity, it is futile to expect that we could attain perfect oneness with the Divine. We have to dress in these colors if we want to draw near to what we have been called to embrace from eternity: "loving and delightful union with [our] Beloved" (DN II:21 [12]).

To enable us to wear such clothing is the first and foremost sign of God's affection for us. Putting on these vestments is not our doing, it is the work of "ah! the sheer grace!" that does not relent until we come to rest in harmony with the love of God.

Lifted to Liberation

St. John finds in this line of his poem validation of his conviction that without grace we could neither have departed for the land of likeness to God nor escaped the wiles of the devil, the ways of the world, and the bewitching guile of sensuality separated from spirituality. How fortunate we are to have reached "the happy freedom of spirit desired by all" (DN II:22 [1]). The landmarks of this way are these:

1. We went from what was lowly or pretranscendent to what was sublime and transcendent—thanks to grace.

2. We went from being mere earthly creatures to becoming heavenly, divinized people of God—thanks to grace.

3. We went from being all too human to becoming conversant with the ways of heaven (cf. Phil 3:20)— thanks to grace.

These characteristics are proper to one who has attained the state of perfection. It represents for creatures of the night the dawning of a new day. Describing this process has been the master's purpose. As he already pointed out in the prologue, many who pass through this night of purgation, illumination, and union do not understand it at all. This passage, painful as it is, is replete with blessings. What happens here must never be taken for granted. It is the greatest of graces to enter the night and its terrors and not to grow discouraged; to see in the danger of this profound transcendence crisis a distinct formation opportunity.

St. John has taken the time to write of the benefits of the night to assure people on the way not to be frightened by so many trials. They ought to take courage and keep nurturing hope precisely because of the many advantages they shall attain in God's good time. The night yields in the end a veritable banquet of graces for the soul who labors through it. But there is one more condition to be met on this way of liberation: we must proceed "in darkness and concealment" to God's door (DN II:22 [2]).

19

The Hidden Life

(*The Dark Night*, Book Two, Chapter 23)

In this chapter St. John reveals a secret worth telling: Due to the soul's concealment under the cover of darkness, the devil as a rule cannot find us. We are hidden from his seductions and deceits because our attention is focused solely on God. For this reason we proceed more securely to where the Beloved awaits. There in that place we know so well we receive the graces of infused contemplation.

No evil power can penetrate this secret place of encounter with the Divine. There God's grace comes to us as pure gift. Without the use of exterior means or interior senses, it penetrates our consciousness at the highest level of graced intuition or of really "seeing into" (intimacy) who we are and who God wants us to become. The sensory side of our love and knowledge is tainted by the weakening of free will by original sin. This gives the demonic access to our spirit.

Now this deceptive power can no longer slow our pace. Drawn by grace into hiding, we escape the self-centering contamination of our lower loves by the evil one. The prince of this world cannot find us nor can he monitor our ascent for the sake of delaying it. He cannot distort what is happening in us through divine infusion. St. John concludes, "Accordingly, the more spiritual and interior the communication and the more removed it is from the senses, the less the devil understands it" (DN II:23 [2]).

Secrecy Offers Security

To go forth to the place God has prepared for us, we must not be afraid. Our security is extremely important to St. John. We must remain with God in an inner exchange of love wherever we are and whatever we do. It is best if this sacred communion goes on in secret, hidden from our own pride, from possible misunderstanding by others, and above all, from demonic temptations to despoil what belongs to God alone.

To commit ourselves to concealment, so much so that if anything shines forth from us it is clearly of God and not our doing, we must, so to speak, be willing to obey a few "ground rules."

1. First of all we have to keep a veil of darkness, that is to say, a disposition of detachment, over our senses so that we allow nothing (no-thing, *Nada*) to take the place of God. Divine self-communication is wholly spiritual in nature. We must resist making it pedestrian and corporeal in such a way that we call more attention to ourselves than to God. In short, on the sensory level, we have to let go; we must cease striving to prove our spirituality by grabbing on to any sign of self-aggrandizing glory.

2. We have to recognize that we are weak in this regard. We are always in danger of trying to press the transcendent under the canopy of the pretranscendent instead of the reverse. Briefly, if we do not allow our sensory self to dominate, we will enjoy more freedom of spirit and make room in our hearts "for a more abundant spiritual communication" (DN II:23 [3]).

3. By following these first two rules, we will have established the best defense against demonic erosion of the process of divinization. For this reason alone we can journey to God more securely. The words of the Lord advising us not to let our left hand know what our right hand is doing (cf. Mt 6:3) take on a whole new meaning. St. John's translation of this text is worth quoting, perhaps even memorizing:

This is like saying: Do not allow the left side, the lower portion of your soul, to know or attain to what happens on the right side, the superior and spiritual part of the soul; let this be a secret between the spirit and God alone (DN II:23 [3]).

Reception of Secure Joy

The closer we come to freedom of spirit in Christ, the more active is the demonic, whose lies are legion. He seeks to veil and distort the communications God wants to impart. The latter are sufficiently interior and secret enough to frustrate such ploys, especially if the receiver's sensory levels remain silent and attentive to God. While the devil can attack the edges of our consciousness, he cannot gain access to the inner abyss where the Holy abides in us and we in him. We can be sure that no trick will be spared to excite our senses, to disturb our gentle, quiet concentration, or to conjure up before our mind's eye fears of suffering, horrors that could happen, or anxieties that leave us in a sweat. The evil intention here is to shake up the superior part of our distinctively human spirit, to block our capacity to receive and enjoy the marvels of God's indwelling presence.

Despite these manipulative and seductive attacks, there is no cessation of divine communication. It is as if we shine from within, so much so that others may notice at times a mysterious glow in our countenance. We also gain the strength we need to resist temptation. Clever as the tempter is, assiduous as are his attempts to deter our progress, it is to no avail. Our friend and defender, Jesus, offers us all the help we need if we but call on his name. We receive a bouquet of benefits, the best of which is a felt sense, a more secure conviction that God is near. As St. John exclaims, "What a wonderful thing it is!" (DN II:23 [4]).

The more troublesome our adversary is, the stronger becomes our line of resistance. We are in the thick of the battle. Spiritual warfare is being waged in more souls than we know. The more rumbles the devil stirs up on the battlefield, the more entrenched we become in our line of graced defense by God and his angels. We recede to inner depths where the divine strategy works best.

We may not make any special efforts of our own to feel safe, but we do. Even with war raging around us, we know we are being led almost effortlessly to a safe haven, a refuge as neutral as a heavenly Switzerland, where we are hidden from the enemy and withdrawn from danger.

> There the peace and joy that the devil planned to undo increase. All that fear remains outside; and the soul exalts in a very clear consciousness of secure joy, in the quiet peace and delight of the hidden Spouse that neither the world nor the devil can either give or take away (DN II:23 [4]).

What a beautiful description this is of transformation. So changed is one that the proclamations of the bride in the Song of Songs make perfect sense. Enemies surrounding her evoke no fear for she is under God's valiant protection (cf. Sg 3:7-8). Just as in its depths the sea is calm despite the storm churning on the surface, so even if flesh and bones are subject to torment, nothing can dispel the strength and peace we feel in the depths of our being.

The converse is also true. When spiritual communications are received by the senses rather than exclusively by the spirit, it is easier for the evil one to create a disruption. The agitation can reach horrendous proportions. The torment and pain the devil can cause is as immense as it is ineffable. The evil spirit can wreak havoc in good spirits through the inner and outer senses. The closer the devil comes to our essential self, the more unbearable is the pain.

A reference point for this disturbance is found by St. John in one of his favorite scriptures, the Song of Songs, where the bride confesses at one and the same time her desire to enjoy perfect oneness with her Beloved in a garden like that of the first paradise (cf. Sg 6:11-12) and the troubled nature of her spirit due to the roaring of the devil. Spiritual warfare does not cease despite the progress one has made.

The Soul as a Battlefield

St. John's description of the conflict that can tear us apart is as vivid and symbolic as the battle plan of a great general. On the one side are God's own messengers, the good angels, who mediate divine communication to our human form. On the other side is the devil who detects this action and hisses with fury.

Seeing the favors God wants to bestow upon a soul on fire with love, the adversary acts—in accordance with God's allowing will—to block these holy communications. As we read in the Book of Job, Satan makes things miserable but in the end he cannot conquer the inmost citadel of the soul (cf. Jb 1:9-12; 2:4-6). Our life may be the battlefield on which good and bad angels wage war, but the victory belongs to God who guards and protects our soul.

In the light of the Job story and his own life experience, St. John has no trouble believing that God permits Satan to have his way with us once in a while. While true visions—those that are intellectual and substantial—may be mediated by good angels, God may allow the devil to present inauthentic versions of the same to see if we are able to be deceived.

In a similar vein, St. John recalls what happened to Moses, as recorded in the book of Exodus, for example, in 8:1-3, when he called down upon the Egyptians a plague of frogs. Almost immediately Pharaoh's magicians dispelled them. When Moses turned water into blood (cf. Ex 7:20-22), they performed what for them was a similar trick. The difference between Moses and the magicians is that sorcerers fall for the deception that they can control the Mystery at will. Moses knew that the power behind his miraculous acts was not his own but God's.

By the same token, the devil is adept at imitating corporeal visions. The unpurified pockets of our faith, together with our penchant to seek signs and wonders, can obscure or block the genuine spiritual messages mediated to us by God's angelic emissaries. Good and bad angels alike see "every high thing" (cf. DN II: 23 [8]).

While the evil one feigns an appearance of the Most High under the guise of some apparition or figure, he cannot cause or form genuinely spiritual communications. These are—by virtue of their transcendent origin—without form or figure. They are pure spirit. This fact infuriates the devil who may appear in some frightful guise so as to attack the recipient of a true communication of the Divine.

The devil's aim is to use his spiritual powers to destroy a spiritual person. At the thick of the battle, our inner life feels torn asunder. The good angel, the emissary of infused contemplation, communicates this grace to our inmost center. We run to hide under the shadow of her wings (cf. Ps 36:8; 63:8), but, alas, not swiftly enough to slip past the devil, who will use any means to despoil God's work. He may inflict on our otherwise calm heart some terribly disturbing news of a real or imagined calamity. The specter of some sort of worldly horror looms up from we know not where—as, for example, the possible destruction of our life's work by a jealous colleague or an envious co-worker.

Depending on the depth of our prayer and self-surrender, we may be able to run fast enough from this temptation not to give the spirit of evil a chance to disturb our inner peace. Our contemplative capacity to "forget it," to press everything under the "cloud of forgetting,"[1] may force the demonic to retreat because he knows he cannot get past the fortification of infused faith. In that case we can recollect ourselves in short order by means of the efficacious grace God sends to us through his guardian angels.

When and if evil does prevail and abject disruption manages to wedge its way into an otherwise faithful heart, "This terror is a greater suffering than any other torment in life" (DN II:23 [9]). The horror of what is happening stems from the fact that these conflicting communications snap us back and forth like a rubber band between the good that we would do and the evil we would not (cf. Rom 7:19).

We feel the warfare within because we are clearly not our joyful, appreciative selves at such crisis moments. We cannot exactly pin down the cause of why we feel this way because it is too incorporeal. It goes beyond the kind of sensory pain that can be relieved by a tranquilizer. This goes far deeper. It is more a disturbance of the soul than of the body.

Thanks to all we have gone through in the dark night, such spiritual suffering, according to St. John, does not last for long. He is convinced that if it did, the dismay it causes might be so intense—the spiritual warfare so violent—that death or the departure of the soul from the body might result. Even when we have recovered from such an incident, due to the diabolic nature of this communication of near despair, its remembrance still evokes great suffering.

The terrible thing is that all that transpires on this battlefield happens passively without our doing or undoing anything. As in the story of Job, the good angel allows the devil to test and try the innocent, to bring into actuality the absolute devastation life can be, not to destroy but to evoke the depth of our strength to keep the faith.

The battle is allowed because it prevents us from remaining naive about the reality of evil in this world. It further purifies our heart to love and trust God alone, and it prepares us—as does a time of vigil—for the feast of favors God has in store for his faithful ones. The scriptures make clear that God never mortifies without also giving life; he never humbles a good person like Job or any prophet unless he plans also to exalt him (cf. 1 Sm 2:6-8). Suffering is the way to wisdom when it frees us to walk in the truth and to make the world a better place.

When the turning point comes—and St. John assures us it will in a while—the delight of the spiritual favors God then bestows is a hundred times more ineffable and sublime than were the terrors of the dark night of purgation we had to undergo. When "perfect love drives out fear" (1 Jn 4:18), we are at peace. Having withstood so many persecutions and mean attacks, we appreciate with humble elation this vision of the good. It both prepares us for and forecasts the Beatific Vision that will be ours in the life to come.

Substantial Touches of Union

Divine visitations mediated by the angels of God are like lights that guide our walk through the darkness. They show us places where we can hide from the enemy and where his cohorts cannot find us. We feel safe there, especially on those rare occasions when God may visit us directly without any emissary. When a person of good will and true prayerfulness receives such favors from on high, one can be sure this will happen only under the cover of divine concealment. One receives something Satan can never hold: the key to liberation.

Why is the hidden life so essential at this stage of our formation journey? It has to do with the fact that the Mystery dwells substantially "in that part of the soul to which neither the angel nor the devil can gain access and thereby see what is happening" (DN II:23 [11]). The evil one, who would be victorious, is himself left in the dark. He cannot gain access to the intimate interchanges that happen between us and God. These remain secret. They are granted directly. They are holy and sublime with a sovereignty no enemy can overcome.

St. John says that the "substantial touches of divine union between God and the soul" grant us the highest degree of prayer possible in this life (DN II:23 [11]. One such touch has enough power to change our life forever. By it one receives more good than through any other practice or prayer, however perfect.

Of these substantial touches of infused contemplation the bride in the Canticle says, "Let him kiss me with kisses of his mouth" (Sg 1:2). This kiss symbolizes the closest intimacy with God one can ever hope to experience. This kiss responds to our deepest yearnings and fulfills them wholly. Little wonder that one esteems, even covets, such a touch of divinity more than all of God's lesser though always efficacious favors put together.

The bride in the Canticle received lavish favors from the Beloved but none satisfied her. She asked for the "kiss" that would transform her and save her from the devil's taunts (cf. Sg 8:1). The bride knew that God alone could give her this grace. It was not something that could come to her from the outside nor from any creature. However much she felt nourished by satisfied appetites or affections fulfilled on the sensory level of her life, she was never really content. She knew all of these goods would one day dry up. The only thing she could rely on were the blessings and graces granted by God. These alone would free her whole being from the hindering tactics of her pretranscendent desires and from the devil who played on them.

Why is it that the evil one retreats at a certain point? Unable to understand the power of these blessings and the divine favors that accompany them, there is nothing left of us to assail. He simply cannot grasp "the loving substance of God in the substance of the soul" (DN II:23 [12]).

How does the attainment of such blessings come about? There is only one way: that of intimate nakedness or pure faith. This is the path we must take: that of purgation or pure trust in and abandonment to the Mystery. This is the safe road: that of spiritual concealment or release from creaturely controls that open us to pride-filled illusions and demonic seductions.

The truth St. John has been trying to convey throughout his treatise is from beginning to the end paradoxical. We can only reach this place of utmost clarity in the darkness of not knowing. We can only attain this delight of revelation in concealment. We can gain strength only in union with God in hiddenness. We can escape the hatred that would destroy us only through love.

Such favors, exactly because God issues them without our knowing how and without our autonomously acquiring them, belong to the superior or spiritual part of our transcendent self. As such they are not to be captured and confined by our lower or pretranscendent nature.

At times of intense presence to God, one feels as if he or she is two persons, and for good reason. In the case of any activity initiated by God for our sake, the infusion is entirely spiritual. There is no direct communication with our sensory self, though indirect reverberation may effect the very stilling we have sought for so long.

When, thanks to pure grace, a person becomes in St. John's terms "wholly spiritual," when, to use Adrian van Kaam's terms we become "transcendent-functional" and "transcendent-vital," erratic passions and pretranscendent pulsions and ambitions are placed in a servant posture in relation to our superior, distinctively human, transcendence dynamic.[2] Unitive contemplation becomes our hiding place, peace our lasting disposition. It is the place from whence— our house being now all stilled—we can go forth to serve the Lord without fear. Though storm clouds gather around us, on a higher level we have evidence to prove beyond a shadow of a doubt, as did the English mystic, Julian of Norwich, that "all will be well."[3] In St. John's words:

> This is like saying: Since the superior portion of my soul is now, like the lower, at rest in its appetites and faculties, I went out to divine union with God through love (DN II:24 [1]).

20

The Solitary Bird

(*The Dark Night*, Book Two, Chapters 24 and 25)

In the previous chapter St. John described the way in which one who is at war undergoes buffeting and purging in both a sensory and a spiritual sense. In these chapters the reverse is his focus. He wants to show how war gives way to peace, agitation to rest.

For divine union to become a possibility, both parts of the soul, lower and higher, have to be reformed in the dark night. Our life has to be put in order, returned, as it were, to "A condition of complete simplicity (Costing not less than everything)."[1] We have passed through the pain of purgation only to arrive at a kind of second naivety.[2] The stilling of our house has to be first sensory and then spiritual, a work accomplished in the active and passive nights through which we have passed. Here, in summary, is what has transpired:

1. Insofar as the human condition allows, one arrives in a habitual and perfect way at a spiritual house at rest.

2. The cause of this quietude and the freedom of spirit it brings are infused, substantial touches of divine union.

3. These hide one from diabolic disturbance and conceal one from the erratic ebb and flow of the senses and passions.

4. Sustained by such touches, the soul comes to deep rest, gains renewed strength, and finds stability even in the midst of change. As the saint declares in his *Sayings*

of Light and Love, "Well and good if all things change, Lord God, provided we are rooted in you."[3]

5. One is now in a position—indeed a permanent disposition—of "form-receptivity." That is to say, one is able to "receive permanently this divine union, which is the divine espousal between the soul and the Son of God" (DN II:24 [3]).

The sensory and spiritual parts of the soul are now constantly in tune with one another as is a good servant toward a loving master. Such rest, like a good night's sleep, makes one feel stronger. This consonance extends to all the members of our household—to body, mind, and spirit, to all of our faculties and appetites. Inner and outer warfare ceases. What ought to be asleep is asleep. What ought to be awake is awake.

Tying the Knot of Love

Functional effectiveness proceeds from transcendent attention to God's will and to his unique communal call for our life. Peaceful silence in regard to earthly woes and heavenly hopes encompasses every aspect of our being. One is simultaneously a care-giver and a care-receiver. It comes to pass in due course that wisdom divine, the word made flesh, unites himself to us in a new bond called by St. John the "possession of love," a description of which can be found in the book of Wisdom:

> For when peaceful stillness compassed
> > everything
> > and the night in its swift course was half
> > spent,
> Your all-powerful word from heaven's royal
> > throne
> > bounded, a fierce warrior, into the
> > doomed land … (Wis 18:14-15).

Further testimony to this "possession of love" can be found in the Song of Songs. The bride says that after she passed by those who wounded her and removed her veil (cf. Sg 5:7), her lover revealed himself to her in a new way. She was reunited in splendid wonder with him she loved so well (cf. Sg 3:4).

As St. John observes, one cannot reach this level of union unless one has attained profound purity of heart. Such purity is out of reach unless one is willing to be led by grace onto the rigorous road of daily dying in faith and detachment from all that is less than God. Only then can one hope to see and love all things in God.

The symbol of removing the bride's veil is a way of saying that progress without mortification is impossible. Wounding her in the night signifies the pure faith that compelled her search and the depth of her desire for her spouse. She could not put on the bridal veil that would please him unless she was first willing to have the veil removed that covered her sensuous heart.

St. John is as firm on this point at the end of his treatise as he was on its first page:

> Persons who refuse to go out at night in search for the Beloved and to divest and mortify their will, but rather seek the Beloved in their own bed and comfort, as did the bride (Sg 3:1), will not succeed in finding him. As this soul declares, she found him when she departed in darkness and with longings of love (DN II:24 [4]).

On a Glad Night

With this emphatic declaration, the saint moves on in the last chapter of *The Dark Night* to the third stanza of his poem which is:

> On that glad night,
> in secret, for no one saw me,
> nor did I look at anything,
> with no other light or guide
> than the one that burned in my heart.

St. John begins to explain why it is so that the night of the spirit is ultimately not sad but glad. By dwelling on this metaphor he hopes to enumerate its good properties and why it leads to so lofty a goal as union with God. He begins by listing three reasons for the gladness he felt:

1. The first has to do with the fact that God takes the lead. He guides us to a sacred, secret place, remote from the limiting perception of the senses, where we are able to gaze contemplatively on our life as a whole. No longer held back by mere sense knowledge or any creaturely attachment as ultimate, we are freed to follow the road leading to the union of love. Now nothing can detain us.

2. The darkness of the night also shadows our spiritual faculties. We find our intellect, memory, and will less sharply focused on this or that event or annoyance. This obscurity offers us a rare opportunity to avoid ruminating on the past or fantasizing about the future. All we want to focus on is our journey to God—not on outside forces, no matter how badly they seem to want to deter us. Our advance is now wonderfully free of any major hindrance. Until now forms and figures arising from our natural powers of apprehension stood in the way of our ascent to God. Now these no longer prevent us from "being always united with the being of God" (DN II:25 [3]).

3. While we cannot count on any support as such from the intellect—no particular lights flash on to stave off the cloud of unknowing—still we make progress. While no exterior guide satisfies our restless hearts, we continue to pursue the lofty path to heaven's door here on earth. Since the darkness is dense, love alone is our guide. It is this kind of love—passionate, courageous, intense—that attracts the heart of the Beloved.

The "Love that moves the sun and the other stars," to quote the poet Dante,[4] makes the soul soar like a solitary bird in free flight. The way may be unknown, the flight pattern initially unclear, but we continue to travel "on that glad night" with a sure speed set by the Holy Spirit.

Coming Home to God

So ends this magnificent text of St. John. No one can read it without coming away with a new view of the spiritual life. Do we not long to unloosen the latches of our narrow cages and fly free over clear waters and above the clouds? At some point we can no longer bear being enslaved by mundane demands and pedestrian appetites. We want to fly away from these limited lives of ours, tear through the veil that shrouds us from beholding God's face, and alight on the warm breast of our Beloved.

If we have learned anything from St. John, it is this: Daily we must attempt to detach ourselves from whatever hinders our homecoming to God. Only as God gives us the grace to soar above transitory things will this good intent succeed. We must not despair or give up when we find ourselves falling backwards or not soaring as high as we know we could, had we the courage to follow the lead of grace. We must continue to do the best we can, not pushing against the pace of grace but flowing with the energy God gives us to make the ascent. By ourselves we would never reach the goal we have set, but God will draw us as far as he wants us to go. All we can do is try to fly as high as we are able.

Whatever holds us down, a thin thread or a heavy chain, has to go. The less heed we pay to these things—the more we treat them as if they do not exist—the higher we will fly. Slowly and gradually we will be able to reorder our priorities. The rise upward may seem interminably slow but, if we are faithful, grace will help us to soar higher and higher on eagle's wings.

Transitory demands at times do hold us down. We have no choice but to attend to them. Still we must rest secure in the knowledge that the "eternal now" of God's all embracing love will sustain us at every turn of the road. We shall rise and not grow weary; we shall fly until we are free.

In the end the glad night becomes one grand song of love to God, a hymn of praise no amount of earthly suffering can silence. This song bursts forth from a heart afire with love that orders all things finely. It forecasts an era of compassion, gentility, and peace where life itself becomes a lullaby and we can leave our cares "forgotten among the lilies" (DN, Prologue, Stanza 8).

Endnotes

Introduction

1. For an example of foundational theme tracing through formative reading, see Susan Muto, *Blessings That Make Us Be: A Formative Approach to Living the Beatitudes* (Petersham, MA: St. Bede's Publications, 1982).

2. All references to *The Dark Night* and the other major and minor works of St. John cited in this book are taken from *The Collected Works of St. John of the Cross*, trans. Kieran Kavanaugh and Otilio Rodriguez (Washington, DC: Institute of Carmelite Studies, 1991). Hereafter *The Dark Night* is abbreviated *DN* followed by an indication of the book, chapter, and paragraph number(s) quoted either directly or indirectly. I urge every reader to keep the original text on hand, to read and study it, side by side with this companion.

3. See William Butler Yeats, "The Second Coming" in *Chief Modern Poets of Britain and America*, ed. Gerald Sanders (New York: Macmillan, 1970), p. 121.

Chapter 1

1. For these and other terms from the science of formation, I am indebted to the pioneering work in this field done by Adrian van Kaam. The thought expressed here is fully developed in his book, *Fundamental Formation*, vol. 1, *Formative Spirituality* (New York: Crossroad Publishing Company, 1983). For further clarification, see the Glossary of Terminology following these Endnotes.

2. For an in-depth analysis of the disposition of awe, see Adrian van Kaam, *Human Formation*, vol. 2, *Formative Spirituality* (New York: Crossroad Publishing Company, 1985), pp. 177-250.

3. *The Dialogue of Catherine of Siena*, trans. Suzanne Noffke (New York: Paulist Press, 1980), pp. 325-326.

4. Such seeing often happens only during or after what Adrian van Kaam calls a "transcendence crisis." For a detailed analysis of this inevitably "religious experience," see van Kaam, *The Transcendent Self: The Formative Spirituality of Middle, Early and Later Years of Life* (Pittsburgh, PA: Epiphany Books, 1991).

5. A detailed discussion of how to appraise life appreciatively can be found in Adrian van Kaam and Susan Muto, *The Power of Appreciation: A New Approach to Personal and Relational Healing* (New York: Crossroad Publishing Company, 1993).

Chapter 2

1. See "The Book of Her Life" in *The Collected Works of St. Teresa of Avila*, vol. 1, trans. Kieran Kavanaugh and Otilio Rodriguez (Washington, DC: Institute of Carmelite Studies, 1976), pp. 44-45.

2. For a fuller description of the saint's understanding of "participant transformation," see *The Ascent of Mount Carmel* in *The Collected Works of St. John of the Cross*, pp. 163-165. I explain this notion more fully in Susan Muto, *John of the Cross for Today: The Ascent* (Notre Dame, IN: Ave Maria Press, 1991), pp. 42-45.

3. See, for example, "Introduction to the Letters" and "Letters" in *The Collected Works of St. John of the Cross*, pp. 735-764.

4. See *The Ascent of Mount Carmel* in *The Collected Works of St. John of the Cross*, pp. 150-151.

5. For a contemporary look at these ancient yet ever present aberrations, see Henry Fairlie, *The Seven Deadly Sins Today* (Washington, DC: New Republic Books, 1978).

Chapter 3

1. Anonymous, *The Cloud of Unknowing*, ed. James Walsh, *Classics of Western Spirituality* (New York: Paulist Press, 1981), pp. 222-223.

2. See "The Way of Perfection" in *The Collected Works of St. Teresa of Avila*, vol. 2, trans. Kieran Kavanaugh and Otilio Rodriguez (Washington, DC: Institute of Carmelite Studies, 1980), p. 94.

3. See, for example, *The Sayings of the Desert Fathers: The Alphabetical Collection*, trans. Benedicta Ward (London: A. R. Mowbray, 1975); and Thomas Merton, *Wisdom of the Desert: Sayings from the Desert Fathers of the Fourth Century* (London: Sheldon, 1974).

4. See, for example, *Francis and Clare: The Complete Works*, trans. Regis Armstrong and Ignatius Brady in *Classics of Western Spirituality* (New York: Paulist Press, 1982); and Adrian van Kaam, *A Light to the Gentiles: The Life Story of the Venerable Francis Libermann* (Lanham, MD: University Press of America, 1985).

Chapter 4

1. See also *The Ascent of Mount Carmel* in *The Collected Works of St. John of the Cross*, pp. 331-332; and Susan Muto, *John of the Cross for Today: The Ascent*, pp. 170-174.

2. See "The Book of Her Life" in *The Collected Works of St. Teresa of Avila*, vol. 1, p. 56.

3. Ibid., p. 58.

4. See Adrian van Kaam and Susan Muto with Susan McBride, "Say Yes Always" in *Formation Guide for Becoming Spiritually Mature* (Pittsburgh, PA: Epiphany Books, 1991), pp. 95-120.

Chapter 5

1. Murray Bodo, *Tales of St. Francis* (Cincinnati: St. Anthony Messenger Press, 1988), pp. 134-135.

2. For an astute analysis of the dynamics of envy and originality, see Adrian van Kaam, *Living Creatively* (Denville, NJ: Dimension Books, 1978).

3. *The Philokalia*, vol. 1, trans. G. Palmer, Philip Sherrard, and Kallistos Ware (London: Faber and Faber, 1979), p. 87.

4. See Susan Muto and Adrian van Kaam, *Commitment: Key to Christian Maturity* (Mahwah, NJ: Paulist Press, 1989), p. 121 ff.

5. For further meditations on the richness of the ordinary, see Susan Muto, *Renewed at Each Awakening* (Denville, NJ: Dimension Books, 1979).

Chapter 6

1. See Adrian van Kaam, *Fundamental Formation*, vol. 1, *Formative Spirituality* pp. 65-67.

2. Ibid., pp. 55-65.

3. Ibid., pp. 143-144.

4. For a further elucidation of these dynamics and their universal human implications, see Adrian van Kaam, *Transcendent Formation*, vol. 6, *Formative Spirituality* (New York: Crossroad Publishing Company, 1995).

5. *The Story of a Soul: The Autobiography of St. Thérèse of Lisieux*, trans. John Clarke (Washington, DC: Institute of Carmelite Studies, 1975), pp. 211-212.

Chapter 7

1. Two centuries later another spiritual master, Francis de Sales, expresses similar concern for the dearth of qualified spiritual guides or directors: "For this purpose choose one [spiritual guide] out of a thousand, as [Teresa of] Avila says. For my part I say one out of ten thousand, for there are fewer [people] than we realize who are capable of this task. [One] must be full of charity, knowledge, and prudence, and if any one of these three qualities

is lacking there is danger. I tell you again, ask God for [such a guide], and having once found him, bless his Divine Majesty, stand firm, and do not look for another, but go forward with simplicity, humility, and confidence for you will make a most prosperous journey." St. Francis de Sales, *Introduction to the Devout Life*, trans. John Ryan (New York: Doubleday, 1966), p. 47.

2. See "The Book of Her Life" in *The Collected Works of St. Teresa of Avila*, vol. 1, pp. 46-47.

3. See Jean Pierre de Caussade, *Abandonment to Divine Providence*, trans. John Beevers (Garden City, NY: Doubleday, 1975).

4. From "A gloss (with a spiritual meaning)" in *The Collected Works of St. John of the Cross*, p. 71.

5. *The Confessions of St. Augustine*, trans. John Ryan (New York: Doubleday, 1960), pp. 254-255.

6. See Adrian van Kaam, *Human Formation*, vol. 2, *Formative Spirituality*, pp. 69-70.

Chapter 8

1. Dag Hammarskjöld, *Markings*, trans. Leif Söjberg and W. H. Auden (London: Faber and Faber, 1964), p. 56.

2. See Frederick Franck, *Pilgrimage to Now/Here* (Maryknoll, NY: Orbis Books, 1974).

3. See *Teresa of Avila: The Interior Castle*, trans. Kieran Kavanaugh and Otilio Rodriguez, *Classics of Western Spirituality* (New York: Paulist Press, 1979), p. 165.

4. Evelyn Underhill, *Practical Mysticism* (Columbus: Ariel Press, 1942), p. 188.

5. See *The Teaching of Christ: A Catholic Catechism for Adults*, eds. Ronald Lawler, Donald Wuerl, and Thomas Lawler (Huntington, IN: Our Sunday Visitor Publishing, 1976), p. 479.

Chapter 9

1. See Richard Hardy, *Search for Nothing: The Life of John of the Cross* (New York: Crossroad Publishing Company, 1982).

2. *The Story of a Soul: The Autobiography of St. Thérèse of Lisieux*, trans. John Clarke, p. 277.

3. Walter Ciszek with Daniel Flaherty, *He Leadeth Me* (Garden City, NY: Image Books, Doubleday, 1975), pp. 89-90.

4. For an analysis of these ways of faith deepening, with reference to St. Thérèse of Lisieux, see Susan Muto, *Steps Along the Way: The Path of Spiritual Reading* (Denville, NJ: Dimension Books,

1975), pp. 116-133. With reference to Brother Lawrence of the Resurrection, see Susan Muto and Adrian van Kaam, *Practicing the Prayer of Presence* (Mineola, NY: Resurrection Press, 1993), pp. 47-58.

5. *The Spiritual Canticle* in *The Collected Works of St. John of the Cross*, p. 44.

Chapter 10

1. For a further exploration of the misleading power of supernatural phenomenon, see Susan Muto, *John of the Cross for Today: The Ascent*, pp. 76-98.

2. For an in-depth description and analysis of this accommodation process, see Adrian van Kaam, *Transcendent Formation*, vol. 6, *Formative Spirituality*.

Chapter 11

1. See *Pseudo-Dionysius: The Complete Works*, trans. Colm Luibheid, *Classics of Western Spirituality* (New York: Paulist Press, 1987) and Anonymous, *The Cloud of Unknowing*, ed. James Walsh, *Classics of Western Spirituality*, p. 256. For further insight into the apophatic tradition, see also Susan Muto, "The Way of Unknowing" in *Steps Along the Way: The Path of Spiritual Reading*, pp. 73-90.

2. See Barbara Dent, *My Only Friend Is Darkness: Living the Night of Faith* (Notre Dame, IN: Ave Maria Press, 1988).

Chapter 12

1. See Adrian van Kaam and Susan Muto, *The Power of Appreciation: A New Approach to Personal and Relational Healing*, pp. 103-109.

2. See Sören Kierkegaard, *Purity of Heart Is to Will One Thing: Spiritual Preparation for the Office of Confession*, trans. Douglas V. Steere (New York: Harper Torchbooks, Harper & Row, 1956).

3. See Ruth Burrows, *Guidelines for Mystical Prayer* (London: Sheed and Ward, 1976).

4. This text can be found in Adrian van Kaam and Susan Muto with Susan McBride, *Formation Guide for Becoming Spiritually Mature*, p. 163. It summarizes in a simple and beautiful way the section of this book entitled, "Flow with Grace," pp. 147-171.

Chapter 13

1. See *From Glory to Glory: Texts from Gregory of Nyssa's Mystical Writings*, trans. Herbert Musurillo (Crestwood, NY: St. Vladimir's Seminary Press, 1979).

2. See Adrian van Kaam, *On Being Involved: The Rhythm of Involvement and Detachment in Daily Life* (Denville, NJ: Dimension Books, 1970).

3. See *The Ascent of Mount Carmel* in *The Collected Works of St. John of the Cross*, p. 150.

4. See *Catherine of Genoa: Purgation and Purgatory, The Spiritual Dialogue*, trans. Serge Hughes, *Classics of Western Spirituality* (New York: Paulist Press, 1979).

5. See Douglas Groothuis, *Unmasking the New Age* (Downers Grove, IL: InterVarsity Press, 1986).

6. See Paul Vitz, *Psychology as Religion: The Cult of Self-Worship* (Grand Rapids, MI: Eerdmans Publishing Company, 1977).

Chapter 14

1. The entire poem is cited in *The Family Book of Verse*, ed. Lewis Gannett (New York: Harper and Row, 1961), pp. 141-146.

2. See Adrian van Kaam, *Transcendent Formation*, vol. 6, *Formative Spirituality*, Part II.

Chapter 15

1. See Antonio de Nicolas, *St. John of the Cross: Alchemist of the Soul* (New York: Paragon House, 1989), pp. 27-28.

2. See Adrian van Kaam and Susan Muto with Susan McBride, *Formation Guide for Becoming Spiritually Mature*, pp. 166-168.

3. See "A gloss (with a spiritual meaning)" in *The Collected Works of St. John of the Cross*, p. 72.

4. See Adrian van Kaam, *Religion and Personality* (Pittsburgh, PA: Epiphany Books, 1991), pp. 91-141.

5. See *Symeon The New Theologian: The Discourses*, trans. C. M. deCatanzaro, *Classics of Western Spirituality* (New York: Paulist Press, 1980), pp. 368-378.

6. See *Meister Eckhart: Teacher and Preacher*, ed. Bernard McGinn, *Classics of Western Spirituality* (New York: Paulist Press, 1986), pp. 171-174.

7. See Susan Muto, *Meditation in Motion* (Garden City, NY: Image Books, Doubleday, 1976), pp. 75-97.

8. See Adrian van Kaam and Susan Muto with Susan McBride, *Formation Guide for Becoming Spiritually Mature*, p. 36.

9. See "The Book of Her Life" in *The Collected Works of St. Teresa of Avila*, vol. 1, pp. 89, 107.

Chapter 16

1. See G. K. Chesterton, *Saint Thomas Aquinas: "The Dumb Ox"* (Garden City, NY: Image Books, Doubleday, 1956).

2. See "The Way of Unknowing" in Susan Muto, *Steps Along the Way: The Path of Spiritual Reading* pp. 73-90.

3. For a thorough description of the ways of purgation, illumination, and union, see Susan Muto, *Blessings That Make Us Be: A Formative Approach to Living the Beatitudes*, pp. 16-128.

4. See "A gloss (with a spiritual meaning)" in *The Collected Works of St. John of the Cross*, p. 70.

5. See *Walter Hilton: The Scale of Perfection*, trans. John Clark and Rosemary Dorward, *Classics of Western Spirituality* (New York: Paulist Press, 1991).

6. See Adrian van Kaam, *Dynamics of Spiritual Self Direction* (Pittsburgh, PA: Epiphany Books, 1993).

7. For information on their works as used by him, see Footnote 1 in *The Collected Works of St. John of the Cross*, p. 440.

Chapter 17

1. For a further explanation of this concept, see Adrian van Kaam and Susan Muto with Susan McBride, *Formation Guide for Becoming Spiritually Mature*, pp. 115-117.

2. See Irenee Hausherr, *Penthos: The Doctrine of Compunction in the Christian East*, trans. Anselm Hufstader, *Cistercian Studies* (Kalamazoo, MI: Cistercian Publications, 1982).

Chapter 18

1. Sören Kierkegaard, *The Point of View for My Work as an Author: A Report to History*, trans. Walter Lowrie (New York: Harper Torchbooks, Harper and Row, 1962), pp. 87-95.

2. See *The Ascent of Mount Carmel* in *The Collected Works of St. John of the Cross*, pp. 154-155.

3. See *The Spiritual Canticle* in *The Collected Works of St. John of the Cross*, pp. 574-580.

Chapter 19

1. Anonymous, *The Cloud of Unknowing*, ed. James Walsh, pp. 128-130.

2. See Adrian van Kaam, *Transcendent Formation*, vol. 6, *Formative Spirituality*, Part II.

3. *Julian of Norwich: Showings*, trans. Edmund Colledge and James Walsh, *Classics of Western Spirituality* (New York: Paulist Press, 1978), pp. 152-153.

Chapter 20

1. T. S. Eliot, *Four Quartets* (London: Faber and Faber, 1965), p. 59.

2. See Paul Ricoeur, *The Symbolism of Evil* (New York: Harper and Row, 1967).

3. See *Sayings of Light and Love* in *The Collected Works of St. John of the Cross*, p. 88.

4. Dante Alighieri, *The Divine Comedy*, vol. 3, *Paradise*, trans. Mark Musa (New York: Penguin Books, Viking Penguin, 1986), p. 394.

Glossary of Terminology

The glossary of terminology that follows is derived from Father Adrian van Kaam's fifty-year development of formation theology with its auxiliary pretheological formation anthropology and formation science.

The glossaries themselves will reappear in a more complete collection to be found in forthcoming volumes of an extensive dictionary van Kaam plans to publish with Epiphany Books (1994-1996) on formation theology and its pretheological auxiliary disciplines. Under his supervision these entries have been adapted slightly to accommodate their use in this book and to define some of the terms used in the text.

The copyright for each glossary is the sole property of Father van Kaam and the Epiphany Association. I respect his moral right to be identified as the author of these definitions and all his original ideas and expressions therein.

Abandonment—In English "abandonment" or to "abandon" may connote a state of mere apathy or passivity, but such is not its deepest meaning. For this reason the word "abandonment" ought to be connected with the word "option." Christian abandonment suggests, therefore, that one is free before God to make a decision or choose an option, albeit with much struggle and uncertainty. (In this sense an option means to surrender oneself with Christ to the will of the Father as it is disclosed in our life and world.) During his last agony Jesus prayed to his Father: "... if it is possible, let this cup pass from me; yet, not as I will, but as you will" (Mt 26:39). His prayer becomes our prayer when we sincerely hope that what we decide will be in accordance with the mystery of God's will for us. Only in this spirit of abandonment can we "Rejoice always. Pray without ceasing. In all circumstances give thanks, for this is the will of God for you in Christ Jesus" (1 Thes 5:16-18).

Appraisal—The grace of appreciative abandonment to the Mystery is a source of growth in the art and discipline of formational appraisal. Its aim is to help us to live in fidelity to our unique-communal life call in praise of the Lord. To come to know or to appraise what makes our life more formative or consonant with Christ, we must align our powers of appraisal with the wisdom of our faith and formation traditions; with the highest pneumatic-ecclesial dimension of our life; and with the probable disclosures of our call by the Holy Spirit at this moment of our still unfolding formation history.

Appraisal Process in the Christian Tradition—Appraisal in the light of our deepest worth and value as persons created in the form and likeness of God is a lifelong process. It includes different acts and dispositions. The main ones are: abiding in awe and attention; apprehension; appreciation; affirmation; and application. Once we awaken to the specific Christ-form of our life, we have to abide in awe-filled attention to the directives that come to us from daily experiences as appraised in the light of the Holy Spirit. We need to apprehend the direction in which they are pointing us. We must try to practice appreciative abandonment; to affirm our call in the light of the Holy Spirit and the church; and to apply our decision in the conviction that God has our best interests at heart.

Appreciation—Appreciative acts and dispositions with their consonant yet subordinated depreciations are the outcome of the appraisal process. The more we grow in fidelity to the Christ-form of our soul, the more likely we are to attain a joyous, peaceful state of mind and heart. These are the marks of a consonant style of life characterized by an overall feeling of well-being if God grants us this gift. In formation theology the disposition of appreciation is based on the praiseworthy, appreciable presence of the Holy Trinity in our inmost being and in our field of formation. To live in appreciation is to trust God totally, even when we do not fully grasp what is happening to us here and now. In times of darkness, hope does not desert us. In every obstacle we try appreciatively to see a formation opportunity and to move toward consonance with the Divine Forming Mystery.

Appreciation in the Christian Tradition—Graced appreciation reminds us that "whatever you do, in word or in deed, do everything in the name of the Lord Jesus, giving thanks to God the Father though him" (Col 3:17). This disposition enables us to enjoy the epiphanies or manifestations of the Eternal in the church, in nature, and in our everyday life. Our whole life becomes a quest to acknowledge, "How great are your works, O Lord!" (Ps 92:6).

Appreciative Abandonment—Once we are graced with an appreciation of God's presence in every situation, we become filled with joy and peace, fully abandoned to the mystery of God's love, the wisdom of God's ways. "For my thoughts are not your thoughts, nor are your ways my ways, says the Lord. As high as the heavens are above the earth, so high are my ways above your ways and my thoughts above your thoughts" (Is 55:8-9). Above all, for us Christians, the word "appreciation" means abandoning ourselves in praise of God's glory and accepting in awe God's nearness to us in the ups and downs, the joys and sorrows, of daily life.

Awe—As a graced disposition of the abandoned heart, awe inclines us to be present to the mystery of the Trinity in its every manifestation or epiphany. Awe creates a space for silence in our hearts so we can be open to the still small voice of the Spirit in wonder and adoration.

Christ-Form—Christians believe that through baptism we receive the image or form of Christ Jesus (cf. Gal 3:27; 4:19). Our human spirit, illumined by the Holy Spirit, thus gains the freedom to live in union with Christ our guiding source. "He will change our lowly body to conform with his glorified body by the power that enables him also to bring all things into subjection to himself" (Phil 3:21). Over a lifetime Christians are called, in cooperation with the Holy Spirit, to allow this unique image of Christ within us to give form to our entire life and world. "Let us not grow tired of doing good, for in due time we shall reap our harvest, if we do not give up" (Gal 6:9). The Christ-form given to us at baptism frees our founding form from its captivity to original sin. Grace abounds as well to help us overcome the bondage of our personal and communal sinfulness.

Consonance—God ultimately intends for us lives that are whole, complete, peaceful, consonant. This happiness can only be ours if we follow the lead of the Holy Spirit and begin to sound together (*con-sonare*) with the Divine Forming Mystery at the center of our life and world.

Consonance in Christian Life—Our empirical human life form attains Christian consonance insofar as it is in tune with the manifestations of the Christ-form of our life; the works of the *Pneuma* or Holy Spirit in our human spirit; the hidden holy wisdom of our highest pneumatic-ecclesial life dimension; and the mystery of grace and redemption in church and humanity. This divine consonance heals and elevates our human condition. The grace of God lifts people of good will and true faith—in all their formation dimensions—into a pneumatic-ecclesial life fully consonant with the Divine Forming Mystery. Hence our Christian formation tradition holds before us the hope of "transforming union," or a life wholly at one with the Lord.

Depreciation—To depreciate or devalue who we most deeply are and what we ultimately desire—union with God—is a source of unhappiness. It can be more or less severe depending on how depreciative our lives have become. Depreciative thoughts can lead to depressive feelings. What alters this process of depreciation before it leads to the misguided option to feel that we are abandoned by the Mystery? The answer is the power of faith-filled appreciation of the Mystery as benevolent, whether or not we feel and sense that benevolence personally and intimately.

Depreciation in Service of Appreciation—To appraise and affirm what is transcendently calling us may lead to praiseworthy rejection of what is not to be appreciated because it interferes with God's call for our life. What we reject as dissonant calls forth in our higher transcendent self acts and dispositions of enlightened depreciation. What we have wisely rejected and depreciated, however, can attract us again and again. Therefore, acts and dispositions of firm rejection and depreciation of what is incompatible with God's will for our life must remain available to us. We must activate these dispositions when our lower pretranscendent "I," losing touch with our transcendent "I," is in danger of succumbing to dissonant attractions and temptations. We foster depreciation of the latter in order to foster appreciation of what God really wants for us.

Dissonance—The term "dissonance" is the opposite of "consonance." In pretheological formation science, dissonance refers to the lack of responsible attunement to the Formation Mystery in our human field of formation. Insofar as it can be known and appraised by human knowledge without the help of Christian revelation, such dissonance can signal a shift to depreciative thinking or a general lack of fidelity to our founding life form or call.

Dissonance in the Christian Tradition—We become "dissonant" Christians when we are not living in consonant appreciation of Christ and the will of the Father for us. We, as dissonant Christians, literally do not allow God's will to "sound through" our life. We are not "appreciatively tuned in" to the Christ-form of our existence. The awareness of being "out of tune" with God's allowing and/or challenging will is appropriately called "dissonance," or what Timothy refers to as making a "shipwreck" of our faith (1 Tm 1:19). Often sin blinds us to our unfaithfulness to the Christ-form. At times we have intimations, little flutters of fear or pinches of guilt, that may signify that our lives are no longer in appreciative conformity with the promptings of the Holy Spirit. "For I do not do the good I want, but I do the evil I do not want. Now if [I] do what I do not want, it is no longer I who do it, but sin that dwells in me" (Rom 7:19-20). Essential for committed Christian living is our willingness to pay attention to these dissonances and to ask the Holy Spirit to enable us to change them into consonant opportunities to grow in spiritual maturity.

Divine Forming Mystery—This phrase signifies God revealed as the Holy Trinity of Father, Son, and Spirit in whom we are sourced and from whom our life receives its direction. God, by whatever name we call the Divine Forming Mystery, is the unfathomable other in whom we live and move and have our being (cf. Acts 17:28). The Mystery is the source and center of the entire world in which we find ourselves. This is the Forming Mystery that Genesis reveals to us, the mystery of our having been preformed in the mind and heart of God, of our having been made in God's image and likeness (cf. Gn 1:26).

Formation Tradition—A formation or form tradition is usually an implicit personal, familial, or cultural way of living in daily life what we believe. Thus a form tradition is an embodiment—with all its possible disruptions and misinterpretations—of a faith tradition, be it religious or ideological. The only way to appraise and to purify a formation tradition is to raise it to a focal or focused level of consciousness. Then we can begin to assess its impact: What in it is foundational? What is accretional? What represents cultural, familial, or personal distortions? What in it is consonant with our basic ecclesial faith and formation tradition? Making form traditions focal can enhance the consonant role they are meant to play in our entire formation story.

Formation Tradition as Transcendent—A specific transcendent formation tradition cannot communicate its message unless it collaborates with the grace-inspired awakening of the transcendence dynamic. This is a gift of our Creator inherent in human nature. Usually such an awakening occurs in the light of either a specific ideological or a religious transcendent faith tradition. Often what opens people to their transcendent longing for the "more than" is the gift of disappointment and suffering, that is the gift of a true "dark night" experience.

Formative—This term suggests that we are always being "formed by" or "giving form to" people, nature, events, and things in our day-to-day world. We are always in ongoing formation. At any moment we are receiving and/or giving form in some way within our providential formation field.

Foundational Life Form—Our foundational life form is the unique-communal call we are meant to disclose and implement during our lifetime. Each of us is called to be an unrepeatable expression of the great mystery of love that fills and forms the universe. This basic unique expression is also always communal. The forming mystery calls each of us to express our love in communion with other unique human beings in mutual care and appreciation.

Founding Life Call—This is our original call in the Divine Forming Mystery; it is the guiding principle that gives unity and coherence to every facet of our life and world. Contained in this providential seed is the mystery of who we are and who we are to become. It is not fully and immediately available to direct experience; yet it continuously inspires and guides our ongoing formation.

Foundationals of Faith Deepening—Certain essential or basic spiritual dispositions, directives, and disciplines point the way to maturity in the life of faith. Together they constitute the foundational formative conditions for the possibility of any faith-deepening whatsoever. Examples of foundational dispositions are candor, commitment, courage, compatibility, compassion, humility, detachment, and charity. Examples of foundational directives are the teachings of the Beatitudes. Examples of foundational disciplines are spiritual reading, meditation, prayer, liturgical celebration, and contemplation.

Functional Dimension—This dimension of the human life form enables us to implement effectively, skillfully, technically, organizationally, and/or bureaucratically our practical decisions. When our functional potency awakens, we can start to bring order to our life and world. We begin to choose the practical directives that give functional form to our life call. This awakening of the functional dimension is accompanied by an emerging awareness of our individual skills and talents. We accept the responsibility to develop these gifts in service of our call as situated and guided by any sphere or dimension of our formation field.

The functional dimension is also the link between the sociohistorical, vital, and transcendent dimensions of our life. It functions as the bridge between our pulsations, impulses, aspirations, and inspirations and our everyday life situations. In other words, the functional dimension translates sociohistorical pulsations, vital impulses, and transcendent aspirations and inspirations into workable, flexible and satisfying call-obedient ambitions. These consonant ambitions can be executed effectively in our factual and traditionally appraised formation fields while remaining in tune with our unique-communal life call and consonant with our basic faith and formation traditions.

"More Than"—Because we are spirit through and through, we are able to be open to all that is "more than" we are. What is distinctively human is, therefore, transcendent. This capacity to go beyond accounts for our treasure of possibilities. Because we are human spirit, our formation is always "more than" a fatalistic pattern of unfolding or a passage through the pretranscendent stages of human development described by the social, clinical, and educational disciplines. By the same token, we need "more than" functional satisfaction or vital gratification to still our deepest longings; we seek transcendent joy.

Mystery—The mystery of formation preforms our foundational life form with its inherent unique-communal life call and direction. The same mystery also gives form to the formation traditions by which we should live insofar as they are consonant. Hence a hidden divine consonance underlies the seemingly disparate directives we disclose and follow over a lifetime and the consonant decisions we make.

Pretranscendent—According to pretheological formation anthropology, the human form of life is pretranscendent insofar as its sociohistorical, vital, functional, and functional-transcendent dimensions are not yet sufficiently elevated and permeated by the posttranscendent traditional "transcendent-functional dimension." In formation theology the "pneumatic-ecclesial dimension" is the crowning or highest dimension. It elevates and deepens immensely the transcendent dimension that is merely known by human reason without the light of Christian revelation.

Pretranscendent "I"—Pretheological formation anthropology describes how human life is encapsulated in a central pretranscendent "I" to the degree that it cannot see or go beyond a merely or mainly socio-vital-functional or functional-transcendent life. It is to some degree a life subordinated to our quasi-foundational autarkic pride form. This subordination is expressed in self-preoccupied attachments or addictions. These self-attachments engender routinized form directives that give rise continuously to coercive robot-like processes of thought, affect, imagination, memory, anticipation, and action.

Our central pretranscendent "I" binds together the subordinated pretranscendent "I s" embodied in our plans and projects; for example, our medical, scholarly, literary, vitalistic, social, athletic, and business "I s." Often these "I s" may try to usurp the dominant position of our central pretranscendent "I."

We are on the way to full consonance insofar as we allow the present disclosures of our divine life call to give form increasingly to our unfolding higher transcendent "I." Our transcendent "I" in turn ought to give form to our lower pretranscendent central "I"; and through the central pretranscendent "I" to the subordinated "I s" that should be related to it in a "servant" fashion.

Pride Form—The autarkic pride form controls formation by evoking fear, defensiveness, and resistance the moment its stranglehold is threatened by lucid and sober appraisal of the "oughts" and "shoulds" of our formative conscience. Exalted form directives of the pride form may be deeply entrenched in the intrafocal layers of our consciousness, thus blocking transfocal directives. They may have their origin in primal reactions when the still naive, vulnerable, and not yet controllable pride form of life was threatened during early periods of our formation history.

Formation theology holds that the original fall led to the emergence of this quasi-foundational or counterfeit form of life. The autarkic pride form thus gives us a false sense of total independence that veils the truth of our being made in God's image and likeness (cf. Gn 1:26). It obscures the dynamic call of our true founding life form; it tempts us with the illusion that we can do it alone; it encourages us to deny our dependency on the Mystery that makes us be. The pride form interferes with our disposition to listen to and obey the consonant dispositions of the Spirit-enlightened heart; it replaces them with such dissonant counterfeit dispositions as underestimation or even depreciation of faith and formation traditions as interpreted by church authority; it leads to envious comparison, judgmentalism, or the misuse of gifts and talents for merely self-centered or functional-transcendent projects.

Transcendent—The traditional transcendent-functional dimension of human life is the distinctive mark of our humanity and formation. It helps us to know ultimately what to do and where to go with our life. It provides the deeper direction for our actual life as always linked in faith to our founding life form. From our traditional transcendent dimension there emerges the potency and tendency of our heart to be formed by and to give form to aspirations and inspirations. From the viewpoint of formation theology, the transcendence dynamic frees us over a lifetime to discover our specific eternal call in Christ through the Holy Spirit. This call is manifested in our pneumatic-ecclesial life dimension. It illumines for us in turn the deepest meanings of our formation field.

Transcendent Formation—The pretheological auxiliary science and discipline of foundational human formation develops criteria to research and reflect upon the tradition-al-transcendent-functional formation of the human race. These criteria apply to the basic common potencies for transcendent-immanent formation that can be disclosed in all human forms of life. This research puts into brackets the claims of specific faith and formation traditions without denying or confirming such claims. In this respect it follows the pretheological scholastic philosophical tradition. This philosophy intended to put momentarily into brackets any theological considerations so that insights would emerge about what human speculative reason could disclose concerning human nature. Pretheological formation science analogously asks what empirical-experiential reason can tell us about the empirical-experiential aspects of any traditional-transcendent-functional formation of the human race, even if it is not yet enlightened, corrected, and deepened by the fullness of Christian revelation.

Transcendent "I"—Our transcendent higher "I" is the "I" that unfolds itself in the light of our obedience to our founding life form or, dynamically speaking, to our unique-communal life call. This form or call is our deepest mysterious identity. In Christ our transcendent "I" is hidden in the Radical Interforming Mystery of the Holy Trinity. Christ is the Divine Word Incarnate. He is the Forming Word that contains within himself, as little words, all basic forms in universe and humanity.

In relation to the relatively free human form, the Forming Word, who is Christ, is also the Calling Word. Christ continually calls to our freedom. He invites us to listen attentively and wisely to all events of our factual, or personally, ecclesially, and traditionally appraised fields of formation.

The deepest call or word that we are is not at once disclosed to us. It is revealed to us over a lifetime. The first condition for disclosure is that we, empowered by the Calling Word, who is the Lord, try to seek and implement through the Holy Spirit what the full formation field seems to be disclosing in our successive here-and-now situations as the most probable appeals of our divine life call.

Transcendent "I" in Relation to Affirmation—In contrast to confirmation, affirmation of our unique-communal life call represents our own provisional, tentative assertion of any possible disclosure of direction. Affirmation presupposes that a disclosure shows sufficient probability to be implemented, at first tentatively and then empirically, in our life through the use of our pretranscendent servant "I." To the degree that we implement such disclosures of God's will in our core or character dispositions, we strengthen and give form to the directions and inspirations of our higher "I."

Transcendent "I" in Relation to Detachment—A main condition for trustworthy disclosure of our call is that we maintain sufficient detachment from probable, provisional disclosures until they are fully appraised. Detachment enables us to disregard, correct, or complement such disclosures in the light of our basic faith and formation traditions, as interpreted by the church. New events in our formation field may contain new disclosures. These will demand that we repeat the process of appraisal.

Transcendent Transformation as Subordination—Traditional-transcendent-functional transformation does not change the nature of our socio-vital-functional or functional-transcendent life; rather it subordinates it to itself, thus enhancing this life in its own unique assets. This life used to be subordinated, totally or in part, to our autarkic idolatrous pride form through absolutized directives of pretranscendent development. This life becomes liberated, enlightened, and elevated in itself by our founding life form as gradually disclosed in and through the traditional-transcendent-functional dimension of our life form.

Transformation—Only with grace is a divine change possible, that is a transformation in Christ of our deepest self. Only with the help of grace can our spiritual journey approach its final destiny. Graced-transformation is the ultimate answer to our aspiration for wholeness, completeness, and spiritual maturity in Christ through the Holy Spirit. It is our entrance into an intimate relationship with the Trinity. However blocked our power of listening may be by the confusing voices of the autarkic pride form, God offers us the opportunity to be transformed. Through the power of the Holy Spirit, Christ shows us the way to let go of what is dissonant and to listen to what gives us new life in him and his church.

Vital Dimension—This dimension of our everyday life in the world accounts for our bodily constitution—our neuroform or biogenetic makeup—as well as our temper form or temperament. These facets of the vital dimension enable us to react instinctively where appropriate and to respond in a vital-emotional way to our surroundings. We receive and give form on a day-to-day basis in the light of the changes that occur in our body as we grow physically and mature spiritually.

Bibliography

Alighieri, Dante. *The Divine Comedy.* Vol. 3 of *Paradise.* Trans. by Mark Musa. New York: Penguin Books, Viking Penguin, 1986.

Anonymous. *The Cloud of Unknowing.* Ed. by James Walsh. *Classics of Western Spirituality.* New York: Paulist Press, 1981.

Bodo, Murray. *Tales of St. Francis.* Cincinnati: St. Anthony Messenger Press, 1988.

Burrows, Ruth. *Guidelines for Mystical Prayer.* London: Sheed and Ward, 1976.

Catherine of Genoa: Purgation and Purgatory, the Spiritual Dialogue. Trans. by Serge Hughes. *Classics of Western Spirituality.* New York: Paulist Press, 1979.

Chesterton, G. K. *Saint Thomas Aquinas: "The Dumb Ox."* Garden City, NY: Doubleday, 1956.

Ciszek, Walter with Daniel Flaherty. *He Leadeth Me.* Garden City, NY: Image Books, Doubleday, 1975.

The Collected Works of St. Teresa of Avila. Vol. 1. Trans. by Kieran Kavanaugh and Otilio Rodriguez. Washington, DC: Institute of Carmelite Studies, 1976.

The Collected Works of St. Teresa of Avila. Vol. 2. Trans. by Kieran Kavanaugh and Otilio Rodriguez. Washington, DC: Institute of Carmelite Studies, 1980.

The Collected Works of St. John of the Cross. Trans. by Kieran Kavanaugh and Otilio Rodriguez. Washington, DC: Institute of Carmelite Studies, 1991.

The Confessions of St. Augustine. Trans. by John Ryan. New York: Doubleday, 1960.

Collings, Ross. *John of the Cross: Way of the Christian Mystics.* Collegeville, MN: Liturgical Press, 1990.

Cronk, Sandra. *Dark Night Journey: Inward Repatterning toward a Life Centered in God.* Wallingford, PA: Pendle Hill Publications, 1992.

Culligan, Kevin G. *Saint John of the Cross and Spiritual Direction.* Vol. 20 of *Living Flame Series.* Dublin: Carmelite Centre of Spirituality, 1983.

Cummins, Norbert. *Freedom to Rejoice: Understanding St. John of the Cross.* San Francisco: Harper Torchbooks, Harper and Row, 1991.

de Caussade, Jean Pierre. *Abandonment to Divine Providence.* Trans. by John Beevers. Garden City, NY: Doubleday, 1975.

de Nicolas, Antonio. *St. John of the Cross: Alchemist of the Soul.* New York: Paragon House, 1989.

Dent, Barbara. *My Only Friend Is Darkness: Living the Night of Faith.* Notre Dame, IN: Ave Maria Press, 1988.

The Dialogue of Catherine of Siena. Trans. by Suzanne Noffke. New York: Paulist Press, 1980.

Dombrowski, Daniel A. *St. John of the Cross: An Appreciation.* Albany: State University of New York, 1992.

Dorgan, Margaret. "Thérèse, a Latter-Day Interpreter of John of the Cross." *Carmelite Studies* (1990): 97-118.

Dubay, Thomas. *Fire Within: St. Teresa of Avila, St. John of the Cross, and the Gospel—on Prayer.* San Francisco: Ignatius Press, 1989.

Eliot, T. S. *Four Quartets.* London: Faber and Faber, 1965.

Fairlie, Henry. *The Seven Deadly Sins Today.* Washington, DC: New Republic Books, 1978.

The Family Book of Verse. Ed. by Lewis Gannett. New York: Harper Torchbooks, Harper and Row, 1961.

Francis and Clare: The Complete Works. Trans. by Regis Armstrong and Ignatius Brady. *Classics of Western Spirituality.* New York: Paulist Press, 1982.

Francis de Sales. *Introduction to the Devout Life.* Trans. by John Ryan. New York: Doubleday, 1966.

Franck, Frederick. *Pilgrimage to Now/Here.* Maryknoll, NY: Orbis Books, 1974.

Frohlich, Mary. "John's 'One Dark Night': Romantic, Political or Mystical." *Spiritual Life* 37, no. 1 (Spring, 1991).

From Glory to Glory: Texts from Gregory of Nyssa's Mystical Writings. Trans. by Herbert Musurillo. Crestwood, NY: St. Vladimir's Seminary Press, 1979.

Giles, Mary E. *The Poetics of Love: Meditations with John of the Cross.* Vol. 18 of *American University Studies.* New York: Peter Lang, n.d.

God Speaks in the Night: The Life, Times and Teachings of St. John of the Cross. Trans. by Kieran Kavanaugh. Washington, DC: Institute of Carmelite Studies, 1991.

Groothuis, Douglas. *Unmasking the New Age.* Downers Grove, IL: InterVarsity Press, 1986.

Hammarskjöld, Dag. *Markings.* Trans. by Leif Sjöberg and W. Auden. London: Faber and Faber, 1964.

Hardy, Richard. *Search for Nothing: The Life of John of the Cross.* New York: Crossroad Publishing Company, 1982.

Hausherr, Irenee. *Penthos: The Doctrine of Compunction in the Christian East.* Trans. by Anselm Hustader. *Cistercian Studies.*Kalamazoo, MI: Cistercian Publicaions, 1982.

John of the Cross: Conferences and Essays. By members of the Institute of Carmelite Studies and others. Ed. by Steven Payne. Washington, DC: Institute of Carmelite Studies, 1992.

Julian of Norwich: Showings. Trans. by Edmund Colledge and James Walsh. *Classics of Western Spirituality.* New York: Paulist Press, 1978.

Kierkegaard, Sören. *The Point of View for My Work as An Author: A Report to History.* Trans. by Walter Lowrie. New York: Harper Torchbooks, Harper and Row, 1962.

_____. *Purity of Heart Is to Will One Thing: Spiritual Preparation for the Office of Confession.* Trans. by Douglas Steere. New York: Harper Torchbooks, Harper and Row, 1956.

Larkin, Ernest. *John of the Cross.* New York: Crossroad Publishing Company, 1993.

Mallory, Marilyn May. "John of the Cross and the Green Vestment of Hope." *Spiritual Life* 38, no. 2 (Summer, 1992): 107-113.

Meister Eckhart: Teacher and Preacher. Ed. by Bernard McGinn. *Classics of Western Spirituality.* New York: Paulist Press, 1986.

Merton, Thomas. *Wisdom of the Desert: Sayings from the Desert Fathers of the Fourth Century.* London: Sheldon, 1974.

Muto, Susan. "Asceticism in St. John of the Cross: Wisdom for Every Person of Good Will." *Word and Spirit* (A Monastic Review) 13 (1991).

_____. *Approaching the Sacred: An Introduction to Spiritual Reading.* Denville, NJ: Dimension Books, 1973.

_____. *Blessings That Make Us Be: A Formative Approach to Living the Beatitudes.* Petersham, MA: St. Bede's Publications, 1982.

_____. *John of the Cross for Today: The Ascent.* Notre Dame, IN: Ave Maria Press, 1991.

_____. *The Journey Homeward: On the Road of Spiritual Reading.* Denville, NJ: Dimension Books, 1977.

_____. *Meditation in Motion.* Garden City, NY: Doubleday, 1976.

_____. *Renewed at Each Awakening.* Denville, NJ: Dimension Books, 1979.

_____. *Steps Along the Way: The Path of Spiritual Reading.* Denville, NJ: Dimension Books, 1975.

_____ and Adrian van Kaam. *Commitment: Key to Christian Maturity.* Mahwah, NJ: Paulist Press, 1989.

_____ and Adrian van Kaam. *Practicing the Prayer of Presence.* Mineola, NY: Resurrection Press, 1993.

Nemeck, Francis Kelly and Marie Theresa Coombs. *O Blessed Night: Recovery from Addiction, Codependency and Attachment Based on the Insights of St. John of the Cross and Teilhard de Chardin.* Staten Island, NY: Alba House, 1991.

O'Donoghue, Noel Dermot. *Lovelier Than the Dawn: Four Meditations on the Mystical Teachings of St. John of the Cross.* Vol. 27 of *The Living Flame.* Dublin: Carmelite Centre of Spirituality, 1984.

Payne, Steven. *John of the Cross and the Cognitive Value of Mysticism.* Norwell, MA: New Synthesis Historical Library, 1990.

The Philokalia. Vol. 1. Trans. by G. Palmer, Philip Sherrard and Kalistos Ware. London: Faber and Faber, 1979.

Pseudo-Dionysius: The Complete Works. Trans. by Colm Luibheid. *Classics of Western Spirituality.* New York: Paulist Press, 1987.

The Sayings of the Desert Fathers: The Alphabetical Collection. Trans. by Benedicta Ward. London: A. R. Mowbray, 1975.

Ricoeur, Paul. *The Symbolism of Evil.* New York: Harper Torchbooks, Harper and Row, 1967.

Simsic, Wayne and Carl Koch. *Praying with John of the Cross.* Winona, MN: St. Mary's Press, 1993.

The Story of a Soul: The Autobiography of St. Thérèse of Lisieux. Trans. by John Clarke. Washington, DC: Institute of Carmelite Studies, 1975.

Symeon The New Theologian: The Discourses. Trans. by C. de Catanzaro. *Classics of Western Spirituality.* New York: Paulist Press, 1980.

The Teaching of Christ: A Catholic Catechism for Adults. Ed. by Ronald Lawler, Donald Wuerl, and Thomas Lawler. Huntington, IN: Our Sunday Visitor Publishing, 1976.

Teresa of Avila: The Interior Castle. Trans. by Kieran Kavanaugh and Otilio Rodriguez. *Classics of Western Spirituality.* New York: Paulist Press, 1979.

Underhill, Evelyn. *Practical Mysticism.* Columbus: Ariel Press, 1942.

van Kaam, Adrian. *Fundamental Formation.* Vol. 1 of *Formative Spirituality.* New York: Crossroad Publishing Company, 1983.

_____. *Human Formation.* Vol. 2 of *Formative Spirituality.* New York: Crossroad Publishing Company, 1985.

_____. *Transcendent Formation.* Vol. 6 of *Formative Spirituality.* New York: Crossroad Publishing Company, 1995.

_____. *Dynamics of Spiritual Self Direction.* Pittsburgh, PA: Epiphany Books, 1993.

_____. *The Transcendent Self: The Formative Spirituality of Middle, Early and Later Years of Life.* Pittsburgh, PA: Epiphany Books, 1991.

_____. *A Light to the Gentiles: The Life Story of the Venerable Francis Libermann.* Lanham, MD: University Press of America, 1985.

_____. *Living Creatively.* Denville, NJ: Dimension Books, 1978.

_____. *On Being Involved: The Rhythm of Involvement and Detachment in Daily Life.* Denville, NJ: Dimension Books, 1970.

_____. *Religion and Personality.* Pittsburgh, PA: Epiphany Books, 1991.

_____ and Susan Muto. *The Power of Appreciation: A New Approach to Personal and Relational Healing.* New York: Crossroad Publishing Company, 1993.

_____ and Susan Muto with Susan McBride. *Formation Guide for Becoming Spiritually Mature.* Pittsburgh, PA: Epiphany Books, 1991.

Vitz, Paul. *Psychology as Religion: The Cult of Self-Worship.* Grand Rapids, MI: Eerdmans Publishing Company, 1977.

Walter Hilton: The Scale of Perfection. Trans. by John Clark and Rosemary Dorward. *Classics of Western Spirituality.* New York: Paulist Press, 1991.

Watson, Stephen. "St. Francis of Assisi and St. John of the Cross." *Carmelite Digest,* 8, no. 2 (Spring, 1993): 54-64.

Welch, John. *When Gods Die: An Introduction to John of the Cross.* Mahwah, NJ: Paulist Press, 1990.

Yeats, William Butler. "The Second Coming" in *Chief Modern Poets of Britain and America.* Ed. by Gerald Sanders. New York: Macmillan, 1970.

Index

imperfections of proficients
160
impure feelings 58
indiscreet zeal 62
inebriation 222
inflow of grace 172
informational 247
infused contemplation 100,
104, 112, 123, 132, 145, 172,
173, 252, 282, 256, 289
inordinate affections 182
inordinate appetites 236
inordinate attachments 51,
61, 77, 198
intellect 169, 191, 196, 203, 279
interior detachment 51
intimacy 94, 220, 282
intimacy with the Trinity 87
invitation of grace 221

J

Jacob 264
Job 127, 205, 216, 286, 288
journey into the night 18
joy 169, 197, 236, 239, 266, 277
Julian of Norwich 291
justice 164

K

Kierkegaard, Sören 184, note
2, Chapter 12, 273
knowledge of self 124

L

lack of satisfaction 91
ladder of contemplation 257,
262
ladder of love 26, 259, 260
land of likeness 31, 61, 202,
227, 248 280
land of unlikeness 26, 227
leap of faith 31

liberation 84, 118, 119, 225,
280
Libermann, Francis 47
libidinal energy 57
Liebermann, Francis 47
life-transforming dispositions 263
limits of progress 101
limits of sense-bound perception 230
livery of hope 277
locution 252
loneliness 177, 180
longing of love 216
love 90, 180, 199, 209, 218,
260, 288
low-grade depression 73
lower appetites 230
lower level appetites 232
lukewarmness 94
lust 53, 134, 229

M

material poverty 95
maternal love 122
maturity of spiritual in-
timacy 260
meditation 32
meekness 45, 63, 138
melancholia 57, 95
memory 169, 171, 184, 191,
196, 202, 279
memory of God's presence 93
mercy 124
Michelangelo 205
Milton, John 124
miracle of transformation 229
mortality 85
mortification 31, 43, 68
Moses 127, 238, 251, 252, 286
Mother Teresa of Calcutta 124